Colonial Encounters in a Native American Landscape

Colonial Encounters in a Native American Landscape

THE SPANISH AND DUTCH IN NORTH AMERICA

Nan A. Rothschild

Smithsonian Books
Washington and London

Copy editor: Vicky Macintyre
Production editor: Robert A. Poarch
Designer: Brian Barth

Library of Congress Cataloging-in-Publication Data
Rothschild, Nan A., date
Colonial encounters in a Native American landscape: the Spanish and Dutch in North America/Nan A. Rothschild.
p. cm.
Includes bibliographical references and index.
ISBN 1-58834-1380-0 (alk. paper)
1. Mohawk Indians—History. 2. Mohawk Indians—Government relations. 3. Pueblo Indians—History. 4. Pueblo Indians—Government relations. 5. Indians of North America—First contact with Europeans—Hudson River Valley (N.Y. and N.J.). 6. Indians of North America—First contact with Europeans—Southwest, New. 7. Hudson River Valley (N.Y. and N.J.)—History. 8. Netherlands—Colonies—America. 9. Spain—Colonies—America. I. Title.
E99.M R67 2003
974.7004′9755—dc21 2002042830

British Library Cataloguing-in-Publication Data available

Manufactured in the United States of America
09 08 07 06 05 04 03 5 4 3 2 1

♾ The paper used in this publication meets the minimum requirements of the American National Standard for Information Sciences—Permanence of Paper for Printed Library Materials ANSI Z39.48-1984.

For Mike,
friend, husband, and consummate editor,
who makes all things possible,
with love

Contents

Preface

The idea for this comparison began about 10 or 11 years ago, after I had spent some time working on the Zuni Reservation, where we surveyed five farming villages and excavated Lower Pescado Village, which had a historic as well as a Precolumbian occupation. As I began to learn more about Spanish colonial policy, I was struck by the difference between Spanish intentions and the outcome of the colonial encounter: Native American cultures survive strongly in New Mexico and Arizona in spite of serious efforts from the sixteenth century onward to transform the indigenous peoples into good Christians and loyal members of the Spanish empire. The disparity between Dutch traders' goals and their effect in the Mohawk-Hudson Valley was even more striking. The Mohawk had left their Mohawk Valley home by the late eighteenth century.

As I considered these differences and read historic accounts of the colonial encounter in each region, I came to believe that one unexplored way to understand these two outcomes was to conduct a fine-grained analysis of archaeological data in conjunction with historic information. Using archaeological tools of spatial analysis and material culture offers a unique way to "see" the relationships between two groups on the ground. Where does each group live in relation to the other? How entangled are their respective material cultures? And how do these situations change over time as the encounter proceeds? Combining these data with history and the body of theory about colonialism that has developed in anthropology offers the clearest path to understanding the past.

The book has taken a long time to complete, in part because of other demands on my time, but also because some of the most important sources were hard to obtain. Reports from cultural resource management projects provide the major part of the archaeological information I relied on for the Southwest. Academic archaeologists should make more use of this source of information, and since I had not done any work in the Rio Grande River Valley, these reports were essential to me. I was fortunate that Dean Snow had completed his compilation of Mohawk site information just prior to the time I was doing this research; I had studied the colonial Dutch in New York City but had not conducted archaeological research upstate. I know that in writing a book such as this, in which I compare two regions and people's behavior in them, I lack the depth of expertise possessed by archaeologists who have worked in only one of the two areas. I may have made some errors in fact or interpretation because of this but believe that the distance from each setting may provide an advantage, as I come to them without ingrained bias. In addition, anthropology's use of the comparative method is a strong element in the book.

Even after finishing this project, I do not fully understand some things, such as the social distance between Dutch men and Native American women, especially given the behavior of Dutch men in Batavia. I am also uncertain as to how those who were identified as Hispanic in the Southwest perceived themselves. There were a number of subcategories within the Hispanic rubric, and classifications were made by outsiders, officials of various kinds, who named people in racial terms. However, the material culture at Hispano sites signals a mixture of backgrounds that is difficult to interpret. Were these simply opportunistic uses of what was locally available, or do they signal variable identities?

I come away from the project with an admiration for the adaptability of many of those involved in the encounters: for the indigenous peoples who were invaded but maintained much of their culture intact, even if they had to relocate to do it; and for the colonists, who may have been aware of the grand designs of European elite but had to adapt to unforeseen circumstances in living in the New World. The role of indigenous women has mainly been neglected in historical writings on North American colonization, and I have tried to highlight their importance and present some of their responses to colonial situations as described in historical accounts. Understanding events in the past is a difficult endeavor, but the combination of firsthand descriptions, even given the observers' biases, with archaeological information, which has its own limitations, provides the best chance we have to capture a version of reality.

Acknowledgments

This project has taken many years and considerable assistance from a number of colleagues and friends. First, I have relied on the work of many archaeologists who have been extremely generous in allowing me to use the results of their research, some of it unpublished and some available as primary data from site reports, and other material only available in the Cultural Resource Management (CRM) or "grey" literature. These reports represent an underutilized but significant source of information for archaeologists. Dean Snow (who compiled all known Mohawk site data in a comprehensive and very important data base), Robert Funk, Paul Huey, Robert Kuhn, and Lois Feister gave me crucial information for the Dutch-Mohawk context. Linda Cordell, Winifred Creamer, Jonathan Haas, Jake Ivey, Mark Lycett, James Moore, Ann Ramenofsky, David Snow, and Cordelia Snow provided valuable information on the protohistoric Pueblo and early Spanish/Hispanic material. Kate Spielmann's significant reports on the Salinas pueblos, only available in the grey literature, were especially useful, providing a large body of information from well-excavated sites. Kurt Jordan's dissertation research on the Senecas of the eighteenth century provided an important perspective and interesting discussion. Kathleen Deagan's writings on the importance of a gendered view of Spanish-Indian relationships in the Southeast were central to my initial interest.

I am also grateful to other southwestern researchers, Barbara Mills, David Hurst Thomas, and Lori Pendleton, and to Tim Seaman, Rosemary Talley, and others at the Archaeological Records Management Service in Santa Fe; their site files are a joy to use. And my thanks to Stefan Bielinski and George Hamell of the Albany Museum for assistance, and to Charles Hayes and Martha Sempowski of the Rochester Museum and Science Center for access to Seneca data in the museum's files.

A number of friends, family, and colleagues have read parts of this manuscript at various stages, and all of them offered useful comments and suggestions: Tom Biolsi, Anne-Marie Cantwell, Jeffrey Cooper, Michael Fleisher, David Nugent, Emily Rothschild, Oliver Rothschild, Joan Vincent, and Diana Wall; Paul Huey, Kurt Jordan, Robert Kuhn, Barbara Mills, Dean Snow, and Kate Spielmann read and gave me significant comments on particular segments. Jane Kepp, Lynn Meskell, and Michael Cooper all read the entire work and made quite important suggestions from very different perspectives. I have, in most cases, followed their advice. In places where I have not, they are absolved of blame, and I am responsible for any problems with the final product.

This project has been in progress for longer than I can remember, and a host of undergraduate and graduate students from Barnard and Columbia have had a role in bringing it about: Heather Atherton, Hilary Chester, Jessica Davis, Emily Donald, James Fenton, Katherine Gallagher, Kurt Jordan, Mobina Khan, and Christopher Matthews were particularly involved. It has been long enough that I may have omitted someone, for which I apologize. Mansur Kameletdinov was helpful in many small and large ways. Heather Atherton and especially Kelly Britt were absolutely essential in compiling the bibliography, a particularly onerous task. I am grateful to Chief Irving Powless Jr. of the Onondaga Nation, for permission to reproduce the Hiawatha Belt. Antoinette Wannabo took on a huge task when she agreed to make the maps; neither she nor I understood the enormity of it at the time, and I am incredibly grateful to her for her persistence in completing it. I think it was a learning experience for us both.

Barnard College has supported my completion of this work with resources and leave time; I could not have done it without both of these, and I appreciate Barnard's environment and commitment to faculty research. Smithsonian Books expressed enthusiasm for the project early on, and Robert Lockhart, Daniel Miller, and Scott Mahler have each been very helpful at various stages; Scott saw the process through from the submission of the manuscript to the final product with cheerful encouragement. Emily Sollie, Robert Poarch, and Vicky Macintyre also played important parts in later stages; Vicky copy-edited the entire manuscript with sensitivity and skill.

I

Colonies and the Study of Colonialism

Colonial encounters have been one of the dominant forms of social and cultural interaction over the past several hundred years. Motivated by the political economies of nations with expanding populations and fueled by technological innovation, these events were invariably tied to exploration and conquest, and, as a by-product, to complex interconnections between societies and cultures. Anthropology's belated recognition of the importance of these encounters is reflected in a surge of investigation and thought during the last decade or two of the twentieth century, documenting their intriguing variability despite familiar and predictable outlines of interaction. In its most neutral sense, a colonial setting is one in which, given two groups of people of unequal power, the more powerful one enters the other's territory to obtain material resources, using various forms of force and political/legal control systems to achieve its goal, with an ethnocentric rationale for that invasion. Domination is a crucial component of colonial interactions (for examples, see Beidelman 1982; Dirks 1992), but although it is always present, its form and degree vary between contexts.

The goal of this study is to understand how two specific colonial encounters occurring in North America during the seventeenth century developed as they did, and to unravel the reasons why. Such a comparison is enlightening as it brings out aspects of each situation that may be otherwise overlooked and shows the tremendous variation that may exist in what appear as similar situations at the same time in the same continent. I examine colonial situations in the southwestern and northeastern United States as reflected in documentary and archaeological information, much of the latter from contract reports. These important resources have not been fully exploited for the colonial period. In the first setting, Spanish missionaries and settlers intruded into what is now New Mexico, in search of mineral wealth and native labor. For the missionaries, the rationale was saving Pueblo souls, but they, like the state and the colonists, extracted labor by various means. In the second setting, the Dutch extracted furs—initially from the Mahicans, then from the Mohawks in the Hudson River Valley of New Netherland/New York. Territorial encroachment, though minor in some other colonial situations, was crucial to both cases described here. I chose these settings in part because I have worked in both and was struck by the interesting differences between them. At the same time, the indigenous groups involved shared somewhat similar subsistence patterns and social structures. Other possible comparisons in the Northeast, involving French or British colonists, seemed less valid. The French, for example, did not establish colonies, while the native peoples were not as well documented archaeologically where the British settled.

Ironically, the Dutch, whose goal was simpler and on the face of it less invasive, as they only wanted to acquire beaver skins, ultimately had a more devastating impact on the Mohawks than the Spaniards had on the Pueblos. The latter's ambitious scheme to remake Pueblo religion and culture in ways that suited the colonial agenda failed in many ways, leaving the Pueblos geographically—and to some degree culturally—intact, whereas the Mohawks—while retaining their cultural identity—had vanished from their home territory by the end of the eighteenth century. These different outcomes can be attributed to a number of factors: geography and the difficulty in reaching the Rio Grande Valley, the characteristics of the indigenous peoples and respective European groups involved, and above all the nature of the interactions as they developed.

The crucial elements included material culture flows, the role of women in each setting, differences between Catholicism and Protestantism, and the degree of social proximity between Europeans and native peoples. The Dutch demand for a nonrenewable resource, furs, engaged the Mohawks as producers of a specific article on the margins of the world economy. When the beaver declined and the trade moved beyond them, they had no remaining resources of value to sell to

Europeans save their land, which was already being increasingly invaded by the latter. The Spanish, on the other hand, operated within a still-feudal system and settled among the Pueblos, interacting with them culturally and sexually, producing a mestizo population that combined both material and genetic traits. Ultimately the existence of two separate populations in the Rio Grande Valley—Pueblos and Hispanos—reinforced the survival and identity of each. Environmental differences played a role as well: the Spanish were quite dependent on the Pueblos for basic subsistence in the difficult agricultural setting of the Southwest, while the Mohawk/Hudson Valleys were more productive and able to support additional residents requiring sustenance.

This comparison revolves around two pairs of "partners" in each context: a European nation and a Native American people. The Europeans resembled each other in certain ways, notably in their exploitive intentions, their technological sophistication, and their evolving power—political and otherwise—over the indigenous peoples. The Native Americans' responses to invasion also held significant commonalities, as they actively reorganized and altered European plans rather than passively acquiescing to them. The material record serves as a silent witness to the changing nature of such colonial interconnections. Archaeological data on material culture, subsistence, and the changing social and spatial landscapes in each context are used to monitor the evolving interactions. These data combined with documentary sources and oral history shed light on the views and behavior of both the colonizer and colonized.

The Nature of Colonial Studies

Many studies of colonialism have ignored its complexity and bilateral nature. Some have focused on European agency in these encounters and paid insufficient attention to the fact that while colonized peoples may bear the major impact of contact, the colonizing group (those at home as well as the invaders) is also affected to a great degree. Hence this work includes aspects of colonialism as a general phenomenon, especially the form characteristic of European invasions of other continents between the sixteenth and nineteenth centuries, although the central concern here is the seventeenth and eighteenth centuries.

From the point of first contact, colonial interaction proceeds along a series of familiar pathways with actions and behaviors characterized as domination, collusion, resistance, repression, rebellion, exploitation, extraction, exchange, commodification, and, more recently, globalization. The colonial impact on the Maori, for instance, consisted of "dispossession, depopulation, despondency, desperation and depression," as elegantly noted by Ngata (1994:4–6, cited in Allen 1998:147). Not surprisingly, colonial encounters often modified the landscape, material culture, and political economy of both groups. Linguistic changes were also typical. In many cases, the genetic composition of both peoples was altered, and ethnogenesis was a common byproduct. Change is not a finite or "one-time-only" event, however. Modifications lead to redefinition within the system, and then to the possibility of further change, in a continuing pattern. While modification itself is predictable, its specific forms are not, and the effects of contact are, and were, generally uneven throughout a society and across cultures. As a result, the colonizing society did not anticipate the forms of modification that developed among the colonized or the effects on their own lives. Although changes may not have occurred as expected, they did, for the most part, conform to internal cultural and political-economic logics, with parties on both sides selecting some aspects of what they encountered and rejecting others.

I suggest that a significant part of the complexity and unpredictability in the course of colonial endeavors derives from the culturally constructed misperceptions that characterized both sides of most interactions. Most notably, neither knew who "the other" was, nor what the other desired. Initial encounters, in particular, were marked by profound ignorance. European groups beginning their conquering voyages after the close of the fifteenth century had a notion they might find "savages" or "wilden" in the New World, or more complex "civilized" people in the Far East. Some, especially by the eighteenth to nineteenth century, had seen exotic objects in "cabinets of curiosities" (Axtell 1992:30) and had heard of strange and shocking practices in distant places. In any case, most came armed with a sense of superiority as they expected to find inferiors, barbarians, cannibals, and monsters, or, at the very least, naive and ignorant "children" in need of salvation.

First contacts were mostly a surprise to Native Americans, who seem to have had few categories into which "others" could fit; there were humans (themselves or others like them) and spirits. In some settings, Europeans were initially placed in this latter category on the basis of their strange aspect and their impressive possessions: ships, horses, and "speaking objects," especially guns (Axtell 1992:101). The Aztecs, according to Friar Sahagún, the chronicler of the Spanish-Aztec encounter, believed the Spanish ship was carrying Quetzalcoatl, their feathered serpent deity (Sahagún 1978); other indigenous observers described birds (sailors) perched on masts (Anne Chapman, personal communication 1997). A number of accounts mention shamanic predictions of the arrival of people such as the Spanish; the Hopi claim to have known white men would come (Nabokov 1991:7). According to Coronado, the Zunis told him in 1540, "It was foretold them more than 50 years ago that a people such as we would come, and from the direction we have come, and that the whole country would be conquered" (Quinn 1979 1:428). "Prophecies" such as these recorded after contact must be viewed with some suspicion; they are prime examples of the rewriting of history. Regardless of how these early perceptions of others were constructed, they were soon modified, probably within less than a generation. The awe with which some indigenous peoples initially viewed Europeans soon gave way to a more realistic appraisal, while Europeans were forced to reevaluate both the anticipated simplicity of the "natives" and their eagerness for European ways. The particulars of the reevaluation process in the colonial situations of interest here are discussed in subsequent chapters. The rest of this chapter presents some existing ideas about colonial encounters and a brief outline of those covered in this volume.

Perspectives on Colonial Contact

Colonialism is an old phenomenon, certainly older than its practice by Europeans from the sixteenth century onward. It goes at least as far back as the Roman, Inka, and Aztec empires. Much of the early anthropological literature on colonial encounters and culture change characterized interaction by terms such as "creolization," "acculturation," and "diffusion," while historical (and some anthropological and archaeological) accounts focused on spatial concepts—frontiers and boundaries. Each of these concepts makes useful contributions, but each also raises some questions (Cusick 1998; Deagan 1998; Rice 1998). For example, a number of scholars (Bolton 1921; Jackson 1998; Thomas 1989) refer to the areas along the southern edges of today's North America as the Spanish Borderlands, as though they actually formed a physical frontier or boundary whereas they are more appropriately seen as a cognitive boundary.

When applied to the results of contact, creolization implies the blending and mixing of cultural traits. It is the most useful of the three terms mentioned in the preceding paragraph because it recognizes that traits are not uniformly passed in one direction, from the colonial, or dominant, society to the colonized, dominated one. The classic paradigm explaining the process of creolization is a linguistic model that incorporates traits or elements into a "grammar." The traits may be derived from both cultures engaged in interaction while the grammar is thought to be based on the structure of the colonized culture (Ferguson 2000). Many of the colonial contexts for which this model is used involve racial as well as cultural mixture; most occur in the southeastern United States, especially the Caribbean, and pertain to African Americans and Europeans/European Americans. Some recent work has suggested archaeologically accessible criteria for different forms of mixture (Dawdy 2000). However, these analyses pay little attention to the principles regulating the adoption of some elements and the rejection of others. The factors structuring the adoption of new traits are complex, they are not random, and they need to be considered in the local, historicized context.

The concept of acculturation is flawed too. It implies that change is impersonal and mainly unidirectional, that it takes place in cultures as a whole. It denies or ignores agency, the fact that individuals make changes. Change does not occur uniformly across entire cultures or societies; individuals allow greater or lesser access to strangers and are more or less willing to adopt something new, often depending on their status within the system, a phenomenon recognized by anthropologists in the field as affecting the willingness of some, often more marginal, individuals to serve as informants. Systems are mediated through individuals who meet and negotiate in a continuing process. The idea of acculturation, linked in the literature to a linear form of culture change, also suggests that the less powerful of the interacting groups loses its culture, its traits being replaced by those of the dominant party (Alexander 1998:478), whereas in fact the process of change is infinitely more subtle and complex.

The third concept, diffusion, which derives from physics, states that molecules diffuse through an empty space or across permeable boundaries. Like acculturation, it is a mechanistic description of human behavior, ignoring people's ability to adopt or reject attributes, or rework them to fit into their own cultural and material environments. Diffusionist models suggest that cultural traits can be detached from one system and moved to another but give no thought to which traits are movable. In their extreme form, they may count traits shared by frontier and metropole cultures to evaluate the degree of similarity between the two (Jordan-Bychkov and Kaups 1989) and thereby demonstrate that the frontier culture is simpler than the parent or metropole version. However, labeling and quantifying simplicity does not go very far in explaining how the retained traits are chosen, and their symbolic importance as signifiers of "home." Some traits may be retained, modified, or dropped, purely on pragmatic grounds, while others are maintained regardless of how inefficient or illogical their usage. Like the other two approaches, diffusion overlooks the domination context of colonial encounters, the nonlevel playing field on which colonizer and colonized met. All three concepts were initially proposed for situations of "contact," which scholars now recognize as "colonial" (Biolsi, personal communication 2001).

Many early studies of colonial encounters in North America, following Turner (1986), refer to "The Frontier," which conjures up an image of intrepid Euro-Americans advancing into an empty or barely populated land. Although there were specific moments when, as a result of epidemic disease and other factors, North America had relatively unoccupied lands, these areas were indeed occupied, by Indians. Euro-Americans simply did not acknowledge the legitimacy of that occupation. As Cronon (1983) has noted, the manner of Native American land use, and the ways in which it differed from European use, especially in the absence of permanent settlement, offered a convenient rationale for the usurpation of Indian lands. Turner's characterization of the frontier denied that the invaders could benefit from interaction with indigenous people but rather presented the meeting as one between savagery and civilization, with (what Turner saw as) the inevitable triumph of the latter. The notion of a frontier as the place where two forces—peoples or civilizations—met is normative and static (Forbes 1968:206), glossing over the many kinds of connections between individuals whose identities encompassed not just European and Indian, but also priest, soldier, trader, mother, elder, member of the Bear Clan, and so on.

The frontier concept also confuses cultural and spatial edges: it supposes that there is a physical boundary between those involved (Kopytoff 1986) and that encounters occur only at these edges. Although margins were significant in contact situations, the effects of the encounters were by no means limited to physical or social margins. This is particularly clear in relationships between enslaved Africans and masters in the American South, a repressively extreme form of "contact." Perhaps the image of a mosaic or patchwork captures the essence of these encounters better than the linear boundary sometimes associated with the frontier concept (Starna 1991:22), although I prefer the idea of "frontier-as-process" espoused by a number of writers (Billington 1967:7; Green and Pearlman 1985:5; Kopytoff 1987). This model is flexible enough to allow for differing rates and kinds of connection as well as variable forms of encounter in different parts of the colonial setting, for example, identifiable ones such as edges versus centers.

Frontier-as-process recognizes an important aspect of the frontiers encompassed in European expansion, namely, that they are not boundaries but intersections between the (developing or developed) world system or mini-system (Wallerstein 1974; Wolf 1982) and more isolated cultural systems. White's (1991) concept of the Middle Ground offers an elegant example of this contact in process. The Middle Ground was not a place but an accommodation and a system of meaning that evolved between Algonkians and the French, during the seventeenth and eighteenth centuries, in the "pays d'en haut" from the Great Lakes west to the Mississippi. It enabled the two groups to communicate with each other and overcome their mutual misunderstanding, although it was based to some degree on "creative expedient misunderstandings" of what each society believed the other wanted (White 1991:x). The joint creation was based on each side's beliefs about the values and practices of the other, but it only lasted while there was a mutual need for it and eroded when the power balance shifted in favor of the French. White's (1991:33) chronological description of the events in this area provides a complex picture of various indigenous groups (including Huron, Ottawa, Kickapoo, Miami, Fox, Menomini, and others) moving west, dislocated by the Iroquois Beaver Wars, and trying to forge ways of interacting among themselves while simultaneously balancing Jesuit overtures, French fur traders' demands, and French requisitions for military support against the British.

> The alliance endured not because of some mystical affinity between Frenchmen and Indians, nor because Algonquians had been reduced to dependency on the French, but rather because two peoples created an elaborate network of economic, political, cultural, and social ties to meet the demands of a particular historical situation. These ties knit the refugee centers to each other, and each center to the French. Central to this whole process was the mediation of conflicts both between the French and their various allies and among the allies themselves.

White's model may not apply to all colonial situations, but it outlines a method of isolating the forces involved in many cases and demonstrates how the resulting conflicts were resolved while underscoring the temporary nature of the resolution. It is quite relevant to the two cases described in this book.

Ethnicity, Identity, and Nation-States

As new forms of colonialism continue to emerge and globalization and transnational movements expand in scale, the ways in which small groups maintain their identity within larger ones become significant. One clear feature of this process is that boundaries, both cultural (or ethnic) and physical, are always being negotiated (see, for example, Anderson 1983; Barth 1969; Cohen 1993; Dirks 1992; Stoler 1992). As Anderson (1983) explains, outsiders play a pivotal role in defining any group. This can be seen in the formation of European nation-states in particular. The construction of the nation-state depended on small bounded groups that were incorporated as the state was founded. "Multiethnicity and statehood are two sides of the same coin," notes Cohen (1993:233). In some cases, the skills needed to control small "alien" groups were the same as those that facilitated the formation of the centralized state, in a practice Thomas (1994) describes as internal colonialism. The skills necessary to manage such groups shape the internal workings of the political unit and include the ability to mediate disputes, collect tributes, and, most important, assign ranks and enforce the hierarchy of the various groups constituting a single society (Cohen 1993). Political expansion was useful to centralized states in another way, namely, in the provision of meaningful tasks for state armies. Just as the organization of labor for tribute is justified by an existing need to build roads, waterworks, and ultimately large-scale grand monuments, armies must be kept busy or they become demoralized and disintegrate.

It is an easy transition from a state system, thus characterized, to a colonial system. Outsiders are significant here as well, characterized in opposition to Europeans, helping them to define themselves and their habitus. "We" are people who (for example) wash every day, drink tea, have one wife, and worship the Christian God, whereas "they" have different practices. The existence of people external to Europe with very different habits was crucial in this sense, as seen in many contexts (Comaroff and Comaroff 1992). In some settings, the state was solidified by exaggerating differences between colonized and colonizer, although it remained essential to maintain ranked distinctions of class, ethnicity, and gender within the colonial society (Stoler 1992:321), balancing the need to affirm the elite's position in the hierarchy with a need for the allegiance of all Europeans in opposition to colonized indigenous peoples. In situations such as this, the qualities recognized as distinguishing colonizer from colonized were assigned moral values (civilized versus savage, rational versus superstitious, scientific versus barbaric, and the like), enhancing the continuation of colonial work in the name of modernity (Dirks 1992). Hierarchical and ethnic distinctions were often marked by specific attributes (language, clothing, and foodways), many assigned by the colonizers. The manipulation of some of these identity markers by the colonized indicates their importance. Colonial encounters forged European identities as well as indigenous ones. What are today referred to as "the Dutch people" (Rothschild 1990) and "the Spanish people" (Bustamonte 1989) consisted of a series of separately governed provinces prior to their New World colonial experiments.

Identities continue to be defined and manipulated in the modern world. In twentieth-century North America, there is an interesting tension relating to the use of tribal identities. On the one hand, the U.S. government has assigned increased value to the concept of a tribal identity in conjunction with land claims cases; on the other hand, some Native Americans have found it more useful to replace the European-defined notion of "tribe" with the larger identity of "Indian." Both of these stances are enacted in legal issues and Pan-Indianism has emerged with particular force in reference to the Native American Graves Protection and Repatriation Act (NAGPRA), with Native Americans claiming that specific affiliation between a set of bones or ritual objects and a descendant tribal group need not be established for reburial or repatriation to occur. Pan-Indianism is also relevant in urban settings, where it becomes a unifying device as many of the traditional markers of identity (language, dress, foodways) have been eliminated. It is ironic that some of the power that Indians hold today is the result of their struggles throughout the nineteenth and twentieth centuries, during which the need to fight the federal government strengthened indigenous political structures (Cornell 1988).

Colonial Expansion

Although colonial systems have important political and sociocultural functions, the primary rationale for colonial enterprise is the economic one. Notwithstanding the humanitarian and moralistic rhetoric surrounding such an enterprise, a colony was meant to generate economic profit; if it did not, it would not be maintained (Furnivall [1941]1978). Its basic purpose was to extract various resources using indigenous labor from the underdeveloped periphery for the benefit of the densely settled metropolitan core (Wallerstein 1974; Wolf 1982). The labor and resources normally used for subsistence were allocated to cash crops or support for colonizers (Alexander 1998:382; Santley and Alexander 1992), with a dramatic impact on the colonized, as seen in the details of the two case studies discussed in this volume.

European colonial expansion falls into two types, linked to different periods. The one being considered here was characteristic of the sixteenth to eighteenth centuries and can be portrayed as romantic in contrast to the more rational (Fabian 1983) colonial efforts of the nineteenth to twentieth centuries, which were affected by the Enlightenment, evolutionary theory, and a concomitant racism (Thomas 1994:77). These later efforts were informed by travelers' accounts and anthropological discussions, and they presented a more scientific guise (Dirks 1992; Smith 1992). Colonists and visitors collected things (plants, animals, objects) and information—on customs, geography, population, and the like. Appreciation went hand in hand with appropriation.

Both the Pueblo-Spanish and Mohawk-Dutch cases belong in the earlier period, although they were quite different, especially in their political economies. The Spanish encounter was typical of the Renaissance (and even Medieval) model of conquest and conversion (Farriss 1984; Thomas 1994), or, to use Anderson's (1983) characterization, they were enmeshed in the religious community and dynastic realm, while the Dutch, as merchant capitalists, foreshadowed the modern state, especially in their involvement with the Reformation and print capitalism. In the Renaissance form of expansion, the possibility of saving the souls of heathens made the colonizers, at least potentially, willing to include them in the realm of humanity, as they became brothers and sisters in Christ. The heathens were viewed as missing something—"sans roi, foi et loi" (Thomas 1994:72)—that could be added, although if or when they refused conversion, the view of their humanity changed markedly. Since the Dutch had no interest in conversion at this stage, the colonized seem to have been regarded as alien beings.

These early nations employed a fascinating, and quite revealing, array of ceremonial possessions of new territories to legitimize taking over indigenous lands when first landing in the New World. British ritual focused on settling the land and building houses and gardens. The French relied on grand processions and entrance ceremonies after they had received signs that they interpreted as welcoming. The Spanish *Requerimiento,* read in Spanish to uncomprehending Native Americans upon entering their settlements, was a warlike statement that threatened the Indians with dire consequences if they did not accept Catholicism and the rule of the king (I am sure no one even pretended the auditors could understand any of the long message). The Dutch and the Portuguese had slightly different attitudes toward legitimacy: the Portuguese claimed lands on the basis of having been the first (Europeans) to discover them, whereas the Dutch focused their energies on describing and mapping them (Seed 1995).

Understanding Colonial Interactions

One's view of what happened during these colonial encounters depends on the kinds of information available about them, as well as the sources, their reliability, and their biases. To complicate matters, some kinds of data are more credible than others, but it is difficult to assess their credibility. Historic accounts privilege the European perspective, oral history is often written in symbolic language that outsiders may not understand, and archaeological data are often not as comprehensive in their coverage of multiple aspects of culture as one would wish. All these issues relate to the postmodern question of how (and whether) one can know another. The information that is available comes from a variety of sources: archaeology, historic documents, anthropological accounts, and oral history. Needless to say, each of these has its strengths and weaknesses. For the period covered in this work, there are no ethnographic accounts of colonial impact, although there are reports on subsequent periods.

Archaeological Information on Interaction

Archaeological data on material culture shared by the colonizing and the colonized societies and on the mechanisms of its transmission offer a unique window on the nature of colonial interaction. I concentrate on two classes of archaeological data that manifest aspects of social life in material ways: interaction promoted through the exchange of goods and labor and the alterations of production that inevitably accompany this exchange in a colonial setting; and the spatial distribution of settlements, structures, and activities, including the construction of landscape. It is in the details of daily life that the actual connections between these groups are visible. How did European settlers subsist? Where did Native Americans and Europeans live in relationship to one another? What kinds of mundane objects—such as dishes—did the Dutch and Spanish use, and who made them? What European objects did Native Americans adopt and in what quantities? What kinds of objects (including food and clothing as well as ornaments and tools) were offered, desired, or demanded? Which ones were provided and which not? How was indigenous labor appropriated and what forms (from subsistence to sex) did it take? How were sexual relations between Indians and Europeans enacted? I discuss a number of these issues with the help of anthropological exchange theory and history, which are essential to the understanding of these processes. Other relevant questions I ask are who was involved, and what mechanisms of distribution pertained? Often these channels privilege powerful, usually male, individuals. In the societies considered here, however, power and agency were more widely distributed than in highly stratified systems (Crown 2000), and the manipulation of imported goods may have offered nondominant individuals a means of acquiring power. Goods find their way to women, to low-status men, and others.

The Acquisition of Things and People

Elements of the material world are significant monitors of connection, expressing interaction through exchange or other forms of acquisition. Understanding the mechanisms and meanings involved with the acquisition of objects and associated services is absolutely essential to any study of colonial encounters. The degree to which each party uses goods provided by the other and the manner by which goods are obtained are among the most important variables to consider in studying colonial interactions as they reflect power relations quite directly.

> There was nothing new about the working methods used for establishing more or less humane contact with primitive peoples. . . . To establish one's peaceful intentions one began by gifting. . . . So Cook took with him on his third

> voyage [in 1776] thousands of articles from Matthew Boulton's factory, Soho, in Birmingham—axes, chisels, saws, metal buttons, beads, mirrors, etc—as presents, and for trading. (Smith 1992:208)

In a situation of contact between two groups that lack a common language, the first act between them often involves the offering or exchange of things; this is a form of communication, one of several that evolve in intercultural settings, including the exchange of words, actions, and services or labor. As is appropriate to a system of communication, the things themselves contain a great deal of coded information that pertains to the attitude of the giver and beliefs about the recipients, is relevant to the objects involved, and carries implications about expected reciprocal behavior. However, it is a flawed system of communication as the messages are often not decipherable across cultural boundaries, the objects themselves have different meanings to the peoples involved, and exchange is viewed in contrasting ways in varying economic systems (as gifts that require a reciprocal gift, as tribute, as a rational economic act, or some combination of these). The act of offering and exchanging goods is, by definition, an economic act because it concerns material things. It is also a political act in that it is an attempt by both parties involved, not just the colonizing society, to exert power and create a specific outcome, although the agency of the colonized has not always been recognized. Exchange is also a social act, connecting individuals, expressing and redefining status relationships.

In considering the role of specific items in colonial exchange and their impact as carriers of ideas, Douglas and Isherwood (1996:xv) state, "Goods are neutral, their uses are social; they can be used as bridges or fences." However, the goods exchanged in colonial situations were not all equal, and some played a greater part in interaction than others, because they were more in demand or because they had greater symbolic significance. Objects may reflect ideas and assumed qualities of the culture from which they come, but they are multivocal, and many qualities may be projected onto them. The concept of indigenous choice—which encompasses the ways in which Indians selected specific European objects as well as their reasons for doing so—has received considerable attention (Axtell 1992; Bradley 1987; Hamell 1983; Saunders 1999).

The objects that Europeans initially wanted from indigenous peoples were food, shelter, and labor services, including sex. In each case study, colonists were initially interested in the extraction of specific items—furs in the Northeast and minerals in the Southwest—although food items were also demanded in both settings, and some important objects manufactured by Native Americans such as pottery and textiles were in demand in New Mexico.

THE USES OF GOODS

An important question to ask at the outset is why did either group want the belongings of the other? Furthermore, how were specific items selected? How much choice did each party have in exchange situations? And how similar was the two societies' use of a particular type of object? Thomas (1991) finds a wide variety of objects—from food to women, from valuables to services—exchanged by both sets of participants in colonial systems of the Pacific, for example. He considers the range of behaviors, reuse, and reinterpretations of the belongings of others, whether acquired through trade, purchase, gift, or outright theft. Later on, when museum collecting was under way during the nineteenth century, Europeans and Americans sought other kinds of indigenous objects for their symbolic properties, perceiving them as expressions of the group that made them, rather than as objects with a specific history. Objects were taken as representing a class of things. Most collectors did not record the name of the person who made the item, but only the tribal group name. Missionaries considered them symbols of the barbarian condition that characterized group life (Thomas 1991:163). At this time they acquired market value and in some cases became art objects: "Aestheticizing a spear or club is inevitably a political act that presupposes some denial of former context and of the capacity of indigenous producers to perpetuate their own uses and constructions of things" (Thomas 1991:174). Thomas finds comparable practices within indigenous societies, whereby alienated and alien things are incorporated, redefined, and reconstituted from their previous meaning or use. The cultural and social significance of the ability to keep certain important items is demonstrated in this work too, for it makes clear that every society has things of value that empowered their owners, who would have tried to keep them out of exchange (Weiner 1992), although this was not always possible (Ewers 1981). Today Indian peoples have asserted ownership in relation to cultural heritage and objects with symbolic weight such as Iroquois wampum belts, Zuni war gods, and the like.

The two case studies described in this book reflect contrasting views of exchange nested in colonial systems. Perhaps, then, as Thomas argues, colonial settings, while all different, share the endlessly shifting condition of contact situations, in which events, the actions of individuals, or objects have different meanings depending on the context of the moment. A person or a thing will be readily offered/alienated on an ordinary day but not on a day of ritual significance or in a politically important locale. These statuses also change throughout an encounter situation, in response to particular economic or political factors, local historic circumstances, disease rates, the amount of rain, and an endless list of other variables.

Creating Desire

Colonial powers had to create a desire for the objects that they offered in each setting. To what degree did desire operate on both sides of the exchange? If demand is socially determined (Appadurai 1986:11), what mechanisms of power were brought into play in creating it? Were elites or marginal individuals more likely to be innovators? How does desire/demand evolve over time and place? Hatley (1993:45) suggests that perhaps the wish of the seller was paramount in creating demand for specific items, but most analysts ignore the motivation and agency of natives in their desire for European goods, because they assume that the supposedly apparent technological superiority of the goods was the reason and that indigenous peoples would immediately recognize it; that white commodities are irresistible and immediately desired, regardless of their cultural cost (Thomas 1991:87); and that indigenous peoples, once exposed, would organize their lives so as to obtain more of them. One example is provided by the Inuit, who "forsook their traditional hunting ways (in which trapping was not a dominant activity) to trap the furs that would get them trade goods—guns, bullets, knives, flour, tea and tobacco" (McCreery 1983:4, in Thomas 1991:85). And the Iroquois at the end of the seventeenth century, are claimed as another: "most of Iroquoia had absolute dependence on articles of European manufacture. Once the axes, knives, kettles, shovels, guns, cloth and many other articles became common everyday utilities and necessities, there was no turning back to flint tools and points, stone pipes and axes, clay cooking vessels and bone awls" (Rumrill 1985:1). These statements are not borne out by the evidence.

There is little support for the imagined universal acceptance and immediate demand. The indigenous acceptance of European goods was quite variable and slower than many observers anticipated, and it did not follow a linear trajectory of gradual increase over time in most North American Indian settings. Rogers (1990) and Hatley (1993) describe indigenous desire for European things waxing and waning, and White (1991:131–133) reports that Algonquians made limited use of Euro-American goods, desiring primarily clothing, ornaments, gunpowder, and some metal tools, which they acquired at a relatively slow rate. A period of learning to appreciate objects and understand their usage was necessary, as is evident in the common "misuse" of things or their use in ways other than the offering society intended, so that a tool might be adapted for a completely different purpose: kettles were used as raw material for projectile points (Bradley 1987), hatchets and axes as neck ornaments, and socks as tobacco pouches (Axtell 1992: 160). The Cherokee reworked pieces of cast iron pots into hoes, while fragments of mirrors or pottery became symbols of power, and jewelry was used as grave goods (Hatley 1993:45). European paint, mirrors, and such were quite powerful to the Cherokee—almost as powerful as weapons—and guns were valued for noise and smoke as much as for their shooting ability (Hatley 1993:47).

Once a trading relationship is established and goods are available within an indigenous society, issues surrounding their distribution throughout the group become significant. They may be used to enhance existing status systems or to reorganize them. Hatley considers the formation of indigenous desire for European goods among the Cherokee in the Southeast. Women, as traditional agricultural producers, had authority in trading situations but were apparently rather cautious in parting with subsistence items (Hatley 1993:44). As in many other settings, much exchange took place through intermediaries, who used their position to gain quantities of European objects for themselves and tried to protect their own superior access to goods. These go-betweens, in keeping most villagers from contact with the colonists, separated the kind of trade that occurred within a village—organized by reciprocity and kinship—from commerce. In other groups too, it was common to guard the role of middleman. Mohawks were quite protective of their intermediate position (Richter 1992), and the Arikara discouraged Euro-Americans from going upriver (Rogers 1990). Access to certain European objects are known to have had an impact on social structure, circumventing existing hierarchies.

The groups of interest in this book differed dramatically with respect to shared material culture. In the Hudson and Mohawk Valleys, Dutch traders practiced commodity exchange after a brief period of gift exchange. The flow of goods was substantial and went in one direction only, introducing many European things into Iroquois lives. The Mohawks produced beaver skins, acceding to Dutch, French, and English demand. However, they did not initially regard European goods as commodities; they distributed these objects according to traditional systems of redistribution based on prestige and obligation. Subsequently they came to understand and practice some aspects of commodity exchange.

In this setting, Indians were consumers and had the ability to demand certain kinds of goods. They were reportedly impressed by many European objects, including those that represented magical or quasi-magical powers: clocks, books, guns (which "spoke"). The things that they desired as consumers fell into two classes. The first consisted of items believed to reflect the power, or what is referred to as the metaphysics, of light (Hamell 1983) and its associated supernatural qualities: "Light, dazzling colors and shiny matter indicated the presence of supernatural beings and essence" (Saunders 1999:245). The production of glass, common in sixteenth-century Europe, was "regarded as a supernatural and magical talent" by Native Americans (Saunders 1999:247). Certain colors of glass beads, especially white and blue (Axtell 1988:173; Hamell 1983:6), and mirrors and shiny objects such as buttons or brass were desirable for similar reasons, while red objects such as beads (made of native copper or shell) symbolized life and blood (Hamell 1983:7).

The second class of objects had practical utility for Indians. Foremost among these were cloth (red, blue, and black were favorite colors at different times; Axtell 1988:171) and metal—used for tools such as axes, hatchets, awls, chisels, knives, fishhooks, hoes, and kettles and sometimes reworked into ornaments (Axtell 1992: 135, 139). All of these items offered genuine labor-saving advantages. Duffel cloth was used for clothing and saved women hours of processing deerskin, while metal tools cut trees faster, made formidable weapons, and lasted longer than stone tools. Guns were impractical—they were expensive, unreliable, and reloading was slow (Axtell 1992:142)—but nevertheless desired, perhaps for their loud noise, as already mentioned, and associated symbolic connotations of power. Another commodity often involved in trade was liquor, but it was a different type of commodity, regarded with ambivalence by the Mohawks and devoid of practical value. Hence it is difficult to know whether the provision of liquor to Native Americans was a deliberately malicious act intended to disable them or simply a mischievous one. This trade is a complex subject and not relevant to the discussion here.

The Cherokee in the Southeast had similar desires. In initial exchange they wanted clothing, guns, and ammunition; they offered deerskins and some slaves. Subsequently, horses were offered by Europeans who desired medicinal herbs, cane mats, and chestnuts (Hatley 1993:32–33). Hatley (1993:10) suggests that the Cherokee wish for European cloth indicates conspicuous consumption, but this is a superficial interpretation, neglecting its importance as a status indicator—a man would present himself as "naked" if he lacked cloth. The potency of symbolic factors in exchange is further illustrated by the report that the Cherokee "King" "gave all their lands to the King of Great Britain" in a small leather bag of dirt. Apparently it was received as a literal transfer of property rather than the intended gesture of alliance (Hatley 1993:76). This illustrates again how common cross-cultural misinterpretations were.

Exchange in the Rio Grande Valley was quite different from that in eastern North America. A much smaller quantity of European goods was available for acquisition, and thus material exchange was less common. It began with a short gifting period and was followed by an intense unremitting demand for Pueblo labor, services, and products by a dominating and extractive Spanish system. The Spanish "offered" Christianity and civilization to the Pueblos in exchange for their labor, a further indication of the extent of attempted domination. However, material flows in the Southwest were bilateral, and Spanish and Pueblo material culture showed much greater similarity than was true among the Dutch and Mohawks. In each case, goods from the other society were used variably; some served primarily as identity markers, while others served more utilitarian purposes.

Exchange in the Southwest offered less access to European goods than was the case in many eastern situations, because the New Mexican frontier was distant from sources and provisioning caravans reached the frontier infrequently. Any object that made its way to the Rio Grande Valley had to be transported from Spain to Mexico and then over a long and dangerous route that took between 6 and 18 months to cross (Palmer 1993). After the initial period of gift-giving, goods that arrived were usually required first by the settlers, both clerical and lay, with little left for trade. While the Pueblos may have desired certain European things, they were unlikely to receive them, and it was only when they were able to take them that they obtained items such as sheep (during the Pueblo Revolt) or horses. However, it is easy to imagine things that would have been most meaningful to them, as symbols of Spanish power. During the revolt, some of these symbolic items were destroyed, especially those connected with churches and missionaries; bell clappers were cut up for practical use in at least one instance (Hackett 1937:375). In other Puebloan contexts, resistance to the Spanish is clearly visible in the alteration and destruction of European objects and in the rejection of Spanish ceramic forms (see chapter 5).

To obtain a complete picture, one must study the adoption and uses of foreign material culture in both directions, in both case studies. That is why the comparative approach is taken here. Indeed, it reveals the variable nature of colonial exchange. In the Southwest, for instance, the Spanish adopted many indigenous traits, objects, and practices (food, clothing, pottery, and even lithic tools), probably more than the Pueblos borrowed, but in the Hudson Valley, the Dutch acquired few things, except for food items (deer and corn, in particular), and one Iroquois-made thing, a *notas,* or skin bag (see figure 5.3), while the Mohawks incorporated and used many European objects. The reasons for indigenous people to adopt European goods are complex. At times it was a way to gain power, at other times it had practical value, and at still others it served to mark identity or aspiration. There were fewer power-related reasons for Europeans to adopt indigenous things, and probably more pragmatic ones (chapters 3 through 5 present some examples of objects adopted). Some items clearly served to define identity, clothing being the best and most visible example. I suggest that the southwestern situation, with its biological and cultural mixing and associated racism, is one in which the stabilization of social categories would have been desirable to all parties, but only clear for Pueblo and Spanish groups, whereas the wide range of *castas* (a series of racially defined categories created by the Spanish colonial system) would have been more complexly signaled and more subject to manipulation.

MECHANISMS OF ACQUISITION

Objects of the other society may be acquired through several mechanisms: demand, tribute, trade, barter, gift-giving, and theft. All of these apply to a number of classes of goods and services. In the colonial context, there was a disparity between the models of "fair exchange" held by each group. European traders operated by and large in the rational system of a market economy, whereas Indian peoples were integrated by premarket practices such as redistribution and reciprocity. This disparity was central to many encounters, including those discussed here.

Initial gifts offered by colonizers are meant to show peaceful intentions and be attractive. Characteristically, Europeans began these encounters by offering ornaments, things that were thought to be appealing to "natives" (shiny glass beads and mirrors), while indigenous peoples were more likely to give food and water, greatly desired after long sea voyages, as well as some offerings—the calumet and tobacco (Axtell 1992:45), or a sprinkle of cornmeal (Gutièrrez 1991)—that had ritual significance to them. Columbus noted "they brought [us] skeins of spun cotton, parrots, darts and other trifles" (Todorov 1984:35). Each party behaved according to rules that made sense to it, and there is reason to think that each was trying to incorporate the other into its emic system. Native American offerings of the pipe and tobacco, or the sprinkling of cornmeal, were rituals of humanization; these things were always offered to newcomers. In some settings, indigenous peoples offered their daughters in marriage to the important and powerful European strangers, surely a precious gift, but also a way to incorporate the newcomers into their system and provide potential links between the groups (Axtell 1992:49).

After an initial period of ornamental gifts, the would-be colonizers might offer functional European objects in trade. Some items were withheld in order to maintain control—things such as guns, which represented European "magic and power," or domestic animals, essential for survival. When guns were finally given to Indians in the Hudson Valley it was for reasons that were important to Europeans, either because a competing European colonial group was offering them or because they provided protection to Europeans; in the Southwest, domestic animals were taken by the colonized group. It is often assumed that the provision of various functional goods led the recipients into dependency. By and large, exchange has been construed as creating power for European givers but not for indigenous givers, and as making natives dependent on Europeans for tools (White 1991). By contrast, little has been said about the often equal or greater dependency of Europeans on Indians for subsistence items. This difference in perception is in the eye of the beholder, or writer of contact-period history, and reflects the pervasiveness of colonialism, extending to contemporary beliefs about colonial encounters. Food exchange is a subset of the exchange of other kinds of objects. While foods themselves may be less likely to carry symbolic loads than do other items, the mechanisms of exchange are often the same.

In a similar vein, colonists required services of a colonized people. These varied from subsistence labor to sex, whether voluntary or involuntary. Additional demands existed for guides, soldiers, church workers, allies, and interpreters. Types of labor extended from slavery through indentured servitude to reimbursed work (a rarity), with indirect labor requirements created by the beaver trade or the demand for basic food provisions. Sexual contacts ranged from rape to marriage and family formation, with various intermediate situations. One particularly horrifying version, reported in Todorov (1984:149), is told by a noble from Savona:

> I captured a very beautiful Carib woman, whom the Lord Admiral gave to me, and with whom, having brought her into my cabin, and she being naked as is their custom, I conceived the desire to take my pleasure. I wanted to put my desire to execution, but she was unwilling for me to do so, and treated me with her nails in such wise that I would have preferred never to have begun. But seeing this (In order to tell you the whole even to the end), I took a rope-end and thrashed her well, following which she produced such screaming and wailing as would cause you not to believe your ears. Finally we reached an agreement such that, I can tell you, she seemed to have been raised in a veritable school of harlots.

There is no way of knowing how many times scenarios such as these were repeated or what other forms of exploitation and abuse were practiced, but it is certain that this was not a unique experience. Colonial court records in New Mexico document many instances of the abuse of women, even practiced by friars (Hackett 1937:213, 214, 216, 217, 225). An important and often overlooked mechanism by which similarity in material culture develops relates to the extraction of women's services and the concomitant appearance of women's possessions in domestic assemblages. Colonizing men who do not have consorts from their own culture may form "temporary" connections with indigenous women, beginning with sexual services. Often these become longer-term associations, and women come to provide a range of domestic services (see chapter 4).

Spatial Reflections of Interaction

Another important class of archaeological data involves the distribution of peoples on the land. Beginning with settlement pattern, it is a truism that, at a simple level, settlement structure reflects social structure. This is manifest in these two colonial case studies in the placement of the European community in relation to the indigenous one. Spanish missionaries moved into pueblos and settlers lived nearby; the Dutch built a fort at a distance from the Mohawks. This single fact reflects major differences in attitude. At the level of individual structures, the archaeological analysis of household architecture and deposits may identify the social rank and ethnicity of its individual members, often linked in Spanish America to gender, as convincingly detailed by Deagan (1983).

On a larger scale, the landscape of a people is a cultural construction, and two peoples living in the same physical space will have very different landscapes, organized around resources, needs, production processes, important figures (both human and spiritual), travel routes, and culturally significant places. As complex as the landscape of another may be (Basso 1996), one measure of the degree to which European and Native American lives became connected may be seen in the congruity of their landscapes, or lack of it. Because the indigenous societies studied here did not signal important places with elaborate architecture, many crucial sites may be so ephemerally marked as to be almost archaeologically invisible, unless they were used redundantly. Of course, landscape consists not only of physical places. To understand how a people viewed their surroundings—the natural and the supernatural, the physical and the social dimensions—one must look at different cognitive planes and at past perceptions, as well as activity patterns. As Schama (1995:6) says, "Landscape is a work of the mind. Its scenery is built up as much from strata of memory as from layers of rock." These strata are derived from culture, among other factors: "What lies beyond the windowpane of our apprehension needs a design before we can properly discern its form. . . . And it is culture, convention, and cognition that makes that design" (Magritte, cited in Schama 1995:12). Further, humans do not passively live on/in the land or landscape but are continually manipulating it, modifying it, and reconceiving it.

Although many kinds of information are available on European landscapes, one must be careful not to overemphasize places where power resided and neglect other potentially significant ones. Caution should also be exercised in relying on images from the historic period, which provide valuable data but may be biased. Realistic art and perspective began in the Renaissance in concert with a growing sense of the disengagement of humans from nature, which allowed them to stand back and look at nature, and ultimately try to control it. Quite a different notion of landscape underlies the origin myth of the Zuni people in New Mexico, which has passed down through oral history to modern times and describes their wanderings in search of their "middle place" after emerging through four dark underworlds (Ferguson et al. 1985). The European concept of landscape exists on one plane, that of the earth's surface, and it gives priority to the visual, while the surfaces of Zuni (and many other Indian peoples') imagination included the underworld and ether, as well as the ground.

Changing landscapes can be seen in territorial patterns among mobile hunter-foragers and their reactions to the establishment of a mission, farm, and trading post in the Zeekoe Valley of South Africa (Sampson 1988). As new foci of movement develop and foragers begin to "map on" and incorporate new places in their territory, it is clear that a change in the foragers' landscape is under way. The resulting spatial changes imply changing perceptions of the land, reflecting new social and economic patterns. This relatively subtle form of change is part of a colonial encounter but could be overlooked if attention is paid mainly to the frontiers or the boundaries between an aboriginal society and a European settlement. Indeed, alterations of landscape and the intersection between the colonizers' and colonized landscapes provide important clues to the impact of the colonizing society and should be a part of any examination of contact.

Documentary History, Oral History

One of the advantages of doing archaeology in the colonial period is the existence of many forms of documents that describe reactions to and incidents of the encounters and provide numerous tabulations.[1] These are, of course, incomplete and biased in both predictable and unpredictable ways. The anticipated biases derive

1. Some of the most important sources I used include Charles Gehring's translations of Dutch documents for the New York State Library's New Netherland Project, especially H. M. van den Bogaert's (1988) 1634 trip into Mohawk country; Edmund O'Callaghan's (1849–1851) *Documentary History of the State of New York;* and Arnold van Laer's (1924) translation of "Documents Relating to New Netherland 1624–1626." In New Mexico, a number of scholars have translated imported documents, beginning in the 1920s and 1930s with Charles W. Hackett (1923, 1926, 1937), George P. Hammond and Agapito Rey (1924, 1927), and France V. Scholes (1929). More recently, the Vargas project, led by John Kessell and stimulated by the Quincentenary, has continued systematic translations of a series of works. David Snow (1992a) reprinted many significant documents. And James Ivey has provided two documents relating to the famine in the late 1660s (BNM legajos).

from the writer's specific point of view related to his (these writers are almost entirely men) mission or goal, and the fact that many of the documents only record specific forms of interaction: governmental or administrative, economic extraction and exchange, success in imposing a new religious form or social mores. Some documents were designed to advance the colonial project, offering glowing descriptions of a wonderful land of beauty and plenty: Daniel Denton ([1670]1966:5), for example, wrote of plentiful supplies of horses, cattle, sheep, and hogs and of rivers well furnished with fish. Others were meant to simply record events and transactions. Owing to the loss of records by the colonists or their deliberate destruction by the colonized (for example, during the Pueblo Revolt), they exhibit a random incompleteness.

It is important to note that the two case studies are not entirely comparable. The Rio Grande Valley is a larger area than the Mohawk/Hudson and includes many more archaeological sites from different autonomous groups of people. The Mohawks represented one people, and they were far fewer (approximately 8,000 to 12,000) than the colonized in the Rio Grande Valley in about 1630 (about 60,000). Another contrast is found in the differences between the archaeological and documentary data in the two cases: each has some weaknesses. Dean Snow has compiled the Mohawk data in one place, making them readily available. Archaeological information for the Southwest has been collected under many different kinds of circumstances by different archaeologists, although they are all stored in the New Mexico state site files (Archaeological Records Management Section, or ARMS) and are easy to gain access to. Since the Dutch colonial period was brief in comparison with the Spanish, the records there are somewhat scantier; although some documents from the Southwest were destroyed during the Pueblo Revolt. However, the letters written by some individuals (Oñate and some Spanish fathers) provide a richly detailed picture of interactions from their viewpoint.

Oral history offers an alternative perspective on colonial situations, preserving some of the indigenous views of past situations, including those of contact. Unfortunately, it is rarely available to those who are not members of the tribal group. What there is has been written down rather recently and is not easy to interpret, as it does not reflect the same ideas of causality as European history. Written versions of oral accounts are more readily available for the Hopi than for other southwestern groups, for reasons that are unclear. For the Iroquois, the only oral accounts that seem to have been preserved (or at least that have been published) are speeches made to representatives of the British government rather late in the colonial period. It may be that oral accounts are closely held by modern Iroquois, but I have found no evidence of them.

Another form of vernacular history used in this study consists of "captivity narratives," stories told by Europeans who were captured by Indians and recorded upon their return home. They often describe details of daily life (dress, subsistence practices, and the like), although they are mixed with a great deal of commentary and need to be read carefully to get at the useful information. Most of these narratives pertain to the American Northeast.

ETHNOGRAPHY AND ANTHROPOLOGY

Although it is clear that artists take "artistic license," up to about the 1980s scholars were inclined to believe that anthropological accounts were relatively free of bias. However, as they have since realized, anthropology was inextricably connected to colonial enterprise, with funding and careers built on the observation and description of "primitives" and "others" (Thomas 1994; Vincent 1990). The origins of anthropology as a social science overlap in time and in procedure with nineteenth-century colonial practice. Colonists as well as early travelers provided extensive descriptions, reporting on their observations and collecting activities—some even brought living members of remote societies to Europe and put them on display. To be sure, the goals of colonial agents and anthropologists differed. While anthropologists wanted to understand aspects of social organization (such as kinship and caste), political systems, and other components of culture for intellectual reasons, colonial administrators had a more pragmatic use for the same information. Data collected by anthropologists have served colonial and other political ends; in some cases, anthropologists knowingly passed on their understanding of non-Western cultures to help their governments (Vincent 1990). In others, colonial agents acquired the information, to expedite the efficient extraction of labor and goods and to maintain order and control. European colonial encounters only became anthropological subject matter when there were virtually no exotic preliterate societies left (Beidelman 1983); anthropologists then expanded their gaze to contemporary Western society. Since the mid-1980s, sociocultural anthropology has produced a large literature on colonial encounters, some of which is important to this study (Chrisman and Williams 1993; Cohn 1996; Comaroff and Comaroff 1991; Cooper and Stoler 1997; Dirks 1992, 2001; Prakash 1995; Thomas 1991, 1994; Young 1995).

The Case Studies

THE NATIVE AMERICANS

Although the Pueblos and the Mohawks were both agricultural peoples who lived in large villages structured by matrilineal clan-based descent systems, they differed in important ways, especially in their environmental settings. Agriculture was more difficult in the Southwest than in the Northeast, and overall population density was lower. The period before European contact in the Southwest was one of increasing migration, at a greater scale than anything preceding or following it (Spielmann 1998:16). Peoples in both areas used relocation as an adaptive strategy. Neither group had a rigid sociopolitical hierarchy, but both had men's societies (such as curing societies and kiva groups) that cut across the clan system. Clans were grouped into moieties.

When the Dutch entered the Hudson Valley in 1614, the Mohawks were part of a confederacy of five peoples—the Oneidas, Onondagas, Cayugas, Senecas, and themselves— known as the Great League of Peace and Power. The league existed primarily to maintain peace among its members, who also served as allies for defense, supported each other in treaties, and participated in condolence rituals. It had no centralized political structure, although its functions included the selection of leaders and making of treaties. Interestingly, there is no evidence to suggest that it formed the basis of an economic network; its members appear to have taken part in little significant exchange of goods, except for ritual items such as pipes. The exchange may also have facilitated the flow of raw materials from distant sources.

Spielmann (1994b:45) suggests that there may have been links among some Rio Grande Pueblo groups, creating one or more "clustered confederacies" in the Galisteo Basin and the Salinas and Piro areas, for example. In her view, a Pueblo confederacy would have been similar to that of the Huron, and somewhat less centralized than that of the Iroquois, but motivated similarly by the need for allies. An important distinction between Hudson River Valley and Rio Grande Valley peoples is that the latter area seems to have functioned as an economic-interaction sphere for most of the Pueblo period, visible in the distribution of pottery types, perhaps accompanying the exchange of food and other resources in an agriculturally marginal area, and distributing exotic imported goods (Riley 1987).

THE EUROPEANS

The Spanish were still primarily a medieval, agrarian society, just beginning to enter the modern mercantile world. Their forays into the "New World" took place within the context of empire building; hence they perceived those they encountered as potential vassals, but also as members of the royal kingdom once they had been converted to Christianity and become properly civilized. Missionary activity, backed by a religious structure, was a crucial part of their entire enterprise. A separate secular administrative structure also existed and was responsible for governing the colony and extracting its wealth. From many points of view, the New Mexico experiment was a very minor part of Spain's imperial effort in the New World and a failure. Economically, the colony was a financial drain, costing the crown more than it produced. Further, the conversion of souls could only have been regarded as a mixed success, since missionaries were forced to accede to Pueblo demands after the revolt. Most Pueblo peoples finally incorporated elements of Christianity, but they ended up with a pragmatic religious mixture that included traditional components as well as Christian ritual and focused on specific goals, such as the success of the harvest. The Pueblo Revolt, in 1680, ejected Spanish settlers, soldiers, and missionaries, but after the reconquista the number of settlers increased and the colony took hold, with Spanish governance lasting formally until 1821.

By contrast, the largely urban, worldly, and ambitious Protestant Dutch, having thrown off Catholicism and the Spanish yoke after 70 years of war (Wolf 1982: 119), were at the forefront of the modern world in their global approach to economic expansion. They developed colonial enterprises in a number of places during the seventeenth century, notably the Caribbean, Brazil, and Batavia (today's Indonesia). As mercantile capitalists, they were concerned with the acquisition of raw materials and the accumulation of goods. Four aspects of merchant capitalism as described by Sider (1986) fit the Dutch-Mohawk situation well: (1) commodities were acquired from communities that organized their own labor; (2) domination existed at the point of exchange, not production; (3) the community controlled the reproduction of conditions for production: and (4) producing communities were incorporated into the larger system in a way that made clear to them that they were different from and weaker than those in power. As a result, any decline in the nonrenewable resource being "produced" would have left the community without recourse: no help could be anticipated from its trading "partners," and no other commodity could be substituted for the declining one.

The Dutch colony in New Netherland had a relatively short life (from 1614 to 1664), although it existed long enough to make a huge impact on the Mohawks. Dutch influence extended beyond this brief period, completely altering the lives of not only the Mohawks but also other Indian groups in the Hudson Valley. The colony focused almost exclusively on the fur trade. Its emphasis on trade and commodification is reflected in a wry statement attributed to a Montagnais Naskapi: "The beaver does everything perfectly well, it makes kettles, hatchets, swords, knives and bread; and, in short it makes everything" (Thwaites 1959:6:297).

It is somewhat artificial to consider the Dutch alone among European peoples in the Hudson Valley. The English and French were also present, either directly or indirectly, and shared similar goals; all interacted with and influenced one another. It is also artificial to ignore other Iroquoian and Algonkian peoples in the Northeast, as well as those further south and west in what is today New Jersey and Pennsylvania. For the purposes of this study, however, the primary interest is the Dutch and Mohawks, and to some extent the British after 1664.

The Effects of Geography and Economy

Geographic location had a major impact on colonial settlement. The Hudson Valley was easily accessible to Europeans, and many settled there, although the Dutch did have problems attracting permanent residents. By contrast, the Spanish could only reach the Rio Grande Valley by overland caravan from Mexico City, a long and difficult route. As a result, a much smaller quantity of material culture was brought into the Rio Grande region. The prodigious quantities of European trade goods introduced into the Hudson Valley had a major impact on the types of change occurring there.

The geographic and environmental differences between the two areas had other consequences. The increased population caused by the influx of Europeans required more food, which was provided at least in part by indigenous people. As already mentioned, the Spanish missionaries and colonists made substantial direct demands on local labor, causing more immediate stress. As epidemic disease tore through native populations, labor burdens increased dramatically, to impossible levels. The Spanish did introduce a number of new food sources, notably sheep, which were eventually incorporated into Pueblo subsistence, but these sources also altered and degraded the environment. Dutch demands did not focus directly on food items to a major extent, although there was some trade for deer and corn. On the other hand, Mohawk subsistence and sociopolitical relations were reorganized to meet this need and provide the desired furs. A cycle of disease, which reduced the Mohawk population, and warfare driven in part by competition for furs, caused tremendous stress and ultimately led the population to leave the Mohawk Valley. They were replaced by European settlers.

Culture and Colonial Strategy

One of the major principles structuring the Spanish colonial enterprise was that souls could be saved through conversion. This interventionist scheme, in which missionaries were sent along with soldiers, allowed for the *possibility* of humanizing the savages, of bringing them into the known world through conversion. This was a conventional feudal mechanism that served to harness labor and create obligation to the fathers and the civil government. Having little interest in the salvation of souls, the pragmatic Dutch sent no missionaries. Instead they focused on commodities obtained through trade from indigenous people and did not directly interfere with existing labor patterns. They showed a marked disinterest in the people encountered, in contrast to colonists from Catholic countries. In fact, the doctrines of Calvinism, especially the belief in predestination, provided no incentive for missionization, which did not begin in Dutch colonies until the nineteenth century, during their most aggressive and imperialistic phase, in the East Indies (Kipp 1990:2, 30).

As the case studies demonstrate, economic and cultural differences account for the vastly different behavior emerging in these two situations. Dutch encampments, for instance, were fortified and distant from Native American settlements. Most Dutch men, from all evidence, were equally distant from Indian women, for reasons that are unclear. One possibility is that the Dutch were frightened by "others," although their treatment of enslaved Africans in New Amsterdam was considerably less punitive than that of the British. By contrast, Spanish churches and garrisons were built in the midst of pueblo communities, and Spanish men cohabited with

Indian women, both Mexican and New Mexican, contributing to a complex series of categories of people defined by ancestry of various kinds. Spanish settlers can be said to have exercised control from their location within the community, relying on the domestic and sexual labor of Indian women, while Dutch control took a less personal and more remote form. Behind the seeming intimacy of the Spanish-Pueblo connection lay a strong physical cruelty that was a more consistent component of Spanish colonial rule than of Dutch administration, although there were notable examples of Dutch violence against Native Americans, especially during Kieft's War (Van der Zee and Van der Zee [1977]1978). Violence against the Mohawks would have been counterproductive for the Dutch, interfering with the steady flow of furs to Dutch trading posts.

The social distance maintained by the Dutch in the Hudson Valley was not apparent in their contemporary colony in Batavia, where they lived with indigenous women, sometimes as the result of a specific Dutch East India Company policy (Abeyasekere 1987:20; Bagley 1973:40). Nor was the distance as clearly defined in Capetown, another Dutch colony to which many of the elite brought their wives, although some Dutch men married Khoikhoi women and others fathered half-Dutch children (Hall 1997:230; Schrire 1995:66). It is not entirely clear why there was such a marked distance between cultures in the Hudson Valley, but it is also manifest in Dutch material assemblages, which included only one identifiably Iroquois-made object apart from wampum and Indian-acquired foods: the *notas,* a small bag made of deerskin. The Spanish, on the other hand, incorporated many material elements from indigenous culture, as well as local women, into their lives. I suggest that this practice helped to maintain Pueblo identity.

Outcomes

One of the most noteworthy aspects of the histories examined here is the disparity between the original desires of the colonists and subsequent developments, as Native American resistance to control had unanticipated consequences and the contact experience became increasingly complex. The continued survival of Pueblo peoples in the Rio Grande Valley is in contrast to the disappearance of the Mohawks from their homeland in the mid-Hudson and Mohawk River Valleys after the eighteenth century. This book explores these contrasting situations with the use of archaeological data to monitor the nature of interaction in the two contexts. What makes it difficult to explain such outcomes, however, is the mutability inherent in colonial situations. Most encounters consist of several stages, the first being a brief period during which each people possesses little information about "the other." In some cases this first interaction may be rather peaceful, characterized by a degree of goodwill as well as a lack of knowledge, but it is almost always short and followed by subsequent stages involving greater demands. In the Southwest, one can identify a second and third stage, divided by the Pueblo Revolt of 1680, after which the Spanish relaxed some of their religious demands but shifted their focus from extraction to settlement in recognition of what the environment could sustain. In the Dutch-Mohawk second stage (lasting until around 1640), trading was intense, which was somewhat satisfying to both parties. This was followed by a more complex period in which furs declined, and both sides attempted to manipulate trade to improve their position. To fully understand these cases, then, it is necessary to extend the inquiry into the mid-eighteenth century, to examine Pueblo-Spanish interactions after the revolt and the continuing connections between the Mohawks and Europeans in the Hudson Valley.

2

History and Key Players in the Southwest and Northeast

To obtain crucial background information on the key players here, I turn to both archaeology and history. Archaeology provides a characterization of Pueblo and Mohawk subsistence and social patterns prior to the contact experience. Historical data provide the same for the Spanish and the Dutch and suggest their motives and priorities in sending settlers, administrators, and, for the Spanish, religious personnel. I also discuss the forms of power accruing to each group involved. I then examine the chronology of connections and how modes of interaction changed throughout the seventeenth and eighteenth centuries. For the Pueblo-Spanish interaction, the turning point was the Pueblo Revolt of 1680; for the Mohawk-Dutch, it was the decline of beaver and the consequent impact on Mohawk lives and European trade. The Southwest is discussed first, followed by the Northeast. I have focused on the Pueblo peoples in the central and northern Rio Grande area because that is where the Spanish were most consistently present, and therefore where contact was most intense. I examine the Mohawk rather than the Seneca, Cayuga, or other Iroquois group for the same reason. From time to time, I use information from other Pueblo groups to the west of the Rio Grande, or other Iroquois groups, for comparative insight.

Geography of the Rio Grande area

The unique environment in the southwestern United States has had a significant impact on its inhabitants. For centuries, agriculture has been marginal throughout the region, and societies have had to devise creative and complex responses to sustain life there. If the region had been consistently impossible for any kind of dense settlement, its trajectory of settlement would have been quite different, and, parenthetically, it would have been a less interesting place. However, the challenge of maintaining a complex, horticulture-based society in marginal agricultural conditions has made the area consistently attractive to archaeologists. Pueblo settlement reached its greatest density in the Rio Grande region, which is also where the Spanish concentrated their colonial efforts because of its reliable water supply, large indigenous population, and convenience as a travel corridor. The segment of the Rio Grande Valley of interest to this work runs north from the approximate location of the former pueblo of Senecu as far as the contemporary community of Taos (figure 2.1).

The Rio Grande Valley is not a typical river-related feature formed by the natural flow of waters from upstream. It is the product of a major rift that occurred about 30 million years ago, and the resulting trough has acted as a pathway for waters originating in the sierras of southern Colorado. Other streams and rivers join and widen the Rio Grande as it flows south, and at the southern tip of present-day New Mexico, it expands still further until finally it flows into the Gulf of Mexico (Marshall and Walt 1984; Ware 1984). The deposition of upstream materials has altered the shape of the valley bed and created terraces. The northern Rio Grande is mostly contained between the major ranges of the San Juan and Jemez Mountains to the west and the Sangre de Cristo and smaller Manzano-Los Pinos Mountains lying east. The region's climate ranges from arid in the south to semiarid further north; yearly rainfall is about 200–1,000 millimeters (Riley 1987:219). Rainfall varies by elevation, area, and season, with summer rains often including short, high-intensity storms, while gentler winter rain and snow come from moisture-laden winds (Cordell 1984:25).

The vegetation in this area is diverse and also varies with elevation. It includes spruce-fir-pine forms, with grasses and pinyon-juniper on lower slopes; other grasses, mesquite, soapweed and creosote bush, and various cacti are found in lower semidesert settings. Cottonwoods, sagebrush, and willows (lately replaced

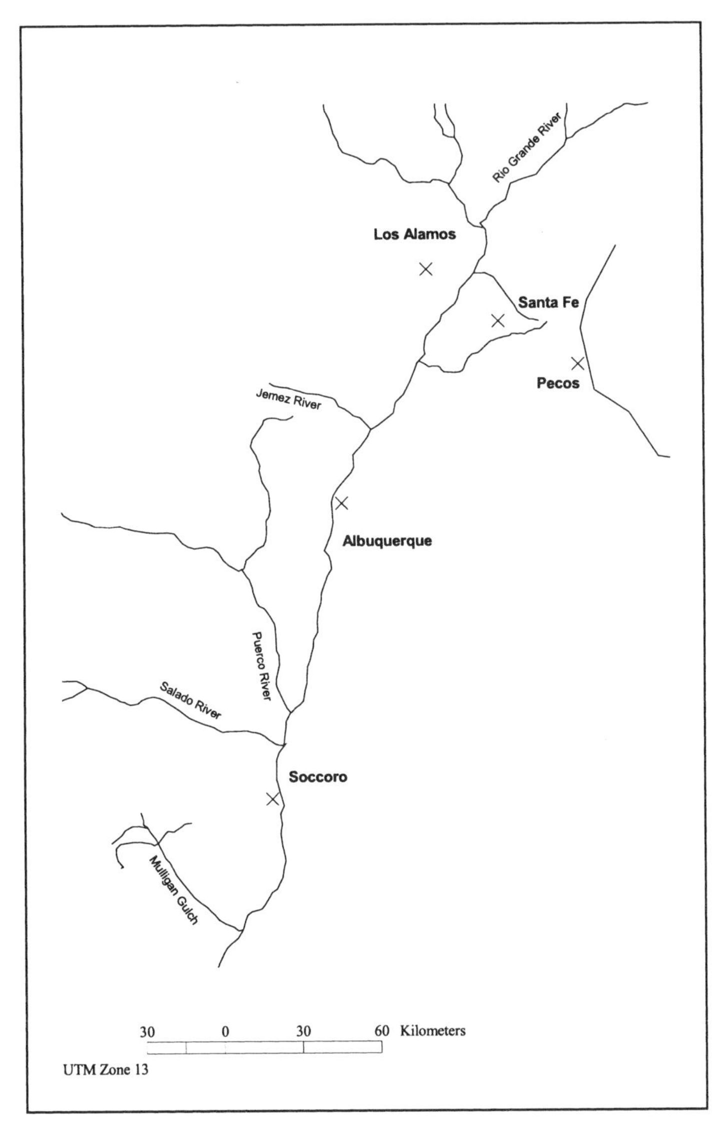

Figure 2.1. Map of Rio Grande area. Courtesy Antoinette Wannebo.

by salt cedar) are found in stream or river beds (Earls 1986; Marshall 1987; Marshall and Walt 1984). A consistent group of animals associated with these plant communities occur throughout the area, although the proportions of each vary greatly from one environmental setting to another. Prominent among the many small creatures present, most of which seem to have been food sources, are cottontail and jackrabbit; prairie dogs and pocket gopher; various rodents; midsized animals such as muskrat and raccoon; and birds, including game, migratory waterfowl, turkey, and others. Larger mammals include whitetail and mule deer, elk, pronghorn antelope, and mountain sheep. Fish were also available in rivers.

The region has been subdivided in different ways. The Spanish established spatially based administrative zones, defining Rio Abajo and Rio Arriba zones, which they subsequently redefined when they moved the border between Abajo and Arriba north after the Piro area was no longer occupied by settled agrarian dwellers. Anthropologists and archaeologists have classified the indigenous inhabitants of the Rio Grande area into seven groups primarily on the basis of language. From the south, these are the Piro, Tompiro, southern Tiwa, Keres, eastern and western Towas, Tewas, and northern Tiwas (Schroeder 1979). Riley (1987) considers geographic factors as well as cultural and linguistic ones to create similar, but somewhat more subdivided clusters during the "protohistoric" (defined in this instance as A.D. 1450–1650), with Pecos linked to the Plains to the east, and western Zuni and Hopi as separate clusters. These classifications include only Pueblo peoples; nomadic groups such as Navajo, Apache, Comanche, and Ute are excluded.

Period of Interest

A combination of archaeological and ethnographic data with information from early Spanish accounts allows a description of Native American life just prior to the moment of contact with European colonial expeditions and the subsequent Spanish invasion, colonizing attempts, and interactions with the Pueblo peoples. Many observers have used the term "protohistoric" to characterize the time just prior to contact. This is a vague term with quite elastic meaning, ranging from 1250–1600 (Snow 1981:368) to 1450–1700 (Wilcox and Masse 1981:378). In other instances the term refers to a time when Europeans had entered the New World but were not in direct contact with the Native American group being examined (Perttula 1992), rather than to specific dates. Usually, such usage implies indirect impact, manifest through the appearance of European trade goods in Indian settings or innovations such as the horse, European-introduced disease, or the movement of peoples who have been displaced as a result of more direct contact (Sutton n.d.). The cases discussed here involve face-to-face contact, and while there was indirect impact on Iroquois peoples before direct contact, there is no evidence of this in the Southwest prior to the Spanish *entrada*.

If, on the other hand, the "historic" period is taken to mean that time when written accounts (or "history") began, then protohistoric would refer to the time just before Europeans arrived and began to record events; in the Southwest, this would end by the mid–sixteenth century (1539). These terms are problematic in their assumption that the only valid form of documentation is the written, thus reinforcing and maintaining colonial premises. "Prehistory" carries the same implication and is replaced here by "Precolumbian." Archaeologists in the Southwest, following Kidder's (1924) work at Pecos, use a relative time scheme for Pueblo ancestral peoples based on pottery chronology and seriation. Following this scheme, I focus on the P V period, beginning approximately A.D. 1540, with the understanding that the reconstruction of life at this time involves extrapolation from P IV (1250–1540) and a fair amount of guesswork. As recent work by archaeologists suggests, P IV may have been a period of unusual migration and aggregation (Duff 1998:43) in the mid and northern Rio Grande Valley, an interesting possibility considering the later Spanish policy that tried to achieve the same goal, although for different reasons.

The Pueblos: Settlement, Architecture, and Population

The inhabitants of the Rio Grande area just prior to the Spanish entrada were broadly similar in many ways yet varied from group to group. The periods referred to as P III, IV, and V are characterized by occupation of aggregated settlement clusters, called "pueblos" by the Spanish. These consisted of contiguous room blocks, sometimes multistory, built of adobe and stone. The rectangular rooms served a mixture of living and storage functions. Castañeda, one of the early Spanish explorers, noted in 1540 that women did the work of mixing the plaster and building the houses, while men brought and laid the timbers (Gutiérrez 1991:15). Room blocks were often built around plazas (at least one P IV site, Arroyo Hondo, had about 30–40 rooms facing each plaza; figure 2.2) that would have been used

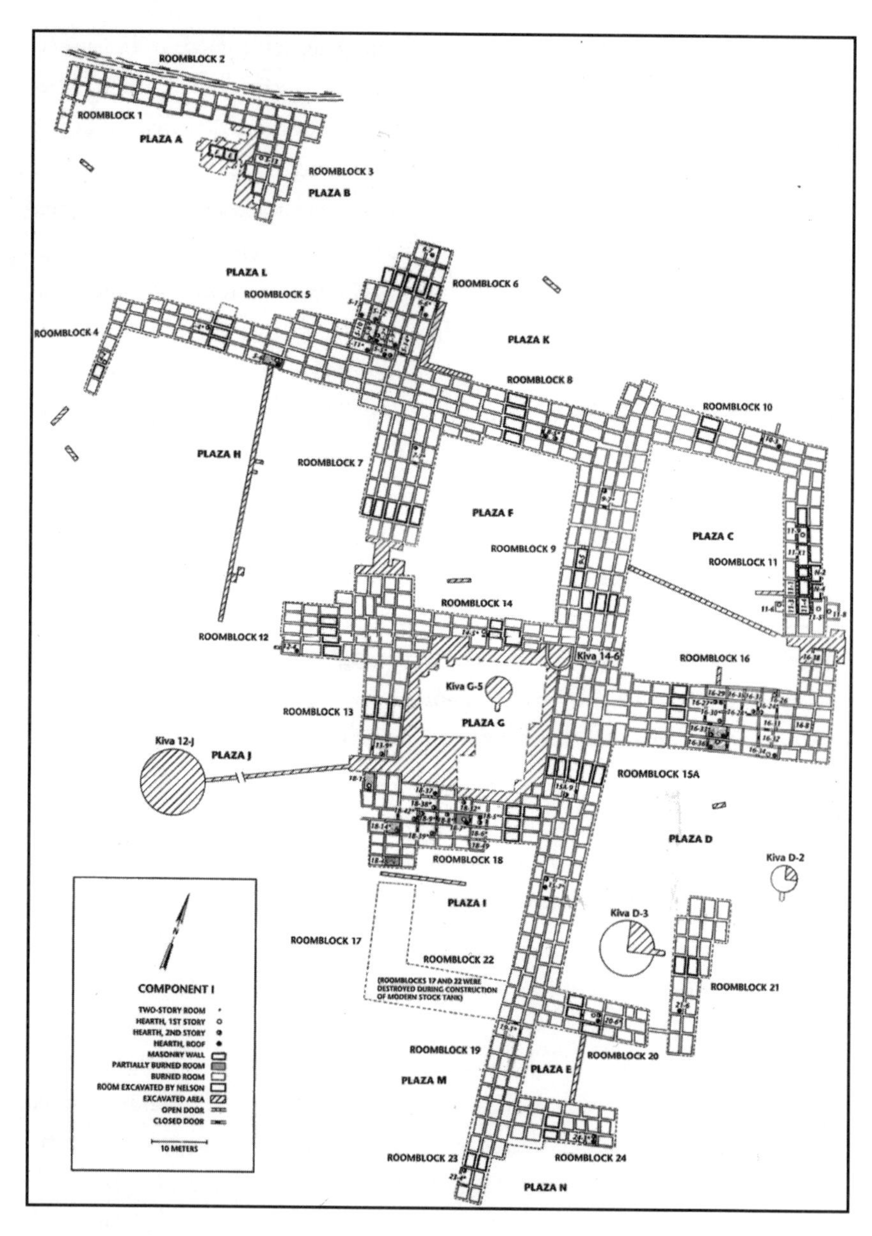

Figure 2.2. Plan view of Component I of the Arroyo Hondo site, a fourteenth-century Pueblo site in the Rio Grande River Valley.

for a number of activities, including food preparation and communal ritual as well as social life. Kivas, serving ceremonial purposes, were either built within rooms or were free-standing circular structures in plazas. Those living in pueblos also used farmsteads or field houses for short-term or seasonal occupation (Abbink and Stein 1977:152). The primary building material was stone or adobe, which makes it possible to date some sites in specific areas. At Paa'ko, for example, adobe construction preceded stone and stone/adobe mixtures and was contemporary with black-on-white pottery, dating to the end of the thirteenth century (Lambert and Rogers 1954:10).

During the P IV period (1250–1540), settlements throughout the Southwest increased in size as a result of aggregation and consolidation, with large pueblos built alongside rivers. This growth correlated with the appearance of large kivas and some agricultural modifications involving terracing and the use of check dams, with some of the well-known so-called abandonments (notably at Chaco Canyon and Mesa Verde), and with the founding of some of the historically known eastern Pueblos (Cordell 1979:142–145; Hall 1989:43; Marshall and Walt 1984:135). The same process of an increasingly aggregated population occupying large pueblos—perhaps for as long as 150 years at a time—is manifest in the western Pueblo area during this period. At about 1400, the Zuni were living in large pueblos along a 25-mile segment of the Zuni River, while the Hopi resided on the mesas, buttes, at Moenkopie and along the Middle Little Colorado River (Adams 1996:48; Kintigh 1990:268).

Both Zuni and Hopi oral history suggest that mobility and migration were consistently important components of past life. Ferguson et al. (1985:10) have collected accounts that may relate to the late Precolumbian period for the Zuni, while Upham and Reed (1989) note a post–Pueblo IV migration. Oral histories are scarce for the eastern Pueblos, but accounts from Santa Ana and San Felipe record their relocations from Paa'ko and Cochiti, respectively (Bayer and Montoya 1994; White 1932). Gutiérrez (1991:xxvii) states that the population was still in flux when the Spanish arrived, but "flux" was part of the normal settlement processes of Pueblo peoples. Given the changing conditions for horticulture, redistribution of people on the land was an adaptive form of behavior, and the clan system would have allowed the flexibility necessary to maintain it.

Archaeologists working with architectural remains from the Southwest have learned to be careful in their assumptions about the population implications of a large "permanent" structure. It is difficult to identify a simple, consistent ratio of people to rooms because pueblos were used and reused, occupants moved in and out for variable periods, at times living only in parts of the preexisting village. Room blocks would be added as needed, and empty rooms were used for trash disposal. This is a clear point of contrast with the Iroquois, who appear to have lived in villages for 10–20 years at a stretch, then to have relocated. The Iroquois pattern is said to relate to soil and firewood depletion; it may also be contingent on the life span of the building materials used. Pueblo architecture would have been somewhat familiar to the Spanish, some of whom came from areas where adobe was used as a building material (Jojola 1997). Some of the early Spanish settlers occupied Pueblo-built structures, so it is difficult at times to differentiate the occupants of these early sites, although a few architectural details may identify the builders of a Spanish house and distinguish it from an indigenous structure (see chapter 3).

Population estimates are predictably quite variable, as Pueblo peoples moved around. A number of early Spanish explorers attempted to record population, but not all of them visited the same pueblos or, if they did, arrived at the same figures. Castañeda's figure of 45,000 people in 1540–1542 may be the closest to an accurate number, while Espejo's figure of 130,000 in 1582–1583 seems too large (Riley 1987:230–231). Other estimates include Velasco's figure of fewer than 20,000 in 1609 (probably too low), while Benavides's 1634 estimate of 80,000 (Frank 1998) may have been exaggerated to show the area as an important one. Population, reduced by epidemic disease and other effects of Spanish expeditions, continued to fall after the revolt (Weber [1992:140] cites figures of 17,000 in 1680 and 14,000 in 1700) and through the eighteenth century (Levine 1996; Ramenofsky 1996). None of these figures include non-Pueblo peoples, who, being nomadic, were more difficult to count. Athapaskans, including several Apache groups, are known to have lived or wintered along the Rio Grande during the late Pueblo period. The Navajo lived west of the Rio Grande, and groups of Plains nomads (notably the Jumanos, Utes, and later the Comanche) were commonly seen at sites such as Pecos or Taos, where the exchange of meat (and buffalo hide) for corn was an important component of the economy (Kessell 1978; Spielmann 1991). This trade is believed to have been conducted between partners whose kin groups maintained long-term relationships (Hall 1989:83); it was disrupted by Spanish demands for corn and hides and by the appearance of the horse.

SUBSISTENCE

The Pueblo were horticulturalists living in marginal conditions, relying in large measure on rainfall and the management of runoff, although those in the Rio Grande River Valley had more consistent water resources than those in other parts of the Pueblo Southwest. Major crops were maize, beans, squash, and cotton, supplemented by a variety of important wild plant foods, such as cholla, cattail, prickly pear, pinenuts, sedge, and yucca. Turkeys and dogs had been domesticated, but hunting provided the bulk of meat, with some groups relying for the most part on large mammals—antelope, mule deer, and white-tail deer—others on small mammals, especially cottontail and jackrabbits, but also gophers, prairie dogs, squirrels, rodents, turkey, quail, other birds, and fish, depending on the precise location, seasonal emphasis, and climatic conditions. Faunal remains from several sites with late Precolumbian occupations in the Rio Grande area—Arroyo Hondo, Piro Pueblo, and Rowe Pueblo—show similarities in their patterns of animal exploitation. At all three, mule deer was the dominant large mammal, with pronghorn antelope frequently present; cottontail and jackrabbit were recovered in large numbers, as were turkeys and a number of small mammals. "There is not an Indian [in Piro country] who does not have his corral in which he keeps his turkeys. Each one holds a flock of one hundred birds" (Hammond and Rey 1924:26). Piro Pueblo (LA 282) is an important site because it was occupied from about 1300 to after the Spanish entry to New Mexico—the entrada—(but before missionization), and it was not reoccupied after the revolt. Precolonial deposits suggest the presence of a wider variety of species, both plant and animal, than colonial ones. Subsistence ratios of small species to medium to large are 3:4:1, where "small" is defined as anything up to a cottontail in size, while "medium" extends from jackrabbit to wolf, and "large" begins with a mountain lion or antelope and goes up to a bison (Earls 1986:255). The faunal species are all local, showing more diversity than Spanish documents record, but the emphasis on rabbits matches the seventeenth-century description of these as "inexhaustable" (Hodge et al. 1945:39, cited in Earls 1986:273).

Rowe Pueblo, a P IV site just east of Pecos, revealed quantities of the above species, as well as pocket gopher and prairie dog, bighorn sheep, and bison. Rabbits (both cottontail and jackrabbit) account for 27 percent of the identified bone sample, while large animals make up 35 percent. It requires 57 desert cottontails to equal one mule deer in weight. Thus this site shows either an emphasis on large-animal hunting or a period of great success. There was evidence of small amounts of bison, but Rowe was not like Pecos, where bison were plentiful and brought back to the settlement as dressed joints (Mick-O'Hara, n.d.).

At Arroyo Hondo, located between Pecos and Cochiti and occupied mainly between 1300 and 1400, a stratified series of deposits yields information on periods of drought, hunting seasons, the frequent use of "low-yield" species by site inhabitants for specific dietary components (e.g., tree squirrels provided fat), and a number of other subtle elements. While rabbits and turkeys were numerically significant, meat-weight analysis indicates the clear preponderance of mule deer as the protein source; artiodactyls (deer, antelope, etc.) and large mammals together provided 87–94 percent of meat, really dominating the diet (Lang and Harris 1984:108).

A specific pueblo's farming success related to the characteristics of the particular econiche, the number of frost-free days, and the availability of water and consequent need for irrigation; the latter involved a number of techniques that were essentially variations on the same system. In some places, the agricultural enterprise of the Pueblos was sufficiently impressive for the Spanish to record, noting considerable stores of basic foods. Castaño de Sosa reports of Pecos in 1591: "There were those who believed that there must have been 30,000 fanegas (a fanega is 2.6 bushels) [of stored corn], since every house had two or three rooms full. It is the best maize seen . . . both maize and beans were of many colors. Apparently there was maize two or three years old" (Kessell 1978:55). This comment may reflect Pecos's particular success, but it also describes the conservation of seed corn and supplies stored against the inevitable sequence of bad years, a practice common to many Pueblos.

SOCIOPOLITICAL ORGANIZATION

In relying on ethnography to elucidate late Precolumbian social organization, it is essential to remember that whereas some aspects of Pueblo society may be similar to those of the past, others will be quite different. The debate about the validity of ethnographic analogy, however, is not central to this work. Pueblo society was organized in a number of nested units, beginning with the household, which consisted of a female-centered extended family occupying a number of adjacent storage and living rooms. Households were organized into villages or pueblos. Pueblo social organization varied considerably, especially between eastern and western groups (Eggan 1950) and among the language groups (Keresan, Tiwa-, Towa-, and Tewa-speakers) of the eastern communities. At the time they were visited by anthropologists, western Pueblos were organized into matrilineages, while eastern Pueblos showed more of a tendency toward patrilineal or bilateral organization, sometimes attributed to the effects of Spanish contact (Eggan 1950:313). Other important social divisions crosscut descent groupings and include men's ceremonial societies (kiva, rain, and medicine) perhaps similar to those of today. The katsina cult is thought to have been developed prior to 1500, so would have been in place during the time of interest here, originating in the western Pueblos, but also found in Acoma, the Tewa villages, and those pueblos to the east and south of present-day Santa Fe (Adams 1991:148). Status reflected age and achievement. Labor was organized and divided by sex, with complementary male and female roles; women were in charge of agricultural and social reproduction, men had responsibility for the hunt, war, trade, rain, and intervention with the gods (Gutiérrez 1991:13–21). Space was gendered, with women controlling houses and men ceremonial space and space outside pueblos, including their mothers' and sisters' fields. Gutiérrez also reminds us of the highly structured universe of contemporary Pueblo peoples, probably best known for the Hopi, centered on the kiva and extending to six cardinal directions (north, south, east, west, up, and down).

Perhaps the greatest debate today concerns the degree of political hierarchy among the Pueblos. In its early stages, the discussion was heavily influenced by evolutionary theory, with some scholars suggesting on the basis of the first ethnographic descriptions that the political system would have fit Fried's model of an egalitarian and relatively nonhierarchical, system. This view has persisted; Gutiérrez (1991:xviii, 12), for example, refers to a two-level system, fitting a chiefdom model, with leadership achieved on the basis of age and success in the hunt, at war, or in ritual activities such as the production of rain. However, a number of observers have recently taken issue with the egalitarian model. From a historical perspective, they argue that what had been observed by ethnographers would not be likely to represent the Precolumbian system and that Pueblo society would have been more hierarchical, especially prior to colonial contact (Upham 1982; Wilcox and Masse 1981). Support for this view comes from the contemporary western Pueblos where power is centrally organized, follows hereditary lines of succession, and is based on the conjunction of authority derived from religious roles and political economy, with privileged access to ritual knowledge an important component, and inequality among clans evident. Critics of a theoretical bent want the focus to shift away from unilinear schemes toward heterarchy, dual-processual theory, complex adaptive systems theory, or other ways of examining the distribution of power (Kintigh 2000; Kohler et al. 2000; Mills 2000a). They recognize that there was probably considerable variability within and between villages of the same Pueblo peoples.

At the same time, there appear to have been some similarities throughout the region. A dual system of war/secular and religious/sacred chiefs was common to many pueblos. Many formal leadership positions were held by men, although some mortuary and other evidence of ritual paraphernalia found in association with women (Hays-Gilpin 2000; Howell 1995) indicates that this was not as dominant a practice as usually assumed. As is clear from historic accounts and ethnography, men and women had complementary roles that were not necessarily arrayed hierarchically. Any status variability that existed does not appear to have extended to differences in living conditions or architectural construction; it might have been expressed in gift exchange (Gutiérrez 1991:9) or mortuary treatment (Howell and Kintigh 1996; Kintigh 2000), but because there are few large cemeteries, no synthetic discussion of these data is available. There are some suggestions of personal status variability (Johnson 1989), but apparently no archaeological or other evidence of inherited status.

TRADE AND EXCHANGE

Another debatable issue is the degree of integration among pueblos. Although seemingly autonomous (Abbink and Stein 1977:152), they were linked by interregional trade. Several archaeologists have discussed the mechanics and function of these links, the size of the linked units, what products were exchanged, and how these changed over time (Riley 1987; Spielmann 1994b; Upham and Reed 1989:70). Riley (1987:7) refers to the greater Southwest as an "Interaction Sphere" throughout which a number of exotic resources were exchanged, including turquoise and other minerals such as obsidian, certain cherts, and hematite; shell (perhaps traded as beads or bracelets); macaw and parrot feathers; and buffalo products. Many of these materials were relevant mostly in ceremonial contexts. The quantities of these items varied according to access by subareas and also fluctuate over time in archaeological assemblages. In the early fifteenth century, the level of interregional trade was particularly high, as visible in the appearance of localized ceramic stylistic groupings in distant places (Upham and Reed 1989:70). Trade seems to have occurred primarily along an east-west axis, from Pecos to Hopi and Zuni and back, with some extensions to the south and the Plains, while a number of settlement clusters represented local alliances or confederacies, some with more concentrated internal trade (Upham and Reed 1989). According to Spielmann (1994b), localized clusters of pueblos such as those in the Galisteo Basin, the Piro, and Salinas areas may have served as units in such a system and may have been characterized by inequality within clusters. There is no archaeological evidence for the hypothesis, she notes, adding that if such confederacies existed they would have been similar to those in the Northeast, but closer to Huron than Iroquois models of confederacy and thus less formal.

Full- or part-time craft specialization may have contributed to exchange interaction as pueblos aggregated and the connection to northern Mexico collapsed. Pueblo artisans would have produced certain "ordinary" items such as ceramics or food beyond the household's needs, prompted by a number of factors, including perhaps the need for exotics in ritual contexts or for elite display, and unequal access to them. Snow (1981:360) bases this idea in part on "the obvious increase in ritual and ceremonial items in the Rio Grande Classic archaeological record" and sees major evidence for the continuation of intraregional exchange after 1400 in ceramics and a decline in the number of villages making large amounts of glazewares, with the appearance of ceramic production centers in the Galisteo Basin, Tunque, the Saline Pueblos, and Pecos. Black-on-white wares were primarily made in a different set of pueblos, including Jemez, the Tewas, and northern Tiwas (Snow 1981:363). Precolumbian ceramic production and the appearance of specialists who manufactured for exchange are central points of interest in this project and have been discussed by a number of archaeologists (Creamer 1999; Habicht-Mauche 1995; Mills 1995b; Spielmann et al. 1999). Clues to the existence of such specialists lie in stylistic design, standardization of form, and other technical elements, while place of manufacture may be assessed through paste composition and glaze recipes. Design elements are often thought to express ideology, identity, or resistance to the Spanish; this topic is discussed in chapter 5.

The Spanish Background

The first question to consider about a colonial encounter is why would anyone travel thousands of miles in dangerous discomfort to an unknown part of the world? For the Spanish of the late Medieval period, several answers come to mind.

The pioneers came to attain wealth, to save souls, and to satisfy a yearning for adventure. Some of them were landless, younger sons in a system of primogeniture that left them few opportunities for advancement. "Spanish conquistadors belong historically to a transitional period between a Middle Ages dominated by religion and a modern period that places gold at the top of its scale of values" (Todorov 1984:42). Another motivation for some was to obtain a reprieve from a previous crime or misdemeanor (Jojola 1997:2). While it cannot be assumed that the Spanish who came to New Mexico in 1539, and then to settle in 1598, had the same orientation and worldview as Columbus a century earlier, there was probably considerable continuity.

Spain was already a major player in the world system in the sixteenth century, competing with other European powers for luxuries and rare resources. As just stated, gold was particularly valued; Cortés is reported to have told Moctezuma that the Spanish had a disease of the heart that only gold could cure (Weber 1992:23). Gold could improve the world trading position of the Spanish (or anyone possessing it), who initially thought that today's New Mexico would have extractable gold and silver. Although northern Mexico did have some deposits of silver and other minerals, it soon became clear that these riches were not available in New Mexico. Even so, Spain was concerned that the British or French not gain this territory, and it colonized the area to prevent other nations from extending their own empires (Hall 1989). This was official Spanish policy, but the individuals who carried it out had other motivations. Some believed that in doing so they would gain not only wealth but noble titles and bountiful land and were willing to use their own capital to finance expeditions. Others saw service to God as a rationalization of the state. Conversions were sure to win the approval of the Pope, and such service merited reward (Weber 1992:23). Bernàl Diaz del Castillo said, "We came here to serve God and the king and also to get rich" (Hall 1989:50).

The voyagers to the New World were not the established elite but a mixture of those who wanted to improve their status and those who sought adventure, independence, and profit. Lesser nobles, younger sons of noble families, and members of the middle class all saw the voyage as an opportunity to improve their own or their family's position through the acquisition of wealth (Hall 1989:53) in a country where land and adventure were becoming scarce. The recapture of Iberia from the Muslims in 1492 under Ferdinand and Isabel had reinforced the importance and power of Catholicism and established a group of experienced soldiers in

Spain who were valued and perceived as romantic figures (Weber 1992:20, 24). While the initial immigrant groups included many identified as soldiers, those who came to settle included many artisans and peasants (Hall 1989:60), who presumably had similar motives. Although Spanish policy encouraged settlers to bring wives and children (Hackett 1923:137), few did; only 13 wives are recorded as coming, along with considerably more women servants (Frank 1998; Gutiérrez 1991:103). Most wives and servants were born in Mexico (D.H. Snow 1992b). This fit the colonial plan, which sought self-sufficient settlements more than simply extractive communities or mining camps, although it is unclear whether these were intended to be permanent. Spain was not interested in conquering people to enslave them, but to acquire more subjects who paid taxes or tribute (Todorov 1984:47).

As Todorov (1984:2–5) says, a conflict was inherent in the Spanish perception of indigenous peoples. On one hand, Catholics were willing to extend their religion to pagans out of generosity; on the other hand, they demanded wealth in return. The implicit assumption here—that these, or any, people were potentially Christian—is a crucial one because it allows for the possibility that, once converted, they would be human in God's eyes and equivalent, in some sense, to other Catholics. However, if/when a people did not offer their wealth "in return" for this "generosity," they would have to be subdued and thus would be unequal by definition. This approach inevitably led to conflict and destruction. The Spanish ritual for entering into a community for the first time, the *Requerimiento* (begun with the eviction of the Moors from Castile), involved the reading aloud (or sometimes whispering) of a long document in Spanish, commanding the group to acknowledge the Catholic Church as the ruler of the world, the Pope as its high priest, and the king and queen of Spain as their rulers. If this pronouncement were accepted, all would be well (although the possibility of its being understood, let alone acknowledged, was almost nil). If not, the document continued, "with the help of God we shall forcefully . . . make war against you . . . take your wives and children and shall make slaves of them . . . and shall do to you all the harm and damage that we can" (Weber 1992:22). The reading of the Requerimiento legitimized for the Spanish many forms of theft and destruction. It is hard to imagine, from a twenty-first century perspective, that this proposition was taken seriously, although ignorance of the law is not today accepted as an excuse for its violation and may not have been then (Thomas Biolsi, personal communication).

ENTRADA

The chronology of Spanish entry into and experience in New Mexico can be divided into three phases, but only two of these can be examined archaeologically. The first began with the entrada in 1539–1540, and continued until 1598. The second extends from 1598, when the first colony was established, to 1680 and the Pueblo Revolt and is marked by missionization and settlement. A third period began at 1692 with the Reconquest and the formation of Hispanic culture and community and continued to the mid–eighteenth century and even longer. Spanish rule ended in 1821 with the Mexican takeover of Spanish territories in present-day Mexico, Texas, and New Mexico. The United States gained control of New Mexico in 1846.

In 1539, Esteban (or Estevanico) reached Hawikuh, a Zuni village, ahead of Fray Marcos de Niza, the expedition leader. Esteban was killed by the Zuni, whereupon Niza decided to turn around, after naming the area Cibola and claiming it for the king of Spain. His glowing reports of the seven cities of gold led to a return trip the following year by Francisco Vasquez de Coronado, who brought to Hawikuh, at his own expense, soldiers, horses, pack animals and arms, and some Christianized Mexican Indian servants, or "allies" (Weber 1992:46). This group included six Franciscan missionaries, so the "conquest [might] be Christian and apostolic and not a butchery" (Beck 1962:45). Having conquered Zuni but finding no gold, some of the company moved on to Hopi where they found some areas they thought might be productive of minerals (Hall 1989:81).

Coronado's group spent the winter at a Tiwa/Tiguex village close to today's Bernalillo. Its inhabitants welcomed them with gifts of cotton cloth, dressed skins, birds, cornmeal, pine nuts, and some turquoise (Adams 1989:81). The Spanish offered glass beads and demanded food, blankets, and "women for their use" and punished uncooperative individuals by killing them, burning some at the stake (Spicer 1962:155), thus negating the notion of the Christian, apostolic conquest. Some of the Spanish went to Pecos, where the inhabitants reportedly tried to lead them onto the Plains with promises of gold, hoping to abandon them there, but while many soldiers died on the Plains, the remainder came back and exploration continued. Coronado's expedition stayed only about a year and brought back a poor report of the area's potential for gold. It left behind a strong impression that the Spanish were ruthless plunderers. A number of Tiwa villages, 10 of the 12 known at the time, were "abandoned" (Spicer 1962:155), but this was presumably a temporary move, part of the phenomenon of southwestern mobility, which had begun earlier in the Pueblo period and lasted after the Pueblo Revolt. They also contributed to a misconception that persisted throughout the early phases of interaction: "What the Puebloans thought they gave as gifts, the *españoles* thought had been surrendered as tribute" (Gutiérrez 1991:52). This conflict in the economic and social meaning of a gift is discussed further in chapters 4 and 5.

Several subsequent forays occurred between 1581 and 1593 (two officially sanctioned ones were led by Rodriguez and Chamuscado in 1581 and Espejo in 1582, and two unauthorized ones were undertaken by Castaño de Sosa in 1590–1591 and by Leyva de Bonilla and Gutiérrez de Humaña in 1593) (Gutiérrez 1991; Weber 1992:78–79). These were apparently more peaceful trips, the Indians (mostly Piro, Tanos, and Keres in the Rio Grande Valley) encountered were "friendly," and food was provided to the Spanish without incident (Cordell 1989; D. H. Snow 1992a, vol. 1; Spicer 1962:56). I suspect that this was possible because the trips were rather brief, some villages had stored food supplies, and the villages encountered had already developed an understanding of ways to avoid conflict.

SETTLEMENT

The second phase of the encounter between the Spanish and the Pueblos began in 1598 when Don Juan de Oñate (figure 2.3) won the right to establish a community along the Rio Grande, besting Don Pedro Ponce de León in a competition in which each man listed what he would provide in the way of supplies and personnel at his own expense (Hackett 1923:227–236). Oñate offered hundreds of soldiers and settlers, including wives and children (Spicer 1962:156; Weber 1992:81); Mexican servants and enslaved people; and Franciscan missionaries. Also included were 1,000 cattle, 5,000 sheep and goats, 80 carts, and a very long and detailed list of provisions, notably foods (principally flour, wine, oil, and sugar); clothing and footgear; paper and medicines; tools and materials for making and repairing them; items for barter (beads, earrings, combs, mirrors, scissors, knives, needles, hawks' bells); religious items (rosaries, beads, medals, images, whistles); and arms, armor, ammunition, and powder. The caravan took three years to reach Yunque Yunque (renamed San Gabriel by the Spanish); when Oñate arrived, the natives left "voluntarily" (John 1975:43).

The first colonial settlement lasted a few years. Only about 50 people remained at the end of 1598 (Weber 1992:85), and most of those left before the winter of

Figure 2.3. Don Juan de Oñate, the leader of the first colonial settlement in New Mexico.

1601, while Oñate was away from the colony looking for wealth and neglecting San Gabriel. The first to leave San Gabriel were those "of distinction" who had wanted a profit and "shiftless" single men looking for fortune. Life in the settlement was hard, it was clear that gold was not to be found, the climate was harsh, and the natives were fierce (Gutiérrez 1991; Spicer 1962:157). The colonists' flight followed the debacle at Acoma, where the Spanish amputated one foot from all men over the age of 25 and imposed 20 years of slavery on the amputees as well as on anyone, male or female, over the age of 12, following an attack on Spanish soldiers who, the Acoma felt, were demanding too much food (Knaut 1995:46). The economic balance of Pueblo communities suffered immediate stress when soldiers and administrators demanded corn, blankets, and firewood from nearby pueblos (John 1975:46), while not contributing to the food supply. During the early years of settlement, a drought in 1600–1601 made corn from Indians scarce and led the colonists to slaughter livestock. Oñate himself left in 1606, but he returned in 1609 with more colonists and missionaries, moving the capital to Santa Fe in 1610 (Spicer 1962:157). Over the next 20 years the settlement along the Rio Grande gradually increased, although the Spanish population of the seventeenth century was never more than about 3,000 people (Weber 1992:90). Church construction was essential to the settlement effort.

THE RELIGIOUS ENTERPRISE

The Franciscan missionaries who accompanied Oñate were interested in the region as a source of possible converts rather than wealth. In 1629 a group of 30 Franciscans arrived, bringing the total to 50 (Weber 1992:92). At that time, 50 churches and conventos (living quarters for church personnel) had already been begun using Indian labor; 25 of these were completed by 1630 (Spicer 1962:158). Missions were expensive to establish and maintain: the initial cost of each was 875 pesos, and three years' maintenance amounted to 300–450 pesos. There were also travel expenses for wagons and mules. As a result, it was decided in 1631 to limit the number built to 66 (Kessell 1987:147–148). Some construction was monumental; at Pecos, for example, each block of the church was made of earth dug from trash mounds and weighed 40 pounds (Kessell 1978:124). Indians were willing to contribute their labor because in return the friars gave them seeds, livestock, manufactured goods, and some ritual paraphernalia, at least initially (Gutiérrez 1991:77). Both women and men took part in construction, with the men doing carpentry and the women doing most of the building (Weber 1992:97).

The Franciscans wanted to save souls, believing that the natives were malleable and could be converted to Christianity. In order to attract them, the missionaries displayed showy church trappings and offered gifts such as bells, beads, hatchets, knives, and food; according to Fray Salvador de Guerra, food gifts were especially effective, bringing Indians in "like fish to the fish hook" (Weber 1992:107). Whether the missionaries initially understood it or not, these gifts required reciprocity, which was useful in supporting the mission staff. When reciprocity did not yield sufficient supplies, the clergy demanded food, labor, and goods in exchange for the salvation they were offering. Claiming success in their conversion attempts, the friars reported that by 1630 they had baptized 86,000 souls (including Pueblos, Apache, and Navajo) (Weber 1992:98). Baptism was easy: it consisted of assigning a new name to the convert, noting the name in church records, and providing a gift of a trinket. What the conversion meant to the supposed convert is difficult to say. Was it simply a means of gaining access to European goods? Was it an act of friendliness or compliance? Clearly it did not have the same meaning to the Indians as it did to the priests, nor did it have the same implications. The lack of a common language and the absence of any comprehension of Pueblo life or culture ensured misunderstandings. The missionaries wanted, expected, and demanded that their converts build temples to their new Christian god, learn catechism, set up and venerate crosses, and learn to live like Spaniards, growing and eating Spanish crops, using Spanish tools, and learning Spanish crafts (Gutiérrez 1991:93; Weber 1992:105). Some initial reactions were enthusiastic and demonstrate the mixing of cultural behaviors (e.g., crosses were sprinkled with cornmeal and feathers). Father Padilla noted of Pecos that "some climbed on the backs of others in order to reach the arms of the crosses to put plumes . . . on them" (Kessell 1978:13).

Not surprisingly, people soon began to realize that the Christian god was not effective in meeting Pueblo needs, so they maintained traditional ritual for curing and for rain, calling on the katsinas in kivas for continuing assistance.

> The Pueblos were not unwilling to accept the externals of the new faith, but . . . Pueblo religion served definite material and social ends, viz., the propitiation of those supernatural forces which they believed controlled their daily existence. They expected the same results from the Christian faith. But they soon realized that the new ways were no more successful in obtaining a good harvest than the old, and they realized too that the effort to abolish their traditional ceremonials and destroy the influence of the old native leaders whose functions were both social and religious raised serious problems concerning the entire fund of Pueblo civilization. (Scholes [1942]1977:16)

As traditional ritual continued, the fathers became angry at their own lack of success, and angry at the people. At Pecos, Father Zeinos said, "I found them so far removed [from the practice of Christianity] that most did not know how to cross themselves" (Kessell 1978:276). For the Franciscans, conformity to specific behavior was crucial; the visible needed to change if the invisible inner person and the soul were to change. However, the disparity between a belief system revolving around animistic spirits that were controlled by behavior designed to harmonize with the natural world and one with a single all-powerful deity and strong polarized codes of behavior leading ultimately to heaven or hell was too great (Gutiérrez 1991:93; Weber 1992:22). Any conformity to Catholicism that did develop was undoubtedly motivated by a combined interest in pleasing the foreigners, a wish to have access to European goods, and fear.

There would likely have been some perception of the priests as shamans, comparable to inside chiefs, who "controlled the sacred, mobilized force, conjured rain, healed the sick, and provided the community with meat" (Gutiérrez 1991:63). The friars took advantage of their knowledge of science to conjure rain when they suspected it was coming and used technology in ways that made it appear magical, but they went beyond these activities, repressing behavior they disliked and using military power. They took young children from their households and attempted to convert them by humiliating and embarrassing their parents (Gutiérrez 1991). There are many accounts of their attempts to quash what they saw as pagan behavior. The incredible cruelty at Acoma is the most extreme example of their repression, but many accounts mention people being flogged, traditional sacred objects being confiscated or smashed, and villages burned. Some of these behaviors are difficult to rationalize with the stated desire for peaceful agricultural communities of converted Indians, and with the fact that ultimately the friars depended heavily on Pueblo labor and support for food. The missionaries were not alone in these demands for sustenance; the political administrators of the colony made similar claims.

THE POLITICAL ADMINISTRATION OF NEW MEXICO

The administrators of the colony during this pre-revolt period included a governor, who was responsible for Rio Arriba Province, a lieutenant governor in charge of Rio Abajo (Simmons 1991:159), and a variety of other officials, mainly *alcaldes mayores* and *fiscales*—community officials responsible for local affairs and financial matters (Hackett 1923; Kessell 1978:177). The settlers included soldiers and civilians. Various incentives were offered to those who remained at least five years: the title of *hidalgo* (noble), which would pass on to a male child and confer aristocratic status on men who would not otherwise have such standing; land, which was also heritable; Indian labor under the *encomienda* system for two generations; exemption from taxes; and freedom from arrest for debt (Gutiérrez 1991:102; Simmons 1991:104).

The administrators' main task was to govern the colony so that tribute could be collected for the king and religious conversions could take place. They were also motivated by personal gain and hoped to become wealthy. To their dismay, the area offered relatively little that could generate a profit: there were few minerals, although some individuals did manage to export sufficient hides, piñon nuts, cattle, textiles, salt, and slaves to become affluent (Hall 1989; Kessell 1987; Spicer 1962). Even modest demands overtaxed the indigenous economy, environment, and labor supply, and since some of the Spanish (both religious and civic leaders) were intent on making a profit through exports, the demands became quite burdensome. Because the administrators also required Pueblo support in the form of limited food and labor, conflict was bound to develop between religious and secular components of the colonial enterprise. The colony was not an economic success and in fact cost New Spain more than it provided in benefits.

Almost from its inception, the colony fomented arguments between the church and secular leadership, with each side angrily accusing the other of empire building, of exploiting and mistreating the Indians (Spicer 1962:158). As documents of the times show, this conflict was often quite vociferous. The records of government representatives described the friars' abuse of Indian labor, who were required to do their personal work, gather wood, weave, and make stockings for the church to sell (Scholes [1942]1977:59), while the religious complained that civil authorities used the Indians as slaves for planting, sowing, day labor, and wood-carrying, making them work even on feast days and in sweatshop-like conditions (Scholes [1942]1977). Administrators were allowed to take orphans as house servants, where they were often exploited (Scholes [1942]1977). Some of the physical abuse was meant as punishment, some was to inspire good behavior, while some was motivated by greed. Women were routinely taken from their pueblos and used for domestic and sexual purposes by civilians and friars alike (Brandon 1990:97).

In some ways the missionaries had greater power than the secular leaders; they were independently financed, and they had (and used) the weapon of excommunication on government leaders, sending some to be tried for heresy at the Holy Office of the Inquisition established in Mexico in 1630 (Knaut 1995). Since there were many friars and they often supported one another in disputes, their claims were a serious matter to administrators (Weber 1992:130–131). The fathers were not supposed to become wealthy and were only entitled to moderate assistance from other colonists, which was restricted to things essential to the church and for their own living quarters (Scholes [1942]1977:79). Some did amass large herds of domestic animals, which were exported in numbers, with adverse effects on the breeding stock and the food supply (Baxter 1993:105).

Church personnel also had power owing to their control over caravans carrying necessary supplies to the missions and colony and scheduled to come every three years, although at times the interval stretched to seven years. Caravans came from Mexico City through Zacatecas and other mining communities in central and northern Mexico, a journey that took anywhere from 6 to 18 months. Their cargos ranged in value from 38,000 pesos in 1620 to 81,000 in 1629 (Scholes 1930:95, 186) and included sacramental wine and mass supplies; personal goods such as sandals, habits, soap, combs, mirrors, scissors, knives, and horseshoes; school supplies; kitchen equipment, majolica, and china dishes; pewter objects; and a variety of foods and spices, such as fine chocolate (the most costly single item on the Pecos inventory), saffron, cinnamon, honey, sugar, and olive oil. Drinking chocolate was an important component of many ritualized meetings, and the spices were used to maintain a semblance of the familiar Spanish taste in foods. The supply caravans also brought mail, passengers, and military equipment. Governors operating as private individuals as well as missionaries often used the returning caravans to export the items that they had collected and planned to sell in Mexico for personal profit. Missionaries had the final say in deciding what was included in the load and viewed the administrators' exports as "fruits of the unlawful exploitation of Indians" (Kessell 1978:149).

THE ENCOMIENDA

The most important institution of colonial administration was the encomienda grant of land and tribute, given by the governors to invaders, colonial settlers, and administrators as an incentive for going to New Mexico. The Spanish rationalization for the institution was that it provided a means of converting and civilizing the Pueblos; in exchange for these gifts, tribute and labor were demanded. All Pueblos had to perform encomienda service unless they worked for the clergy (Trigg 1999:259). An *encomendero* was entitled to receive certain supplies annually from natives: in the 1630s, it consisted of a cotton blanket (or buffalo or deer skin) and a *fanega* (about 2.6 bushels, weighing about 101 pounds) of corn from each household. While this may not seem like a large amount, it could have supplied half of the corn a Spanish settler needed for a year (Ivey 1994; D. H. Snow 1992a:

2:475), and many encomenderos controlled a number of households. Initially, and during years of adequate rain, the demands of the encomienda were probably manageable, but as the numbers of Spanish colonists increased and the number of Pueblo farmers declined—as a result of disease and other factors—when drought and famine occurred, it became an intolerable burden.

A family might hold encomienda grants to more than one pueblo. During the seventeenth century, pueblos were divided into halves, quarters, and other units for encomienda purposes (D. H. Snow 1992a:2:471). Francisco Gomex Robledo held title to "all of the pueblo of Pecos, except for 24 houses held by Pedro Lucero de Godoy; two and a half parts of the pueblo of Taos; half the Hopi pueblo of Shongopovi; [and] half the pueblo of Acoma" (Weber 1992:124). According to royal law, non-Indians of any type—Spanish, mestizo, mulatto or negro, encomendero, soldier, or colonist—were not to settle on Pueblo land or within their land grants, although this rule was more honored in its breach than its observance (Snow and Warren 1969/1973:41). Even when the rule was followed, the definition of "Pueblo land" was narrow and only applied to lands that were under cultivation (Butzer 1992:353). Well-watered land was in relatively short supply, and any that was not being used when the Spanish arrived would have been taken over by the settlers. Encomenderos were supposed to provide food for the priests from their own supplies (Barber 1932:75). In addition to serving the encomienda, Indian labor was to be used for the construction of Santa Fe and missions, among other things. In addition, colonists illegally used Pueblo people as household servants, as cargo carriers (which often took individuals away for long periods), and as herders and farmers. *Repartimiento* labor was another system that demanded Indian labor, often as an assessment levied on the community. Those doing repartimiento were excused from encomienda, and vice versa (Lang 1975). Any work above the required amount of forced labor was supposed to be compensated in wages but rarely was. Labor requirements were also supposedly limited in the amount of time demanded (Weber 1992:126). The encomienda lasted only until the Pueblo Revolt, but repartimiento continued.

An interesting aspect of Spanish colonial rule, similar to Dutch ideas about how colonial life should be managed, is that it tried to define separate Spanish and Indian living spaces. "Mission Indians" (those attached to a specific church) were not allowed to visit another pueblo or Santa Fe without a pass and would receive a punishment of 20 lashes if caught doing so (Simmons 1991:75; Weber 1992:111).

Encomenderos were prohibited from staying overnight in pueblos for more than one or two nights, although merchants were allowed three nights (Barber 1932:74); if they stayed at an inn or boarded with a family, they were to pay for their lodging.

However, the desired separation was not achieved. Pueblo towns appealed to the Spanish for the simple reason that the land was already cleared and housing existed that could easily be modified to suit Spanish preferences (Simmons 1991). The influx of settlers, the invasion of Pueblo land, and the lack of separation had demographic implications, as is evident in the rapid development of a New Mexican mestizo population, following on the heels of the sixteenth-century interbreeding of Mexican Indian women and Spanish men. In response to many instances of the sexual abuse of single women working as domestics, the law stipulated that only married women should be hired to work in Spanish homes and that their husbands should be hired by the same family in order to protect them from sexual abuse (Barber 1932:73). The development of mestizos and *castas* in the colonial New World is a distinctive attribute of Spanish settlement and represents a crucial difference between Spanish and Dutch colonial systems, and, on a larger scale, between Catholic and Protestant systems in the seventeenth century. It produced extensive and interesting problems of identity definition, which are discussed in chapter 5.

MANIFESTATIONS OF SPANISH IDENTITY

The equipment colonists from Mexico brought to New Mexico is fascinating and demonstrates more clearly and succinctly than any other data what the "essence" of being Spanish, especially a member of the elite, meant. Unfortunately, such items are unlikely to survive in the archaeological record, so the documentary record is the main source of information about them. Many brought clothing and elaborate accoutrements appropriate to Spanish and central Mexican social life: velvet suits with lace collars, satin hats, and silk dresses and shoes, all of which must have been put away in trunks or boxes once these colonists arrived in Santa Fe, where settlers wore deer skin and used many of the same materials for clothing that the Pueblos did (Simmons 1991:3–4), though wool replaced cotton, and cow and sheep hide clothing was added to deer skin (Adams 1989:85). Metal tools and other European items, such as writing and recordkeeping supplies, medicines, and the other kinds of equipment mentioned earlier, were also essential. Large kitchen items and household furnishings were probably made after arrival, but some Spanish and Mexican majolica dishes were brought along. Pottery, probably made by nearby Indian or genizaro women, was used for everyday functions.

The colonists saw themselves as bearers of civilization, bringing language and culture, as well as Christianity, to the wilderness. In part, this meant introducing Spanish crops, domestic animals, and farming methods. These crops consisted of apples, peaches, grapes, apricots, cantelopes, watermelons, wheat, barley, cabbages, onions, lettuce, and radishes. Mexican foods (tomatoes, chilis, new forms of beans and corn) also made their way north, as did spices and other items of Spanish cuisine. The acequia system of irrigation was introduced (Simmons 1991:66, 74), as were cattle, sheep, goats, horses, pigs, chickens, and Spanish dogs (primarily mastiffs and greyhounds), which interbred with the Pueblo dogs, previously noted for their ability to climb ladders (Simmons 1991:36–37). The impact of these items varied, the single most important innovation being sheep. Well suited to the New Mexico environment, these animals had a dramatic and rapid effect on Pueblo subsistence and the local ecology, some of it negative: they caused changes in plant communities, environmental degradation, and erosion.

SPANISH TOWN PLANNING

The settlers' concept of a town derived directly from the formal grid used in planning Roman towns. The Spanish were basically town-dwellers, as were the Dutch, used to living in rectangular blocks built around a plaza or plazas containing the important sacred and governmental structures of the community. Private house sites were supplemented by common lands outside of town meant for pasture and other purposes, and by property owned by the municipal government itself (Simmons 1969:8). Town locations were chosen for their agricultural potential and defensibility and were to follow established guidelines about wall placement and the spacing between houses, between houses and church, and between Indians and Spanish residents (Hackett 1923:187). However, Santa Fe, the first such town, expanded from the initial walled town into a more linear form, placing houses relatively close to fields in order to protect crops from hungry animals and raiding Comanches (Bustamante 1989).

Spanish and traditional Pueblo architecture and community layout have some interesting similarities. Both used adobe and stone as building materials, built rectangular structures consisting of aggregated rectangular rooms, and built around plazas where communally important structures (churches, kivas, municipal buildings) were located. There were many differences as well, of course, central among them the governing structure associated with the community form and reflected in its architecture. The Spanish Empire maintained its highly differentiated political hierarchy even in remote outposts, albeit in reduced form. The Pueblo community was much less hierarchical and was connected by loosely associated kin groups and men's societies.

EVENTS LEADING TO THE PUEBLO REVOLT

The Pueblo Revolt of 1680 represents the single known occasion when all Pueblos acted in concert. At that time between 17,000 and 30,000 Indians lived in the Rio Grande drainage, along with some 1,000 to 2,350 Spaniards (Knaut 1995:134; Scholes 1930:96), most of whom lived in Santa Fe. Under the leadership of a medicine man named Popé (Hall 1989:90; Knaut 1995:167; Gutiérrez 1991:132; Weber 1992:134), and several others who "understood the Spanish mentality" (Sando 1979), a group of Pueblo leaders rose up and killed or drove out all Spanish residents, sacred and secular, and their dependents and servants. The rebellion focused on religious issues but in reality sprang from many factors. During the revolt, the Indians destroyed the missions, burned Santa Fe, and killed 21 religious and between 200 and 400 colonists. The rest of the colonists, administrators, and missionaries were allowed to flee from New Mexico and headed south to the area of today's El Paso, where they stayed until the Reconquista of 1693. The revolt occurred in the wake of 15 to 20 years of drought (resulting from little rainfall and high temperatures) and increasing food shortages (Gutiérrez 1991:130; Weber 1992:133). Agricultural difficulties and the increased pressure on the food supply from the combined effects of Spanish demands, Athapaskan raiding that made harvesting difficult, and the declining size of the Pueblo population aggravated by epidemic disease led to starvation. A letter from Fray Bernàl in 1669 said, "The whole land is at war with the widespread heathen nation of the Apache Indians . . . for three years no crops have been harvested. In the past year, 1668, a great many Indians perished of hunger, lying dead along the roads, in the ravines, and in their huts" (Ivey 1994:1). While food shortages played a large role in the revolt, Spanish settlers and the Pueblos shared these hardships to some degree. It seems as though the Spanish could have eaten mutton, but records indicate the settlers had little food: "For two years the food of Spaniards, men and women alike, has been the hides of cattle which they had in their houses" (Ivey 1994:76).

Mission-controlled fields and flocks fed soldiers and guards and supported military campaigns, before being shared with settlers or Indian people.

The Pueblo population had declined as a result of war and disease, the effects of which were amplified by the Spanish policy of aggregation. Supposedly meant to improve defensibility but designed to simplify control of the natives, it facilitated the spread of certain epidemic diseases (Ramenofsky 1996). When the Spanish entered New Mexico, 100–150 Pueblo villages existed; by 1643 only 43 remained (Hall 1989:76, 88) (see chapter 3). As corn supplies dwindled, the traditional trading relationships with Athapaskans were disrupted by raids of Apaches, Navajos, and Comanches, many of whom had acquired horses and guns early in the seventeenth century. When raiders could not get food, they took whatever else was available—sheep, horses, and Indians to be sold as slaves—triggering what has been described as a cycle of endemic warfare (Hall 1989:83–85).

Another significant factor leading to the revolt was the missionaries' efforts to squelch native religion. The scarcity of rain would have made it clear that the friars' claims to control of the supernatural were invalid. A number of repressive incidents led to isolated rebellions from the 1630s onward. In a particularly harsh reaction to "idolatry," three Indians were hanged in 1675, and more than 40 "leaders" suffered lashing for sorcery and sedition (Knaut 1995; Spicer 1962:162; Weber 1992:133). While the revolt is said to have been organized as a reaction to religious oppression, it was really an outgrowth of the malfunction of the political economy (Hall 1989:90) and represents the culmination and best-organized expression of a series of efforts to reject Spanish control (Preucel 2002). It had a number of consequences, the most long-term, perhaps, being that the Indians gained control for the first time of significant numbers of sheep. Despite the success of the revolt, the cohesion of the Pueblos did not last long, factionalism reemerged shortly thereafter (Preucel 2002). Some Pueblos, especially those whose villages lay further south, such as the Piros and Southern Tiwa, did not join the revolt but allied with the Spanish and moved south with them, founding Isleta del Sur (Spicer 1962:163), while others moved west or into refuge areas, in anticipation of military reprisals by the returning colonial administrators and as a result of intra-Pueblo factional strife. Although the strife resumed, the revolt accomplished a great deal. When the Spanish returned they, modified their demands and reached a compromise on several critical issues, especially concerning Pueblo religion. Indeed, today's

Rio Grande Pueblos credit the revolt with having saved Pueblo culture (Frank 1998:52).

THE RECONQUISTA AND THE SECOND COLONIAL PERIOD

The Reconquista in 1693 was not difficult. After an initial foray in 1692, Don Diego de Vargas entered each pueblo, sometimes alone, and told each group that the Spanish were not angry. He subsequently reported that the Indians "were happy to see me" (Kessell 1989:130). The friars rebaptized the Pueblos and began the construction of 40 new missions. A second attempt at a revolt in 1696 failed, in part because the invaders were able to exploit rifts between Pueblo factions that appear to have disagreed on issues including cooperation with the colonists (Kessell 1989:130). Factions such as these have been described historically and are also known to exist in many pueblos today. While members may be described as "traditional/conservative" or "liberal," the labels often represent a number of differences related to age and access to power, land, ritual offices, and other sources of prestige. Vargas played on these rivalries by honoring Indians who helped the Spanish with guns, horses, and titles (Weber 1992:131), while enslaving or executing those who stubbornly resisted. For some, the best response to the reentry of the Spanish was to leave the Rio Grande Valley and head west to Hopi, Zuni, Acoma, or the newly formed Laguna; Vargas never regained control of any of these western areas during the Reconquista.

An important aspect of the second colonial period was the effort to bring greater numbers of Hispanics to settle in New Mexico. Each colonist who came was given tools and settled on land outside the pueblos. The relatively small number of pre-Revolt haciendas was replaced by a larger number of ranchos, smaller in scale. Many of those who had left for El Paso during the revolt returned to the same land (Snow 1984:100). From that point on, the Hispanic population began to increase, while the native population declined. The Pueblo population, estimated by missionaries at as many as 80,000 people in 1630, shrank to about 14,000 at the turn of the eighteenth century (Weber 1992) and dropped to about 9,000 in 1776, leaving the Pueblos behind the Spanish population (table 2.1).

The Tano, most of whom lived in the Galisteo Basin, were almost completely decimated by war, disease, and emigration, some going west to Hopi or Laguna. Pecos held only a handful of residents, the population of Taos was 700 in 1707

Table 2.1
Pueblo and Spanish/Hispanic Population, Sixteenth to Eighteenth Centuries

Year	Pueblos	Spanish/Hispanic
1540	45,000 (Castañeda)	0
1630	80,000 (Benavides)	1,000 (Gutiérrez 1991:106)
1680	17,000 (Frank 1998:66)	2,380 (Frank)
1800	9,400 (Frank)	4,850 (Frank)

and 505 in 1765, while Zia dropped from 2,000–3,000 to 508 in 1765; in the same year, San Ildefonso had 484 residents, half of its size 100 years earlier (Spicer 1962:166). Continuing hostility between Indians and Spanish, a number of severe smallpox epidemics, increasing Athapaskan raiding, and Indian poverty all took their toll on Pueblo communities. Hispanic immigrants began to move into depopulated pueblos such as Taos, San Juan, and San Ildefonso, and by the 1790s New Mexico's Rio Grande Valley had three Spanish towns of at least 2,000 people: Santa Fe, Albuquerque, and Santa Cruz de la Cañada , plus El Paso to the south. Abiquiú, Belén, Tomé, San José de las Huertas, San Miguel del Vado, and Ojo Caliente were all small genizaro and Hispanic settlements constructed as buffers to protect Santa Fe from raiders. Defense against Athapaskans, who attacked settlements and supply trains alike, was one of the priorities of the second colonial period, requiring an organized military presence, as did the defense of Spanish colonial territory against possible encroachments by the British and the French in the eighteenth century (Gutiérrez 1991:148).

A number of things were different during this second colonial period. Some are manifest in population differences and others in attitudes and behavior. This period marks the beginning of the Hispanic culture, although Spain remained the formal administrator of the colony. Perhaps the most significant change was a change in Hispanic attitude toward Pueblo religion such that some previous views of traditional ritual and kivas were softened to characterize them as less dangerous than had previously been thought. By 1776, Fray Domìnguez had likened kivas to "chapter, or council rooms" and suggested that rituals practiced were "not essentially wicked" (Kessell 1989:127). The focus on conversion characteristic of the early phase of the colony had also diminished by the eighteenth century (Simmons 1991:55), although maintaining Catholicism was still a priority and the costs of the religious enterprise remained high. The church's economic power had diminished somewhat, as had its control of the transport system between Mexico and New Mexico; the church now had to make its own arrangements for receiving shipments of supplies (Kessell 1987:302). Conflict between church and state continued but may have been less bitter because of the weakened power of the church and fewer friars (Webster 1997:187). It is unclear to what degree Pueblo religion had been integrated with the Catholic faith. Priests continued to draw parallels between the two and incorporate symbols important to Pueblo religion into Catholicism (Gutiérrez 1991:163), but most Pueblos did not seem to confuse the two. It is more likely that many accepted the foreign faith to varying degrees while still practicing their own. What seems to have changed in this second period is that the friars were more accepting of this situation than they were before the revolt.

The Bourbon reforms abolished the encomienda obligations of food and cloth but replaced them with Repartimiento, forced labor, although some officials continued to demand tribute in cloth (Webster 1997:41). Any Indians who worked longer than the required amount were to be reimbursed. The official tone seemed somewhat more conciliatory toward the Pueblos now, and a number of Hispanic institutions, such as *compadrazgo* (godparent ties) and *vecindàd* (shared community ties) were used to unite settlers and indigenous people (Kessell 1989:19). The development of Hispanic culture reflects the connections between these groups, and the material culture in particular shows both indigenous and Spanish influence. There was no question, however, of what the dominant culture was in the colonists' eyes; the Spanish language was essential for identity, as were some symbolic objects manifesting the—at this point almost mythical—connection to Spain. A negotiated peace with the Comanches in 1770 and a program of smallpox vaccination in 1805 meant easier conditions for settlement and more immigrants from Mexico (Frank 1998:49).

Peoples of the Hudson and Mohawk River Valleys

THE GEOGRAPHY OF THE HUDSON RIVER VALLEY

The Hudson and Mohawk River Valleys are different from the Rio Grande River-Valley in several respects, perhaps the most significant being annual rainfall and agricultural conditions. These river corridors looked attractive to European settlers for another reason—they provided easy access between a deepwater port in New Amsterdam/New York and the interior of the country, where beaver pelts and other skins could be obtained. The Hudson River runs north-south through a glacially formed narrow valley. North of Albany, the area around the river widens out and is relatively flat, while to the south it is wide until about today's Catskill Mountains, where the valley narrows and continues between terraces and hills (Cressey 1966:29). The river is divided into two parts, the lower navigable section that flows from Troy to New York Harbor, and the smaller segment above Troy. The lower part is an estuary (Tarr 1902:184) that supported considerable oyster beds until well into the eighteenth century, thus providing a food source to indigenous inhabitants. The Mohawk River Valley runs westward from its intersection with the Hudson at Albany. Most Iroquoian settlement in the area between the Hudson and Genessee Rivers gravitated to the well-watered lowlands (Cressey 1966:26).

New York State is characterized as having a "humid continental climate" (Carter 1966:72). This means reasonably cool temperatures, although there is considerable seasonal variation. Agriculture in the areas settled by the Iroquois would have benefited from about 180 frost-free days. In contrast to the southwestern United States, the Hudson-Mohawk area is relatively cloudy, with cold snowy winters and warm dry summers. Equally important, the annual rainfall of 35–50 inches is distributed fairly evenly over the year, averaging about 2.5–3.5 inches per month (Carter 1966:67–75). The forest cover consists primarily of oak and northern hardwoods. Soils are alluvial, with good agricultural potential.

THE PREHISTORY OF THE IROQUOIS

When did the Mohawks come to the Hudson Valley? For many archaeologists, the important question is not whether the ancestors of the Iroquois migrated into the area west of the Hudson River between Albany and Buffalo, where they were when the Dutch arrived (Snow 1994), but whether their culture developed there—as proposed by the in situ hypothesis (MacNeish 1976; Tuck 1971). Wherever it originated, the Iroquois culture of interest here developed in the area between the Hudson and the Genesee Rivers from Late Woodland ancestral groups beginning around A.D. 900. Initial archaeological research defined a series of phases: those prior to contact included Owasco (900–1150), Oak Hill (1350–1400), Chance (1400–1525), and Garoga (1550–1575), although there was some disagreement as to the order, existence, and dates of these (Bradley 1987; Guldenzopf 1984; Lenig

1977; Ritchie and Funk 1973; Snow 1994, 1996). With the aid of an impressive series of 14C dates and historical references for Mohawk sites, Dean Snow has redefined the chronology and established individual sites and groupings that are especially relevant for the later part of the Mohawk sequence.

Since the story in this book begins in the seventeenth century, I use information derived from archaeological sites and some ethnohistoric accounts to compile a picture of Mohawk life just prior to and at the time of contact, in the late Precolumbian. Many archaeologists have conducted research on Iroquois groups, including the western Senecas of the Genesee Valley (Hamell 1980; Niemczycki 1984; Wray et al. 1987, 1991) and the centrally located Onondaga (Bradley 1987; Tuck 1971), as well as the Mohawks (Guldenzopf 1984, 1986; Kuhn 1985, 1986a; Kuhn and Funk 2000; Ritchie and Funk 1973; Snow 1994, 1995). Iroquois groups differed from one another, especially after contact with European peoples and their goods had begun. For the Mohawks, as keepers of the eastern door, their experience with European colonists and access to their goods was very different from that of the Senecas, keepers of the western door. However, a composite picture may be valid for some aspects of culture and society, especially in reference to late Precolumbian life. It seems extreme to state that "the culture of Onondaga *as it is today,* and as it was described by explorers, missionaries, and travelers *during the early decades of European contact,* differs little from that of the surrounding Five Nations tribes" (Tuck 1971:2, emphasis added). Surely the groups differed from one another, and the Onondaga today are rather different from their ancestors at contact.

The Mohawks traditionally made their home in the mid–Mohawk Valley, from the Schoharie Creek west to East Canada Creek, a distance of 30 miles. All known Mohawk sites are found within a core area that stretches 4 miles to the north and south of the Mohawk River, and between today's Amsterdam and Little Falls (D. R. Snow 1992:4), although they are known to have had a larger hunting territory, which extended north into the Adirondacks and south down the Susquehanna River almost as far as Oneonta (Guldenzopf 1984) (figure 2.4).

SUBSISTENCE

The Iroquois had a mixed economy: they practiced shifting horticulture, based on the cultivation of corn, beans, and squash, with sunflower and tobacco as other domesticates. Land was cleared by men, but farming was primarily women's work,

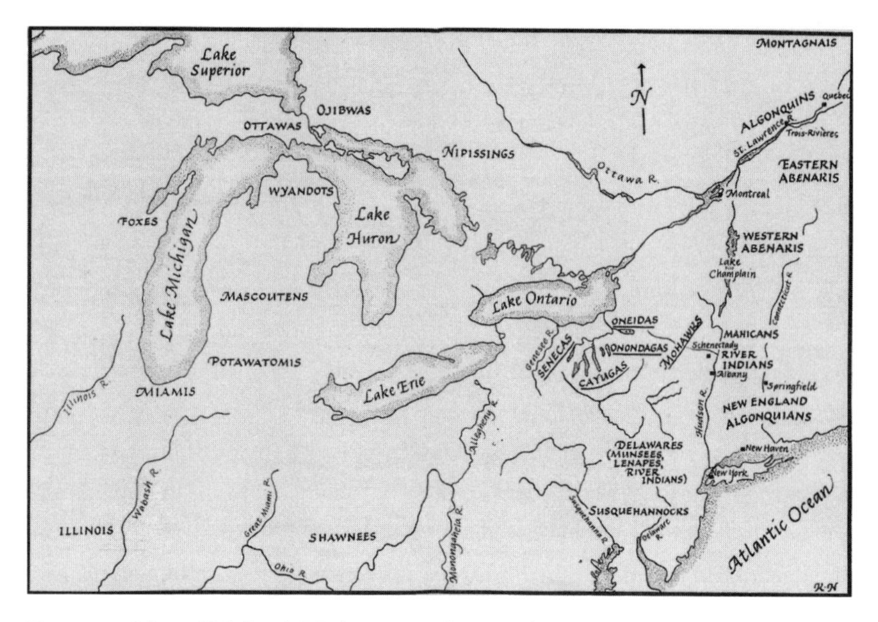

Figure 2.4. Map of Mohawk-Hudson area, showing the Iroquois and neighboring groups in the mid–seventeenth century.

with the women from a matrilineage forming the effective unit of labor (Snow 1995:129). They also collected plants—those noted by early visitors include wild berries, fruits (grapes, plums, and mayapples), and chestnuts, walnuts, and probably hickory nuts (Tuck 1971:4). Hunting was an important seasonal activity for men, focused on deer, small mammals and water birds, with beaver and bear significant at various times. It was the men's job to fish, make war, and conduct the community's political life; they also grew tobacco (Snow 1994:70). Van den Bogaert's 1635 journal notes that one village was empty in midwinter because everyone was out hunting (Bogaert et al. 1988). Late Precolumbian faunal assemblages at Otsungo and Elwood (1300–1525) were dominated by deer (more than 80 percent), with only 2–3 percent beaver present; dog made up 6 percent and bear 3 percent of bone count frequencies (NISP). Dogs may have been eaten primarily during ritual feasts (Kuhn and Funk 2000). A wide range of small mammals, rodents, birds, turtles, shellfish, and fish have been recovered and were consumed as food. Apparently fishing was less significant to the Mohawks than to some other groups for there were no large lakes in their immediate area and the falls at the confluence of the Mohawk and Hudson prevented many species of fish from entering the Mohawk (Kuhn and Funk 2000:7). However, Tuck (1971:3) notes the presence of seasonal fishing villages among the historic period Onondaga.

As Iroquois population grew in the sixteenth century and up to about 1635 and the first epidemic, village relocations became more frequent. Although there is some disagreement about the consistency of subsistence and settlement pattern during the long period from Owasco to just before contact at 1600 (Funk 1978: 64), ceramic styles and other aspects of material culture did change. Settlements may have aggregated in response to the Little Ice Age after 1300, which resulted in a shorter growing season and a diminished yield from farming. Settlement location was influenced by land productivity; during other periods, however, defense was a high priority (Snow 1994:33).

Settlements appear to have moved about every 10–15 or 20 years as land became infertile and wood supplies for fuel and construction became depleted (Richter 1992:23; D. R. Snow 1992; Tuck 1971; Wray 1985:102). Since the Mohawks and all Iroquois practiced slash-and-burn farming, when group size was small it was possible to stay within a relatively small area and shift fields without relocating the community. By the sixteenth century, however, more frequent moves became necessary, and during the seventeenth century, the easternmost Mohawks moved quite often, for reasons discussed in the next section (Guldenzopf 1984; Snow 1994). The interval may have been longer in earlier periods—at least among the Onondaga prior to their coalescence into one nation in the fifteenth century, when larger numbers of people created greater pressure on finite resources (Tuck 1971:213–214).

SETTLEMENT AND HOUSING

The Mohawks spent most of their time in stockaded or fortified village settlements, which Europeans called "castles." In addition, there were probably small unfortified sites, perhaps seasonal camps and hamlets, which are not as well documented archaeologically (for example, the Van der Werken site, Cassedy et al. 1996). Many factors affected settlement and house size, including population, defense concerns, and the quality of farmland (Snow 1994:33). While house size varied widely, Iroquoian house form seemed much the same from about A.D. 900 (Owasco) onward. (Funk 1978:64) The earliest "longhouses" were short and unstandardized. By the sixteenth century, those at Garoga averaged more than 56 meters in length and housed about 90 people each (Snow 1996:170) (figure 2.5).

As houses were enlarged, more of their floor space was used for living and less was available for food storage. Women must have been willing to cooperate in a unit of this size, with some senior women deferring to others rather than asserting their own importance (Snow 1994:74); a similar commitment to harmony at the village level would have been essential to a densely packed community of longhouses. Village clusters, houses, and villages all grew larger and fewer in number throughout the fifteenth and sixteenth centuries. This change suggests consolidation, but there is no evidence of population reduction; in fact, numbers seem larger, perhaps partly as a result of migration. Around the time of contact, communities began placing cemeteries adjacent to villages, whereas previously they were separate and perhaps even located in a central place (Snow 1996:171). In some societies, burial of the dead in proximity to residence is used to establish an ancestral claim to particular places (Goody in Rothschild 1991); I do not know if this was true for the Mohawks.

As warfare intensified after 1200, villages were palisaded and fortified for the

Figure 2.5. An Iroquois longhouse, or *cabannes sauvage,* part of a map of Fort Frontenac drawn around 1720.

first time (Snow 1994:30). This practice continued until the formation of the Iroquois Great League of Peace and Power (Richter 1992:30), perhaps toward the end of the sixteenth century or early in the seventeenth (Kuhn and Sempowksi 2001), which increased the feeling of security among all Iroquois groups. Later changes in settlement pattern structure reflect an interest in protecting trade routes as well as defensive concerns. The nucleated pattern of three or four large villages noted by Europeans may have begun shortly before contact with the Dutch, around A.D. 1550. Early in the 1600s, the Mohawks shifted from tightly nucleated and palisaded sites, located on hilltops, to more open ones on terraces overlooking and closer to the Mohawk River, eastward along the major route to Fort Orange (Burke 1991:24; Lenig 1977:72; Snow 1992:14, 1995:53, 1996:172). They may have chosen these new locations closer to the river in order to see and intercept Indian traders heading to the fort with furs, although Snow (1996:173) has suggested that it may relate to a more intensive form of agriculture. Mohawk villages remained within a corridor limited at its eastern and western edges (D. R. Snow 1992:15).

Three or four main Mohawk settlements or castles were recorded at contact, along with several smaller hamlets or satellites (Guldenzopf 1984; Lenig 1977:71). They were spaced apart throughout the Mohawk settlement area and were often moved to the north and south of the river, sometimes retaining the old village name in a new location (although it is hard to tell because the names are spelled quite differently by the various European observers). Van den Bogaert describes eight villages during his 1634 trip into Mohawk country (probably four communities in the process of moving to new locations; D. R. Snow, personal communication 2001), including three large ones abandoned because of smallpox. While I speak of "the Mohawks," each of these castles represents a residential group that is likely to have had a slightly different relationship with the Dutch because of historic circumstances and geographical position. Given these and the likely differences between clan segments and power within communities, trade, sociopolitical, and other relations between different Mohawk settlements and the Dutch would have been quite variable.

Two other Iroquois groups provide good archaeological information on settlement, revealing a similar pattern of living in several major settlements. The Onondaga developed from Owasco to Iroquois in larger, more sedentary groups living in palisaded settlements located on hills (Bradley 1987:22). They lived in two main communities from the mid–fifteenth century until European contact in the seventeenth century (Tuck 1971:20, 216), although they merged into one political unit by around 1500 (late in the Chance phase), forming what came to be known as the Onondaga Nation (Bradley 1987). A century later, in a development that parallels that of the Mohawks, sites were moved from hilltops to plateaus and ridges, perhaps because defense and fortification were of less concern owing to the Great Peace derived from the Five Nations Confederacy, which Bradley (1987:34–35, 43) thinks was formed during this phase.

The Senecas also lived in two large coexisting villages during the seventeenth century, each with satellites within a few miles. There were about 4,000 Senecas in the early 1600s, and their population remained fairly stable throughout the century, despite catastrophic epidemics and warfare with other non-Iroquois groups (Wray 1985:102). They had less contact with Europeans than Iroquois to the east; most of their encounters were with military personnel and Jesuit missionaries. Their experience differed from that of the Mohawks particularly in terms of the proximity and intensity of European contact. For the Senecas, too, the formation of the League likely reduced the frequency of war with other Iroquois groups and affected their settlement placement.

By the early eighteenth century, a large proportion of the surviving Mohawks had emigrated to what is now Canada (see the next section). The few who remained in the Mohawk River Valley were described as living in small "cabins" (Guldenzopf 1984; Snow 1995), housing 5–10 people in two dispersed communities: Fort Hunter, built by the English at Mohawk request to protect them from the French, and Indian Castle. Data from the Seneca region suggest significant differences between the Mohawks and the Senecas at this time, related to the latter's relative isolation from contact. Jordan (2002) has recently recovered the remains of an eighteenth-century Seneca "shorthouse" and offers a convincing critique of the common assumption—based on documentary accounts—that all Iroquois had by that time made a rapid transition from longhouses to European-style cabins. The question of house size is frequently linked to an important assumption that the matrilineal system, which provided the social glue for Iroquois life, disappeared with the longhouse, and Jordan disputes that idea as well.

SOCIOPOLITICAL ORGANIZATION

Mohawk life was characterized by a gendered division of labor that extended beyond subsistence activities to sociopolitical life. Iroquois society is well known for being matrilineal, with matrilocal residence after marriage; longhouses contained matrilineally related nuclear families of the same clan (Snow 1995:44). Marriage involved lineage and sometimes clan exogamy (Snow 1994:39). During times of sufficient population, especially prior to European-introduced epidemic disease, a village comprised all three Mohawk clans. Senior women as well as men had political power and held their own councils, and those from the dominant lineages or clan segments of each unit of the league chose the sachem of that clan (Richter 1992:43; Snow 1994:62). Iroquois women may have been misunderstood and taken to represent both more and less than they were: they "were not matriarchs, or Amazons or drudges" (Snow 1994:65) but were valued especially for their important economic role as food producers (Richter 1992:42), controlling domestic spaces and adjacent agricultural fields (Snow 1994:129).

Village clusters appear to have conducted only limited economic trade or exchange of ceremonial items such as pipes, perhaps in the form of gift exchange between males (Kuhn 1985). Bradley (1987:43) notes an increase on Onondaga sites of exotic materials (marine shell, nonlocal lithic materials, and native copper), which he attributes to league formation. In contrast to the southwest, however, there is no evidence of commodity exchange between clusters, and both trace element analysis and examination of ceramic styles suggest that ceramics were used relatively close to the place where they were made (D. R. Snow 1992:12). Some ceramic evidence in the form of locally produced wares with foreign motifs suggests "foreign" tribes lived with Mohawks in their longhouses, presumably as a result of capture or adoption (Kuhn 1986b). Around the beginning of the eighteenth century, Iroquoian life was not highly stratified but consisted of a three-tier hierarchy with chiefs and clan mothers at the top, ordinary people forming the majority in the second tier, and unincorporated captives at the bottom (Snow 1994:130). Clans linked villages but were not all equal; some were larger than others and had more important leaders and titles. The size of the kin unit was important as it determined the number of individuals that could be mobilized for a given purpose. Clans contained internal factions, although it is unclear when these were mobilized. Leadership positions held by both men and women seem to have provided more political power than economic benefit; the two were linked at events such as feasts.

The crystallization of Mohawk political entities resulted from co-occurring nucleation at regional, village, and household levels. Each of these units was able to (and at times needed to) absorb migrants and refugees as well as captives from other groups (Richter 1992; D. R. Snow 1992). Initially, wars left gaps in the sociopolitical structure, but as European-introduced diseases ran rampant through Mohawk villages, too few people were available at times to fill important positions. The incorporation of outsiders is visible in archaeological assemblages; for example, the presence of Huron pottery in Iroquois sites suggests the adoption of foreigners captured in raids. The pottery at Jackson-Everson, a late seventeenth-century Mohawk site, shows that Huron outsiders were able to maintain their own identity in such settings; 80 percent of the ceramic ware had Huron designs but was locally made (Kuhn 1986b). One Huron is described as telling the Mohawks that he was seeking them in order to find his relatives and friends (Richter 1992:72). Once adopted or intermarried, foreigners became full members of the group and were eligible for office, even a political one (Delage 1991:232).

As was true in the southwest, by the time of contact a number of integrating mechanisms were cross-cutting kinship lines. These included the False Face Society, medicine societies, and the Eagle, Bear, Buffalo, and Little Water Societies. Interestingly, there were no men's houses or ceremonial structures similar to kivas, perhaps because the men were away often and for long periods (D. R. Snow 1992:11). Tuck (1971:213–214) suggests that these societies may have come into existence among the Onondaga during the fifteenth-century period of convergence and then persisted. They would have functioned to exchange information, creating safety mechanisms during times of increasing pressure on resources, when more people were exploiting the same locations for firewood, game, and farmland, and there were more frequent village relocations. The quest for beaver also sparked conflict among Iroquois, especially between them and their neighbors. The formation of the league served to reduce intra-Iroquois conflict by promoting internal peace, although it did not stop war with others. It may have operated more as a ceremonial-ritual institution at its inception, but by the late seventeenth century it had become more political in the face of increasing colonial pressure (Richter 1992:169). A cyclical relationship began in the late 1630s and early 1640s between war and the quest for beaver skins and for new tribal members, the Beaver Wars and the Mourning Wars. Conflict over furs was perhaps less intense than the fighting in response to epidemic disease and death, and the rents in the social structure that these produced as they multiplied. The death of a relative produced an intense reaction necessitating a raid and the taking of a captive, who would be tortured and then killed or adopted, to ease the sorrows of the group (Richter 1992: 32–35, 40). Once the league had been established, the wars continued but focused on non-Iroquois peoples such as the Huron and "virtually every Indian people in the Northeast" after the 1630s (Richter 1992:62; Trigger 1976; White 1991).

THE MOHAWKS AND THE MAHICANS IN THE EARLY SEVENTEENTH CENTURY

At the beginning of the seventeenth century, when Henry Hudson sailed up the river later named for him, the Mahicans—an Algonkian group—were the primary occupants of both sides of the upper Hudson Valley, in an area extending from what is today northern Dutchess County to Lake Champlain (Dunn 1994:50; Gehring and Starna 1992:8). There were about 6,400 Algonkian-speaking Mahicans in 1609 (D. R. Snow, personal communication). They included the Wappingers on the east bank (in what is now Dutchess and Putnam Counties) and the Esopus on the west side of the Hudson; all of them spoke Munsee, a branch of Algonkian (Goddard 1978). Their ancestors had moved north from the Raritan River, and they were affiliated with Delawares (Lenni Lenape and Munsee) to the south (Ruttenber [1872]1971:25). The Mohawks were to their west. The various European accounts of Native Americans are confused and confusing about what groups existed, who was where, what they called themselves, and how they were identified by European observers (Gehring and Starna 1988).

Information on Precolumbian Mahicans is sparse. They have been described as similar in many ways to the Mohawks, with a mixed subsistence based on horticulture, hunting, and fishing and a matrilineal society (Bender and Curtin 1990). A few archaeological sites—such as the Menands Bridge, Winney's Rift, Schuylerville, Hinley, and the Late Woodland Dennis sites—are thought to represent Precolumbian Mahican settlements (Bender and Curtin 1990; Brumbach and Bender 1986; Funk 1965). Archaeologists have found no evidence of Precolumbian fortified or stockaded communities (Bender and Curtin 1990:5). Juet, a member of Hudson's expedition, describes them in 1609 as living along the river and growing corn, beans, squash, and tobacco on cleared land (Dunn 1994:19). They lived in a slightly different environment than some of their neighbors did, as the Upper Hudson was located in a zone of southern hardwoods. This far upriver there were no oysters, but there were spring fish runs (Bender and Curtin 1990:2).

Several writers suggest that the Mahicans were living in three villages at contact, but none of these has been located archaeologically (Gehring and Starna 1992:9). These are thought to have been small semipermanent, dispersed and unstockaded hamlets, similar to a settlement type seen elsewhere in New England prior to contact (Bender and Curtin 1990:4–12). Chiefs' houses were larger than others, decorated with painting and carving, and are believed to have served as ceremonial centers (Gehring and Starna 1992). Reports suggest that in protohistoric and early contact times stockaded villages began appearing on hills, with a few oval, bark-covered longhouses in each. These were smaller than Iroquois structures, but each contained several nuclear families (Gehring and Starna 1992: 9). These fortified villages may have been established as a result of conflict with the Mohawks or European contact (Bender and Curtin 1990:6; Gehring and Starna 1992:10).

No discussion of Mohawk-Mahican relationships is possible without understanding what was going on further to the north, where the French and various Algonkian-speaking groups controlled trade. The latter, fortified with French hatchets and assistance, had evicted the Iroquois from the St. Lawrence Valley by 1610 and from the Ottawa Valley by 1620 (Trigger 1971:277), both prime trading areas. Prior to that time, Tadoussac, 600 miles to the northeast on the St. Lawrence River, would have been the major source of European goods, perhaps acquired as war booty (Trigger 1962:246 in Lenig 1977:73); the Susquehanna River may have also served as a channel for some goods (Bradley 1987). In any case, between 1603 and 1628, the Mohawks were in a poor trade position, and the arrival of the Dutch along the Hudson was crucial in offering them a chance to become involved in the fur trade. In order to gain exclusive trade access to the Dutch, they needed to displace the Mahicans (Trigger 1971:279).

Initially the Dutch established relations with the Mahicans. They were familiar with Algonkian-speakers from the lower Hudson, and they wanted to take over the French-controlled trade. The Mohawks would have been "unnecessary" (Trigger 1971:278). The Dutch had wampum from Long Island, which gave them an advantage over the French, who had no continuing wampum supply. The Mahicans were able to extract tribute from the Mohawks as they visited Fort Nassau (Dunn 1994:6) to trade with the Dutch. Almost immediately, by 1614–1618, a Mahican-Mohawk covenant allowed trade between both parties and the Dutch (Dunn 1994:41, 81). A mere 10 years later, between 1624 and 1628, after a battle between the Mohawks and the Mahicans in which both used guns obtained from the Dutch, the Mahicans were displaced, ultimately moving east into Massachusetts and Connecticut. The Mohawks had gained control of the west bank of the Hudson by 1630, or perhaps considerably earlier (Burke 1991:24–26; Dunn 1994:6; Paul Huey, personal communication 2002). Although the Dutch initially sided with the Mahicans in their conflict with the Mohawks (Rink 1986), they were later able to persuade the Mohawks that their previous alliance had been a mistake, and from 1630 on the Dutch and Mohawks maintained a close alliance; in particular, the Mohawks controlled trading access to the Dutch (Trigger 1971:282).

There is an interesting parallel between Mohawk and Dutch behavior early in their relationship, in that both behaved as brokers, manipulating goods and competing groups to their own advantage. It is axiomatic that the more trading partners available, the more control a trader had. The Mohawks were able to negotiate between French, British, Swedes, and Dutch, while the Dutch tried to obtain furs from both Iroquois and Algonkian peoples. If a European trader had many competing suppliers, fur prices were low, and conversely, prices could be elevated when different colonial traders were trying to get the same limited supplies. These economic factors had a great impact on political treaties and alliances. The French could not afford a treaty that excluded their Algonkian allies, while neither the French nor the Mohawks could allow a peace that would give those allies trading access to the Dutch (Trigger 1971:282). After the mid–seventeenth century, other peoples and factors came into play as local supplies of beaver dwindled and Iroquois, particularly those further west, began to raid other groups and territories for furs. Where Dutch and Mohawk behavior differs, however, is that individual European traders acted individually and competitively, whereas the Mohawks maintained a traditional economic system in which redistribution and reciprocity governed the flow of European goods throughout their society.

POPULATION

The European impact on Native American population in the Hudson Valley is difficult to assess without reliable estimates of the pre-European population. Van den Bogaart's (1635) chronicle of a winter trip to the Mohawk area is a valuable source used by a number of archaeologists. Starna and Snow suggest a pre-epidemic population of about 7,750 (Snow 1995:4). Although population loss after sustained contact was decidedly dramatic, opinions differ as to the rate of decline: Snow (1995:4) suggests that roughly two-thirds of the population died as a result of epidemic diseases after the 1630s, dropping to about 2,800 between 1634 and 1635, and then to 1,100 between 1679 and 1693. Greenhalgh's journal reports 300 fighting men in 1677; if one accepts Snow's estimate that soldiers represented 25 percent of the population, this suggests 1,200 in total (Snow et al. 1996:191). Whichever figures are correct, these losses forced the Mohawks to reconsolidate and reduce the size of longhouses. As this trend continued, and Mohawk population was affected by war, disease, and emigration, houses were reportedly reduced to cabin size after 1700, housing nuclear families (Snow 1996:78). House size thus went from a probable maximum of 90 per house during the Garoga phase to a suggested low of 5 people per house in 1770, although there has been no archaeological confirmation of this estimate (Guldenzopf 1986:87–92). In the wake of continuing disease and emigration to Canada, the population at the beginning of the eighteenth century was quite small (see chapter 3). Eventually the Mohawks left the Mohawk Valley, selling their land to Europeans, who used it quite differently: they established permanent settlements, with intensive agriculture and domestic animals, making it impossible to continue indigenous living patterns.

Some seventeenth-century estimates of Dutch population give a figure of 10,000 given for the 1660s, which is an exaggeration (Boxer 1965:251; Starna 1991:22). More realistic estimates (see table 2.2) would be about 300 in the whole colony in 1630, 200 at Fort Orange in 1643, and less than 1,000 in New Netherland in 1639 (Rink 1986). By 1714, the figure of 3,300 (including enslaved blacks and white settlers) seems reliable. While these figures include all of New York, the population was concentrated primarily in the two major towns, New Amsterdam/New York and Fort Orange/Rensselaerswyck/Albany.

Table 2.2

Mohawk and European Population, Seventeenth to Eighteenth Centuries

Year	Mohawks	Europeans
pre 1630s	< 8,000	
1630s	300–	< 1,000
1698	1,100	
1714		3,300
1756	580	17,400
1770	640	42,700

Source: Snow 1995:4.

The Dutch Background

As a colonial power, the Dutch were very different from the Spanish. They were rich, urban, and explosively mercantile (Rink 1986:17). The Netherlands represented a striking contrast with the rest of Europe in that it did not have a feudal political economy; 50 percent of its peasants were literate, and many were prosperous, having the highest standard of living in Europe (Delage 1991:24, 44). In their incipient capitalist system, even rural peasants represented a class of free workers who were able through their own labor to accumulate enough capital to buy animals and improve the land that they owned. Dutch merchants have been characterized as greedy and aggressive (Rink 1986:18), but also as cautious, calm, and self-satisfied (Boxer 1965:xxii). Their mercantile system, involving trade with many independent "middleman" agents, led directly to capitalism and complex socioeconomic arrangements, including the subsequent development of a class system in colonies such as Batavia that persisted long after the Dutch had left the Hudson Valley.

The Dutch colonial enterprise began as a by-product of a successful war with the Hapsburg Empire and its Spanish king, Philip II, begun in the mid–sixteenth century and concluded with a treaty in 1648 (Boxer 1965:1, 11) that recognized the United Provinces as independent (Rink 1986:53). The war was undertaken by the Calvinist Dutch to support class liberty and the interests of urban-dwelling merchants (Boxer 1965:xxi). The Hapsburgs—especially Philip—were strongly Catholic and wanted to control the Netherland provinces and eliminate local privilege (Gehring and Starna 1992:2). However, these combined economic and religious factors were sufficient to create a nation from a diverse land, with a number of cultural, racial, and geographic divisions (Boxer 1965:xxii; Anderson 1983).

When the war with the Spanish ended, the Dutch were left with a fleet of good ships (figure 2.6) that they put to use for exploration and the creation of trade. They were able to compete successfully for colonial products during this period of capitalist formation because their costs were lower than those of French, English, and Spanish enterprises. In part, their economies derived from the fact that they sent only traders and did not finance any missionaries (Schrire and Merwick 1991:16), but also from their direct control of all aspects of the trade: shipping, warehousing, currency exchange, credit financing, and marine insurance (Rink 1986:18). As Delage (1991:25) notes, the nature of business changed from the sixteenth to the seventeenth century: whereas during the earlier period fishing (for example) was initiated and controlled by captains who owned their boats and hired crew, 100 years later a fishing business hired captains, crew, and boats. The war with Spain had restricted shipping freedom and access to harbors, increasing risk and thus the costs of getting to market and promoted the formation of a group of risk-taking entrepreneurs who wanted compensation for their risk. During the seventeenth century, the so-called Golden Age (Rink 1986), the Netherlands replaced the Baltic as the center of world commerce. Goods came from all over and were warehoused and repacked, prices were set there, and the entire Dutch commercial system was oriented to profit (Delage 1991:27). Whereas the Spanish colonial enterprise was expansive and centered on minerals to a great degree, the Dutch focused on deriving a profit from whatever trade they undertook.

The Dutch needed to create markets for a variety of goods along their trade routes. To this end, they formed two investment companies (Gehring and Starna: 1992:4): the Dutch East India Company (VOC), a joint stock trading venture founded in 1602 to control trade in the area east of the Cape of Good Hope (Boxer 1965:26; Gehring and Starna 1992:4); and the Dutch West India Company (WIC), established in 1621 to oversee trade in the New World and Africa (figure 2.7). When the VOC sent Henry Hudson to look for a northeastern all-water

Figure 2.6. A Dutch ship characteristic of those used in mercantile trading expeditions around the world.

route to Asia from Europe, he landed instead in New York harbor and sailed up the now-famous river in 1609. His discovery occurred at the same time as two events that contributed to trade: a truce between the Spanish and the Dutch and the founding of the Bank of Amsterdam in 1609, which supported trade and regularized currency exchange, giving investors a sense of security (Gehring and Starna 1992:5). Although Hudson's voyage had not uncovered a route to Asia, the Dutch were interested in North America: furs were in demand in Europe, especially for beaver hats (Van den Bogaert 1988:xiii), and Russian activity in this trade was waning because the czars had imposed a 5 percent tax on furs. Moving into the fur trade to the northeast after 1609 (Burke 1991:3), the Dutch found themselves latecomers, since the French had achieved a foothold in North America (Newfoundland) in 1602 and had established an extensive network of relations with Algonkian-speakers (Trigger 1971:277; Vernon 1978:200). While most trade at that time took place to the north, the Mahicans living in the Hudson Valley had apparently had experience with it, for Hudson reports that when he first encountered them, they had the right kind of skins on hand (Gehring and Starna 1992:7).

The WIC was founded by a close-knit, kin-connected group of Lutherans who had migrated from the southern Netherlands to Amsterdam and who had a good

Figure 2.7. The Dutch West India Company headquarters in Amsterdam, in the seventeenth century.

deal of private capital, especially after the truce with Spain in 1609 (Rink 1986:36, 55). They were also free to act quickly as the crown was very supportive, and profits were fed back into trade. After 1609, Adriaen Block made several trips up the Hudson River to Fort Nassau; in 1612, Jan Rodrigues (described as a mulatto) began trading, reporting that he could get beaver and otter from the Mohawks—called "Maquas" by the Dutch—for "trinkets, liquor, cloth goods and firearms" (Rink 1986:34). Initially, Indian-European trade relations were informal, with few traders involved. By the end of the seventeenth century, 12,000 men worked for the WIC on boats, in offices, and warehouses (Delage 1991:26). This sketch of the rapidity with which trade began presents a striking contrast to the protracted negotiations between Oñate, Ponce de Leon, and the Spanish crown: it took three years to decide who would lead the initial group to New Mexico (Hackett 1923).

ATTITUDES TOWARD NATIVE AMERICANS

Being a Protestant colonial power in the seventeenth century carried no mandate (or burden) to introduce Christianity to indigenous peoples. An important doctrinal element of Calvinism was the belief that God's will was the dominant force in a person's entire life; thus having no power over his or her own salvation, an individual should focus on being rational and sober (Kipp 1990:8–19). (It is noteworthy that in the nineteenth century, attitudes toward missionization changed as Calvinism became more evangelical and proselytizing.) The religion attracted adherents not only because of its doctrine, but also because of the separation it maintained between church and state. In other words, the church did not become involved with mercantile interests. It has been said that affiliation with the Calvinist faith was particularly important during the war with Spain because it became a marker of identity around which people coalesced, signaling their opposition to Catholicism and the Inquisition (Bagley 1973:2; Gehring and Starna 1992:2). The lack of interest in conversion had a practical aspect, as missionaries were difficult to recruit and costly to maintain (Boxer 1965).

One trader, Willem Usselinx, did have a vision of colonialism that was close to the Spanish view. He thought Indians should receive a Christian education and be instructed in modern farming techniques and the planting of crops such as sugar. This would establish a climate in which conversion would flourish when accompanied by examples of virtuous lives for natives to emulate and would produce neither slavery nor the defeat of the Indians. Usselinx's radical idea that the real value of America lay in its soil and climate, not its potential for profit (Rink 1986:52), failed to make its way into the WIC charter produced in 1621 (Boxer 1965:27), which emphasized trade and the company's military abilities. Thoughts of colonization came later (Rink 1986:53, 61).

Dutch feelings about the Native Americans they encountered were complex. On the one hand, official policy, seen in letters of instruction to Willem Verhulst, the director of New Netherland in 1625, focused on the design of the fort, the conduct of trade, storage of skins, and ways to accumulate livestock for breeding; there are some cautionary notes on not letting Indians have company horses. A few lines were devoted to religion, saying that indigenous peoples should be instructed in Christianity; that all should be honest in their dealings with them; that no one should harm, deceive, or do violence to them, but allow them to hunt and fish freely (Van Laer 1924). These statements seem to have been rhetorical, and the reference to instruction was doomed to be ignored, since no minister was regularly present, even to serve the Dutch faithful.

The first minister to New Netherland was Jonas Michaelius, who describes the indigenous inhabitants in 1628 as "entirely savage and wild, strangers to all decency . . . stupid as garden poles. . . . They are as thievish and treacherous as they are tall; and in cruelty they are altogether inhuman, more than barbarous, far exceeding the Africans" (Rink 1986:214). He maintained that the only way to convert them would be to begin with the young, and to separate them from their parents, an idea also promulgated by missionaries to New Mexico (Gutiérrez 1991:75). However, he noted, "This separation is hard to effect. For the parents have a strong affection for their children and are very loath to part with them" (Rink 1994:254). Johannes Megapolensis became the regular minister for Rensselaerswyck in 1642, and a year later began to preach to the Mohawks, attempting to learn their language. He began a dictionary but did not get far with it, or with conversions (Rink 1994:254). In 1644 he notes: "When I am among them I ask them how things are called; but as they are very stupid, I sometimes cannot make them understand what I want" (Snow et al. 1996:41). In 1657 he and Samuel Drisius, another minister, wrote a letter to the Netherlands acknowledging their failure: "We can say but little of the conversion of the heathens or Indians here, and see no way to accomplish it, until they are subdued by the numbers and power of our people, and reduced to some sort of civilization; and also unless our people set them a better example, than they have done heretofore" (Jameson [1909]1990:

399). There was no church in Iroquoia, which meant no instruction of the young, no charity services, or hospitals, although it is unclear whether the Mohawks would have used these institutions had they been available.

Along with their lack of concern for conversion, the Dutch showed little curiosity about the Mohawks, practically ignoring them, simply classing them as "wilden" with whom they were involved in an exchange of imported wares for furs. According to one commentator, the Indians were childlike (a typical way of treating "others") and should be kept friendly with kindness and small gifts; a trader should make them think he trusted them fully but maintain a watchful guard at all times (Isaac de Rasière letter of 1626 to the Amsterdam Chamber of Dutch West India Company, in Van Laer, 1924:212). It is unclear whether the Dutch attitude represented a "live and let live" policy derived from Calvinism and the view that individuals were free to act on the basis of conscience (Dennis 1993: 142) or whether the Dutch simply found the Mohawks frightening and wished to keep them at a distance. In the context of the 1625 Law of War and Peace—which stated that man was by nature rational, that brutal behavior was unnatural, and violence was the result of evil (Edwards 1981:116)—some of the Iroquois behavior in war would have seemed horrific. Additional insight into Dutch attitudes comes from the instructions to Verhulst, in reference to the acquisition of land for the placement of the fort. It suggested that those negotiating for Indian land try by "amicable agreement, [to] induce them to give up ownership and possession to us, without however forcing them thereto . . . , *lest we call down the wrath of God upon our unrighteous beginnings,* the Company intending in no wise to make war or hostile attacks upon anyone, except the Spaniards and their allies, and others who are our declared enemies" (Van Laer 1924:106, emphasis added).

An interesting aspect of the Dutch attitude is seen in their behavior toward Mohawk women, which was strikingly different from that of Catholic Europeans, although evidence on this subject is somewhat conflicting. Some observers state that sex with Indian women occurred, but there is little evidence of consistent sexual contact between Dutch men and Mohawk women, and only two Dutch men are known to have fathered children by Mohawk women (see chapter 5).

Dutch attitudes can also be seen in their behavior in Brazil, another colony where they encountered Native Americans. Initially they felt sympathetic, thinking the Indians had been ill-treated by the Portuguese. Dutch painters portrayed them as dignified individuals rather than exotic curiosities (Hemming 1978:289), but after a while they were presented as lazy, with no interest in work: "They show no interest in accumulating riches or other goods. They therefore do not work for themselves or for others in order to earn money—except to get something to drink" (Hemming 1978:287). Nevertheless, the governor-general of Dutch Brazil and other provinces, Johan Maurits, stated that "each [Indian] should be allowed to live in the way he understands, and to work where he wishes like men of our nation" (Hemming 1978:291). Even though this attitude was only partly enacted in behavior, it presents a striking contrast with the clear Spanish agenda of controlling the totality of Pueblo lives.

SETTLEMENT

Within five years of Henry Hudson's voyage, the New Netherland Company, which had been granted a trading monopoly by the States General, established a settlement at Fort Nassau just south of today's Albany, on Castle Island at the Normans Kill (Jennings 1988:4:13). The intersection of the Hudson and Mohawk Rivers was a crucial nexus from Precolumbian times onward, and it was probably no accident that the Dutch located near there (in contrast to Burke 1991:3). New Amsterdam served as a deepwater port, and a break-in-transport point for overseas shipping (Cooley 1894, cited in Rothschild 1990), while the Hudson offered a route to the interior and furs both from the area around present-day Albany and to the west via the Mohawk River. Fort Nassau, a small fortified trade center, was abandoned in 1618 because of flooding, but in 1624 the WIC established two other settlements on the Hudson. One, designed to protect trading and territorial rights at Fort Orange, was just to the north of and a bit larger than Fort Nassau (Jennings 1988:4:13; Rink 1986:73; Trigger 1971:279); the other, at Fort Amsterdam on Manhattan Island, established control at the other end of the Hudson.

The founding of Fort Orange coincided with the beginning of the Mohawk-Mahican war, and some of its inhabitants left when Peter Minuit, the administrator of New Netherland, said that Dutch settlers were too scattered and should consolidate in New Amsterdam in 1626. Thus, the Albany settlers moved to New Amsterdam for a few years, helping to build houses and the fort (Gehring and Starna 1992:18; Rink 1986). The settlement of Rensselaerswyck, associated with Kiliaen Van Rensselaer's patroonship, was established in 1630, while Fort Orange continued to be occupied until about 1676. Beverwyck, which later became Albany, was established nearby in 1652 (Huey 1991:36). As noted earlier, the Dutch initially traded with the Mahicans, who controlled the area around Fort Nassau, and then moved through the "Mahican Channel" to the St. Lawrence Valley (Jennings 1984).

During the early period, WIC traders trapped furs or acted as middlemen in acquiring furs from Indians, but these furs belonged to the WIC. Would-be colonists after 1630 received free passage and land, and livestock at "reasonable prices." The company and its backers sent seeds, tools (for farming and blacksmithing), flour, guns, liquor, cloth, and cheap goods for trade (Rink 1986:78–82). However, in 1626, five years after the WIC was founded, it decided that the trade was unprofitable and abandoned the management of the colony as neither a commercial nor a political success (Boxer 1965:256; Rink 1986:68). The company had depended on government subsidies almost from the beginning (Rink 1986:64). Ships were returning with only partial cargoes of furs, and many of the immigrants who had crossed the ocean were coming back. It was also difficult to recruit migrants following the rapid expansion (and overexpansion) of Dutch colonial outposts, with settlements in the Caribbean, South America, Africa, and the Far East, which they were unable to maintain. Furthermore, residents of the United Provinces were relatively well off and had less incentive to leave home. The polyglot ethnic mixture of French-speaking Walloons and others from the United Provinces was proving difficult for social existence. Most immigrants wanted to trade and make money fast, rather than settle down and farm, so little food was being produced. Even though the WIC failed, individual merchants were financially successful. They controlled provisioning as well as the trade in furs, hides, tobacco, timber, and slaves and thus maintained high prices for these commodities and consumer goods. Despite competition among merchants right from the beginning, some of them were able to monopolize shipping and undersell or buy out their rivals (Rink 1986:87, 92, 175, 265).

Seeing this conflict, the Amsterdam chamber of the WIC decided to promote the use of private capital to manage the fur trade and established the patroonship system in 1628. Patroons were given large tracts of land (four leagues along one side of the river or coast, or two leagues on both sides) and were required to settle 30–50 people there within four years, at their own expense (Rink 1986:105). The patroon was allowed the use of fruit, flora, minerals, rivers, and springs on his land. He had judicial authority (even over capital offenses) and could establish taxes of up to 10 percent on any income from farming, fishing, or mining. Like the WIC, however, patroons had problems finding colonists. Too few were interested in emigrating, and those who were willing were expensive to bring and maintain, continually requiring renewals of supplies such as wooden casks, nails, farming and smithing tools, seeds, and especially livestock: horses, cattle, sheep, and hogs (Rink 1986:99, 108). Shipping space was supposed to be free for livestock but was hard to get, as the WIC had other priorities for its ships.

Kiliaen van Rensselaer was the most aggressive and successful of the patroons, establishing a claim to Rensselaerswyck in 1629 (Rink 1986:107). He differed from other Amsterdam merchants in trying to populate the upper Hudson as well as maintain trade, and he fought with the New Netherland commissioners to keep their pledges. He used a number of strategies to obtain livestock: in addition to paying for livestock transports, he acquired land and bred animals in Manhattan and bought cattle in the Hudson Valley. By 1636, his was the only patroonship still intact, although it was struggling. The company tried to keep emigrants interested, chiefly by controlling rights to the trade in furs. Initially, patroons did not have this right, then shortly after they were granted it, the WIC announced in 1639 that all colonists could engage in the fur trade if they settled down as farmers. With competition driving up prices and company restrictions on private investors making the system unworkable, profits were hard to come by (Rink 1986: 111, 115, 127, 196). The WIC promised low shipping rates but required fur traders to use its ships or those it licensed. As Rink notes, the company had shifted from a monopoly on the fur trade to a monopoly on shipping and the carrying trade. These problems continued, but ultimately Rensselaerswyck survived, and when the British claimed the colony, the Van Rensselaers were incorporated into the British mercantile system and became British citizens (Rink 1986:135, 200), following the pattern set by the Dutch elite throughout New Amsterdam (Rothschild 1990).

SETTLERS

An important part of the argument of this book concerns the story of Dutch settlement and the behavior of unmarried Dutch men. Can the social distance between these settlers and indigenous women be explained by the presence of European women in the early colony? Limited information exists on who came to New Netherland, and in what numbers. However, documents show that between 1630 and 1644, 174 people came to Rensselaerswyck, more than half of them (102) single men (Rink 1986:147). The latter appear to have waited to marry either widows or children raised by the families who emigrated, yet the marked sexual imbalance was the source of unhappiness, as many of those in the New World wrote home complaining of the lack of women (de Sille 1920:101), as discussed in chapter 5. Some of those who came were "ne'er-do-wells, snatched off the streets of the city where they had drifted from the hinterland" (Rink 1986:159), with no occupation listed. It is difficult to know how they fared, although this strategy was used in many colonial situations.

During the period from 1657 to 1664, immigration records were more complete, making it clear that immigration had increased. Of the 1,079 arriving during this period, only 25 percent were single men; some single women also made the journey (Rink 1986:165), as did many families with small children and older families with children of an age to do farm work. The colony's image had improved by this time, owing to what appears to have been a determined effort by the government and the WIC to promote its virtues. Trade goods arriving in New Netherland increased in the 1660s, ironically just before the English conquest in 1664 (Rink 1986:171). In comparison with many of the Dutch colonies in Asia, New Netherland should have been an appealing place and a setting "where men could live, work and worship in much the same way as they had done at home" (Boxer 1965:228). Boxer attributes the sparse population in 1664 to the lack of support from the home government and to the vital fact that the Amsterdam merchants kept all profits in Amsterdam, as well as to the aggressive expansionist program of the British.

Few Dutch settlers appear to have understood the Iroquois and had smooth relations with them. Arent van Curler (or Corlaer) was one such individual. He was a relative of Kiliaen van Rensselaer and was placed in charge of Rensselaerswyck in 1641. His great uncle complained of his sloppy recordkeeping, and the fact that he was "spending too much time in the woods" (i.e., with the Mohawks), but he became an important figure in negotiations between Europeans and Native Americans. He is believed to have had a least one child (a daughter) by a Mohawk woman (Burke 1991:149), but she presumably lived with her mother.

THE FUR TRADE

Before a trading voyage to New Netherland could be undertaken, an agreement had to be drawn up between the person who chartered the ship and the vessel's owner, often its captain. The charterer paid the costs and took the financial risk; the captain bore the physical risks and received a salary. There were other stipulations: the merchant had to make certain the ship was loaded in time for the ship to sail in good weather, had to pay the crew and captain, and had to pay insurance and any wharf labor fees. The ship owner was responsible for the ship and cargo's safety but had no role in the conduct of trade; an individual called a "supercargo" served on board as the merchant's representative. While in theory all shipping was supposed to stop at New Amsterdam, in reality ships with the ability and appropriate reasons (such as contrary currents) could bypass that port and head straight for Europe, a practice that made smuggling relatively easy. As the colony grew, trade in provisions increased, and livestock raising began to supplement fur trading and farming. The situation in New Netherland offered a strong contrast to that in New England, which had ample population but few beaver and otters. English merchants could not easily get furs because the Dutch and the French controlled the important waterways, hence the appeal of New Netherland and the Hudson (Rink 1986:106, 207, 210, 212).

Because the Dutch relied on the labor of Indian hunters to acquire the desired furs, they tried to maintain good relations with their indigenous partners (Schrire and Merwick 1991:14). In particular, they tried to provide desirable trade goods, although they often did not know or understand what these would be. They were surprised when the Mohawks or others attached a value to objects that differed from their own, as they believed that the uses of goods were self-evident (see chapter 5). Rink describes the confusion among traders when they began to import copper kettles and Isaac de Rasière, the secretary of the West India Company, cautioned the Indians would not understand that these were worth more than the iron ones, which Indians disliked because they were heavy (Rink 1986:88). However, the Iroquois did come to use the copper kettles as a source of raw material. Once they understood what kinds of things were desired, traders often tried to manipulate things of value so as to get more furs. Heavy woolen cloth, called "duffel," was highly desired, as was wampum (shell beads). De Rasière suggested trading this cloth to get wampum from Long Island Indians, and then using the wampum in the Hudson River Valley to get furs (Rink 1986:88). In this trade triangle, European goods were shipped to coastal indigenous people in exchange for shell beads/wampum, the beads went to the Iroquois and Mahicans for furs, and these went to Europe in exchange for a new stock of goods (Cantwell and Wall

2001; Richter 1992:85). The trade was successful until the mid–seventeenth century, when the supply of furs declined and wampum was being over-produced (Richter 1992:96) as iron tools had become available for its manufacture (Snow 1994:91). Europeans misunderstood the meaning of wampum, taking it, along with beaver, to be proxy currency and thus using it instead of coins, which were in short supply in the New World. Its original significance as an accompaniment to ritually important transactions was lost in the "factory" overproduction of beads for commercial exchange.

The importance of wampum in trade has been discussed by a number of scholars (Cantwell and Wall 2001; Ceci 1977), but much of the focus has been on where it was produced and who controlled its production. While shell beads existed for several thousand years prior to their use as wampum, their function as mnemonic devices seems to coincide with the origin of the Great League of Peace and Power (Ceci 1977:4). The connection between wampum and the fur trade is seen archaeologically in its association with historic period goods, present in quantity by the mid–seventeenth century (Guldenzopf 1986; Lenig 1977:83; D. R. Snow 1992:7). There is some disagreement as to the quantities of European material present on late-sixteenth-century and early-seventeenth-century Mohawk sites (Guldenzopf 1986:3; Lenig 1977:78), but the issue is not relevant to this work as there are enough goods to indicate contact. The different perceptions of wampum by Europeans and indigenous peoples in the seventeenth century are crucial to my argument, as I explain in chapter 5.

The timing and impact of the fur trade are also revealed archaeologically, through analyses of European trade goods at sites and faunal evidence showing increases in the quantity of beaver present after the mid–sixteenth century (Burke, 1991:24–26). Beaver seems to have been commonly consumed; a recent analysis of faunal remains at 18 Mohawk sites identifies beaver remains at every Precolumbian Mohawk site. At sixteenth- and seventeenth-century sites, the quantities increase, while diversity and exploitation of other species decrease (Kuhn and Funk 2000:6, 27). Beaver were probably consumed at higher rates as the fur trade increased because the Mohawks were bringing the animals home and not only selling the skin but also eating the meat (Lenig 1977:73).

THE LIFE AND DEATH OF THE BEAVER

The beaver, most prized of animals captured for the fur trade, lived in slow-running streams or lakes that were deep enough to have running water all winter and allow beaver to move around (figure 2.8). The animals normally lived for 10 to 12 years, in colonies of 1 to 12 animals consisting of a monogamous pair plus any offspring under about two years of age. They were easy to trap, and were caught from fall through spring, although the pelts were at their best in winter and spring. LeJeune described them in 1635 as fertile, with litters of five or six young born each year. He also noted that they were in danger of being wiped out because the Indians, on finding their homes, were killing all of them (Delage 1991:164). As the population declined, hunting became more time-intensive, requiring longer travel and distorting Native American labor by forcing people to work less for traditional subsistence needs and more for European goods (Delage 1991:168). Settlement pattern may have changed as a result, since hunting camps would be located with reference to beaver rather than other resources. While hunters were responsible for bringing furs back to camp, the trade involved the labor of both men and women, as women were needed to process the skins, in place of their traditional role of deerskin tanning and hide-working (Ceci 1977; Snow 1994). Otter skins were also desired, although the best otter were not found in the Mohawk Valley but in Canada (Dunn 1994). Faunal assemblages at Fort Orange also yielded mink bones, mostly from later levels (Huey 1988:266, 555), after 1640, and the remains of other minor species hunted for fur, such as fisher and marten.

Figure 2.8. An American beaver (*Castor canadensis*).

Documentary information, though inconsistent and from different catchment areas, provides some estimates of the quantities of furs that were traded. Between 1624 and about 1630, 3,000–6,000 skins a a year were reportedly shipped from Fort Orange (Delage 1991:139, 152); from 1630 to 1635–1640, the number increased to about 5,000–8,000 a year (Delage 1991:139; Van Laer 1908). On a larger scale, Delage (1991:139) notes that in 1626 the Dutch shipped a total of 10,000 skins, while in 1635 more than 16,000 skins were collected from New Netherland, although not all of those were necessarily obtained from the Iroquois. Quantities increased to 35,000 in 1656 after the defeat of the Huron and then to 46,000 after the defeat of the Erie. New France covered a larger area than New Netherland, and the French increased their output from 15,000 per year prior to 1630 to 30,000 between 1630 and 1640 (Delage 1991:152). However, WIC profits were particularly impressive, and higher than those of the French. Between 1655 and 1664, the company recorded exports of furs worth 454,127 florins against operating costs of 272,847 florins, leaving a profit of 181,280 florins (Delage 1991:167), or more than 18,000 florins per year.

It is noteworthy that in the 1640s, during Kieft's War in New Amsterdam, the fur trade was unaffected and peace was preserved between the Dutch and Iroquois. Both sides had an incentive for maintaining the trade: the Iroquois were looking for guns, cloth, and liquor, and the Dutch for the furs themselves (Rink 1986:221–222). Midway in the seventeenth century, however, the local animal supply waned and intertribal war disrupted the western trade (Burke 1991:8). The decline in beaver triggered what some refer to as the Beaver or Mourning Wars, a cycle of continuing war that developed around 1640. As a result, there was a need to replace those lost to war and to European-induced epidemic disease, and also to meet the demands of trade (Guildenzopf 1986; Richter 1992). Furs were still available further to the west, but there were now few in the Mohawk area, and work efforts had to be reoriented from hunting to acquiring beaver from others. As a Mohawk man reportedly observed in 1659, "The Dutch say we are brothers and that we are joined together with chains but that lasts only as long as we have beavers. After that we are no longer thought of" (in Richter 1991:295). Only a few years later, in 1664, the Dutch colonial government ceded control to the British.

AFTER DUTCH CONTROL

The period of Dutch colonial rule was, to an archaeologist, an incredibly short 40 years, although Dutch influence persisted along the upper Hudson long after the

British had taken formal control of New Netherland. Conflict between the Dutch and the British in North America began as early as the 1630s in the Connecticut River Valley when the English—who had little access to furs and needed to find a source—circumvented the Dutch by going north to the interior, where they established a trading post (Rink 1986:117, 124) close to modern Hartford and north of the Dutch post. They claimed that the Dutch contributed to Indian immorality by selling liquor while making them dangerous by selling guns (Rink 1986:26). Once the Mohawks were using guns and other European goods, however, they were part of the world economy, and their interests were inextricably linked to those of their European colonial partners. They used a number of means to get European commodities—raiding others; substituting turkey, deerskin or other furs; and traveling further to acquire them—but ultimately they lost access to regular supplies of the goods they wanted, such as cloth and metal tools (Delage 1991:165). Depending on British "gifts," some work as guides and soldiers, and other limited kinds of trade, they had become marginalized and impoverished. The selling of their land was the last step in the process that alienated them from the Mohawk Valley.

The loss of New Netherland was ultimately due to the intensification of Anglo-Dutch maritime competition in the second half of the seventeenth century. The English Navigation Act of 1651 was aimed at the Dutch and interfered with shipping, cutting Dutch merchants off from their clients, customers, and employees (Rink 1986:188, 249–250). Merchants were able to maintain trade for a while, but it became much more expensive. Although the English gained formal control in 1664, this shift in colonial rule was not accompanied by an influx of English settlers. Few families came, and the British presence in Albany consisted mostly of soldiers and their commanders (Merwick 1990: 260), even into the early eighteenth century. The upper Hudson-Mohawk Valley, especially around Albany, remained Dutch in language, cultural traits such as foodways, and religion; the Reformed Church of America dropped the word "Dutch" from its name only in 1867 (Boxer 1965:229). The presence of the English would have had an impact on the construction of the landscape because they had a very different attitude toward land, defining precise boundaries, marking passages overland rather than on rivers, and naming places so as to reflect British rule and incorporate the land into the crown's domain (Merwick 1990). However, the primary focus of the new colonial power was international issues, especially their wars with the French, and they had less interest in local matters.

As the seventeenth century and the fur supply waned, the conjunction of a number of events led many of the Mohawks to leave the Mohawk Valley and migrate north. By 1700, two-thirds of all Mohawks were living in Canada (Snow 1994: 131). The French had begun to seem desirable as alternate trade partners and a better source of European goods than the English and Dutch-Americans in the Albany area, and the Mohawks were heavily solicited by French Jesuits, who promised them an economically comfortable existence. Many went to Canada as converts, but a primary reason that so many migrated, according to Richter (1992: 124, 126), is that groups of related women moved together. In any case, the kinds of communities founded there were traditionally cooperative settlements, welcoming to newcomers, and they were more appealing than the settlements along the Mohawk (Richter 1992:128).

The result in Iroquoia was the existence of separate factions favoring the English, French, and neutrality. The late seventeenth century was a period of intense factionalism and war, sometimes leading kin to fight kin (Richter 1992:128). Relations between local European residents and Mohawks who had not emigrated to Canada were strained. The fur trade had diminished, and the Iroquois tried to stay in a neutral position between the French and the English, although they came under increasing pressure to ally with one or the other (Snow 1994: 137,142). During a series of French-English wars—King William's War of 1689–1697, Queen Anne's War of 1702–1713, King George's War of 1744–1748 , and the French and Indian War of 1754–1763 (Merwick 1990:263; Snow 1994:148)—that took place on American soil, the Iroquois fought on both sides. Much of Mohawk eighteenth-century history, as recorded by the British, is the story of Indian men such as Theyanguin and Tejonihokawara (both called King Hendrick; Snow, personal communication 2001) and Thayenadanegea, or Joseph Brant, brother of Molly Brant, Sir William Johnson's common-law wife. These were men who interacted with the colonial administration as leaders, went to England to meet the king or queen and were important in British eyes, although it is hard to know how they were perceived by their own people. The final blow came with the American Revolution, in which the remaining Mohawks, many of whom were relatively affluent, sided with the British and thus lost property and land and finally left the valley, as Europeans moved in to live there (Snow 1994:151). Property claims submitted to the crown for war losses may be exaggerated, but they detail extensive landholdings, domestic animals, European tools, and blankets held by resident Mohawks (Guldenzopf 1986).

Conclusion

The two colonial histories outlined here are quite different from one another. In the Rio Grande Valley, an inhospitable and economically unrewarding setting, the Spanish pursued a repressive and often violent approach, living closely among the Indians. They were ousted by the Pueblos for a brief time, after which their relationship was altered and indigenous religion was tolerated to a greater degree than previously. After the revolt, immigration from Mexico to New Mexico increased and the Hispano culture developed. In the Hudson and Mohawk Valleys, the Dutch period of occupation was relatively brief. It was marked by competition among traders and little desire by Dutch settlers to remain. The Mohawks had limited contact with the Dutch but altered some of their subsistence in order to gain beaver skins to use in trade. In both settings, epidemic disease caused a major population decline among Native Americans, with drastic consequences. In the Southwest it was difficult for the Pueblos to resist the second wave of immigration. In the Northeast the cycle of Beaver and Mourning Wars was related to the loss of population as much as the loss of beaver.

3

Shared and Separate Landscapes

One of the most important aspects of interaction between peoples in colonial settings is the congruence of their spaces: this is where the social relations of power are diffused and exerted. There is an inherent geography in power relations, seen in attempts either to dominate or to resist control (Sharp et al. 2000). In the cases considered here, interactions differ in two significant ways: first, in the degree to which colonizer and colonized occupy the same physical space, and second, following on the first, in the similarity of construction in their cognitive landscapes. Archaeologists traditionally focus on spatial information, looking at the ways in which past peoples used the land, but it is essential to go beyond that information to examine the layered meanings of space and place. Landscape analysis is related to what archaeologists have typically called settlement pattern analysis, but a focus on landscape requires a more "emic" (internal) view of how a group of people perceived and constructed their own space and their mental maps. These cognitive maps would include immaterial aspects such as feelings about the land and physical features, important activities carried out on the land, forms of transportation available, and other occupants of the land.

Landscape construction is informed by many aspects of the mapmakers' culture, including notions of equality or social hierarchy, gender, the presence of a local or global perspective, and the relative values assigned to activities. Landscape structures are established by the kinds of journeys people make, the frequency, and purpose and season of these journeys, but the understanding of meanings is not simple, as elegantly presented by Basso (1996) in his work with the Apache. Some insight into indigenous landscape may be recovered from oral history and contemporary mythology. A number of southwestern peoples reveal perspectives on important places through these means. The Tewa and the Navajo, for example, believe their space is bounded by four sacred mountains. The Zuni atlas (Ferguson et al. 1985) suggests the complexity of Pueblo landscapes by mapping the variable and overlapping, but distinctive, distributions of crucial resources, both economic and spiritual, among the Zuni. Edmund Nequatewa (1936), a Hopi, in recounting a series of myths from Shungopovi, indicates the importance of the four directions but also notes elevated places and boundaries, and the locations of water, plants, birds, and animals. The Pueblo landscape after contact would have been populated by spirits, totemic figures, elders, and enemies, including Navajos and the Spanish.

In the Southwest, the Spanish made a deliberate attempt to invade Pueblo space, moving their missions into Pueblo settlements; the Pueblos used effective geographical mechanisms of avoidance and resistance even before the Pueblo Revolt in 1680. The Spanish landscape was different from that of the Pueblos; it began as a narrow and linear corridor along the Rio Grande, but over time as more colonists arrived and many of the Pueblos succumbed to disease, the Hispanic landscape gradually expanded while the Pueblos' shrank. The two landscapes remained different in other significant ways. For the Spanish, the landscape was structured by social hierarchy, religious and economic demands, and power as well as military force. Their perception of land and its features implied a sense of control: over nature and non-Spanish peoples. Land was categorized by type and divided and apportioned, as were water rights. Their perspective was very different from that of the the Pueblos, whose social structure was more egalitarian, while landholding was corporate and held by lineage groups and clans. The Pueblo attitude toward nature was similarly cooperative rather than control-oriented, and the earth was depicted as a mother (Ortíz 1969:21). Cognitively, the Spanish had a more extensive view, informed by the knowledge of a world across the ocean, other European peoples, and European ways of doing things. Some of the letters of Vargas and others refer to absent powers such as the king, the Council of the Indies, religious leaders, as well as their families (Hackett 1923; Kessell et al.

1992b). It is likely that the Spanish saw New Mexico as an unwelcoming and difficult place. In *Death Comes to the Archbishop,* Willa Cather (1990:285–287) describes the young priest

> pushing through an arid stretch of country somewhere in central New Mexico. He had lost his way, and was trying to get back to the trail. . . . The difficulty was that the country in which he found himself was featureless—or rather, that it was crowded with features, all exactly alike. . . . They were so exactly like one another that he seemed to be wandering in some geometrical nightmare . . . an interminable desert of ovens.

While this is a fictional account, it may well capture a sense of how the land was perceived by Spanish settlers.

In the Hudson and Mohawk Valleys, the Dutch and Mohawks remained quite separate, in territories with few points of intersection, except for trading places. Relocations of Mohawk sites, however, reveal the impact of colonial contact. Ultimately, both the Dutch and the Mohawks left the Hudson and Mohawk river valleys, again, in contrast to the Southwest, where both Pueblos and Hispanics stayed in the Rio Grande Valley. The Dutch were somewhat similar to the Spanish in their view of land as an entity that could be mapped, subdivided, and owned, whereas the Mohawks shared much of the Pueblos' ideas of communal land use and ownership. However, the Dutch did not share the Spanish intention to colonize the land. As their primary interest was the extraction of beaver skins, they had limited impact on Mohawk lands, although they had considerable impact on Mohawk lives. Maps that demonstrate settlement changes are used to examine the spatial reflections of these two types of interactions.

Changes in Settlement Pattern in the Southwest

Figures 3.1 to 3.10 show the locations of known Pueblo and Spanish sites over time. They focus on that portion of the Pueblo culture area centered on the Rio Grande River Valley. This includes areas to the east of the river, on either side of the Manzano and Los Pinos mountains, and along the Santa Fe River as far as Pecos. The area also includes a small portion of the region west of the Rio Grande, particularly along the Jemez River. The western pueblos (Acoma, Zuni, and Hopi) are not included because the two regions were involved with the Spanish in different ways. The latter were better able to maintain a more independent stance as they were off the main Spanish route of travel and were by and large ignored after the revolt, when they served as a refuge for numbers of people fleeing the eastern Pueblos. They continued to be of some concern for religious purposes but were less subject to the economic pressures that the eastern Pueblos faced. This segregation of east and west was an important difference between Spanish and Pueblo perceptions of their space.

The factors to be considered here include changes in settlement form, function, and their placement on the land. These are amenable to archaeological examination and can be interpreted to offer insight into landscape construction. Of course, both Spanish and Pueblo settlement was structured by basic subsistence requirements. Both societies had an agricultural base. In addition, the Spanish kept domestic animals, which became important to the Pueblo way of life once these people had access to them. However, the Spanish had economic goals beyond subsistence, especially during the pre-revolt period, which were geared toward extraction of food surpluses and exportable products (notably hides and cloth, pinyon nuts and salt). Physical characteristics of settlement location such as elevation and proximity to water are important, but the social aspects of settlement use are equally interesting, specifically, whether they were open and accessible to all or restricted to certain groups or individuals at certain times. Access to both Spanish and Pueblo religious structures was limited. There were rules that purported to protect Pueblo lands from Spanish usage (often violated), and I suspect that each group would have avoided the other's domestic spaces.

The architectural layout of settlements provides the arrangement of domestic space and defines public spaces, plazas, and courtyards, which allowed for the congregation of differing group sizes. Spanish-directed construction had a notable impact in the Rio Grande Valley. Pueblos and Spanish towns shared some architectural attributes (construction materials, interior fireplaces, rectilinear orientations, and the provision of enclosed or semi-enclosed open-air spaces), but differed in important ways. For both groups, settlement construction was influenced by a set of rules that addressed how communities were to look; for the pueblos, these developed in situ, but the Spanish imported their rules as part of their cultural heritage and then modified them. Note that information on Spanish sites is available mainly for missions; residential sites were not always recorded in documents, or their records have been lost, and few have been examined archaeologically. Land grant records do exist for communities settled under Spanish colonial administration, especially Hispanic settlements established in the late eighteenth century and onward.

Both the Spanish and the Pueblos used strategies to control access to land and thereby structure the landscape; the Spanish tactic was *reducción,* by which they aggregated the occupants of several pueblos into one, centered on a mission. This aggregation achieved several objectives: it kept the Pueblo peoples under the fathers' watchful eyes, it ensured an adequate labor supply for mission needs, and it established Spanish dominance, reflected in the construction of the actual mission, the largest building in the community, architecturally unique, and built with Pueblo labor. Other special-purpose structures placed within pueblos included the *convento,* where friars lived, and the garrison for soldiers. The mission-garrison complex was a new form of public building, much of which was not open to Indian use, except at designated times. These structures were placed in the midst of or adjacent to existing pueblos and had a greater and more dramatic visual impact on the Pueblo landscape than anything else the Spanish built.

The Pueblos demonstrate a tendency toward aggregation into large pueblos throughout Precolumbian periods P III and especially P IV, although they were not always totally or continually occupied (see chapter 2). Archaeology reveals this practice in the Precolumbian period, and throughout the historic period there are Spanish reports of empty pueblos or empty room blocks within pueblos. While archaeologists attribute this periodic abandonment to subsistence requirements, it could also have been a result of declining population and a form of escape from or resistance to colonial domination and control. I assume that families, perhaps clan segments, were the mobile units. Shortly after the revolt, there was a great deal of relocation to refuge villages, an explicit avoidance mechanism, but archaeological data and documentary accounts hint that a similar practice existed before the revolt, as some pueblos close to mission churches were emptied. Recent work on the revolt suggests that it was part of a longer process of resistance to the Spanish that was manifest in a number of different ways (Preucel 2002).

Pueblo communities were less affected by notions of social hierarchy than the Spanish were, but one special-purpose structure found within their villages analogous to churches—the kiva—was used by segments of society that cross-cut clan and lineage ties. An interesting phenomenon is the presence of kivas in convento patios at the missions of Abo and Quarai. Ivey (1988) suggests that they may have been built by missionaries and used for Catholic ritual as a means of persuading Pueblo peoples to incorporate the practice of Christianity with native religion. There are other possible explanations for this practice: the Spanish are known to have demonstrated their power in Mexico by building churches over indigenous temples, and a church was built over a kiva at Paa'ko (Lycett, personal communication 2002). In a similar practice, the Pueblo may have constructed kivas in abandoned churches as an expression of *their* power, as they did at Pecos (Spielmann, personal communication 2001). Liebmann (2002:138) suggests that the construction of these kivas in church (sacred) space represents "resistance through inversion," whereby the Pueblo claimed Spanish space and remade it into their own. The unique architectural characteristics of New Mexican mission churches (as discussed later in the chapter) imply some degree of fusion of Indian and Catholic ideas. Whether it represents a superficial accommodation or a genuine integration is hard to know.

SPATIAL DISTRIBUTION

The locations and movements of Pueblo and Spanish peoples are best seen in figures 3.1 to 3.10 (created by Antoinette Wannebo using ARCINFO), which compile information from a number of sources and focus on the Rio Grande Valley during three time periods: prior to the entrada, during the middle of the prerevolt period of Spanish occupation, and after the revolt. They provide information on Pueblo settlements and missions and record mostly large sites, as the task of locating all would be difficult, if not impossible. The maps contain some errors, however, not the least of which derive from the fact that some site locations are based on Spanish accounts while others come from archaeology. A full discussion of the creation of these maps is provided in appendix 1, but suffice it to say here that dating the sites and identifying the span of occupation are difficult. The available evidence for approximate periods of occupation is based on Mera's (1940) ceramic chronology of Glazewares A-F, which was a remarkable effort at the time but has been improved upon in some cases where dendrochronology has provided more accurate information on occupation period and additional chronological information is now available (Creamer et al. 1994). We cannot derive reliable information on population from site sizes because of the common Pueblo practice of mobility.

The location map in figure 3.1 shows pueblos known to exist shortly before Oñate's 1598 invasion, which is designated Period 1. The predominant location of Pueblo occupation sites lay along the Rio Grande and its tributaries. However, there were additional significant population clusters in the area east of present-day Socorro, west of the Rio Grande and north of the Jemez River, and in the Galisteo Basin. Figure 3.2 shows the earliest known missions, begun around 1616. They were constructed near the early location of Spanish settlements, close to Yunque Yunque in the north. The missions were restricted to the Rio Grande corridor, extending south as far as modern Albuquerque. The exception was Chilili, a single mission constructed outside the corridor, to the east of the Manzano Mountains in the East Tiwa/Salinas area (Mera 1940; Schroeder 1979).

Figure 3.3 shows pueblos and missions known to have been occupied around the period 1626–1650, or Period 2. Figure 3.4 indicates those pueblos that were occupied during Period 1 *and* Period 2. Figure 3.5 shows pueblos and missions that had been occupied during Period 1 but were no longer occupied during Period 2. And Figure 3.6 shows pueblos and missions that were settled during Period 2 and did not exist during Period 1.

I do not suggest that Figures 3.5 or 3.9 represent abandoned pueblos. The issue of abandonment in the Southwest has been discussed extensively (Cameron and Tomka 1993). It seems clear that many pueblos went through successive phases of occupation, followed by reduced or no occupation, whereas the term "abandonment" implies a permanent, and likely intentional, leaving of a place. An ethnoarchaeological study of Zuni pueblo farming villages has demonstrated that leaving a home was frequently not planned as a permanent event, and that even when structures were no longer used as full-time residences, they could serve important functions as places for part-time occupation, storage, sources of building materials, and ultimately, for maintaining a claim to a place (Rothschild et al. 1993).

The number of pueblos occupied rose from 93 in Period 1 to 103 in Period 2 (table 3.1). By contrast, the number of missions more than doubled, from 15 to 32, as the Spanish established sites in the midst of dense clusters of pueblos to institute more effective control in the Rio Grande Valley. Of the 103 occupied pueblos, 72 remained in use from Period 1 and 31 were new; 21 of the 93 occupied during Period 1 do not appear to have been in use in Period 2. Of the 15 missions from Period 1, 14 remained and 1 was abandoned in Period 2, while 18 new ones were built or started.

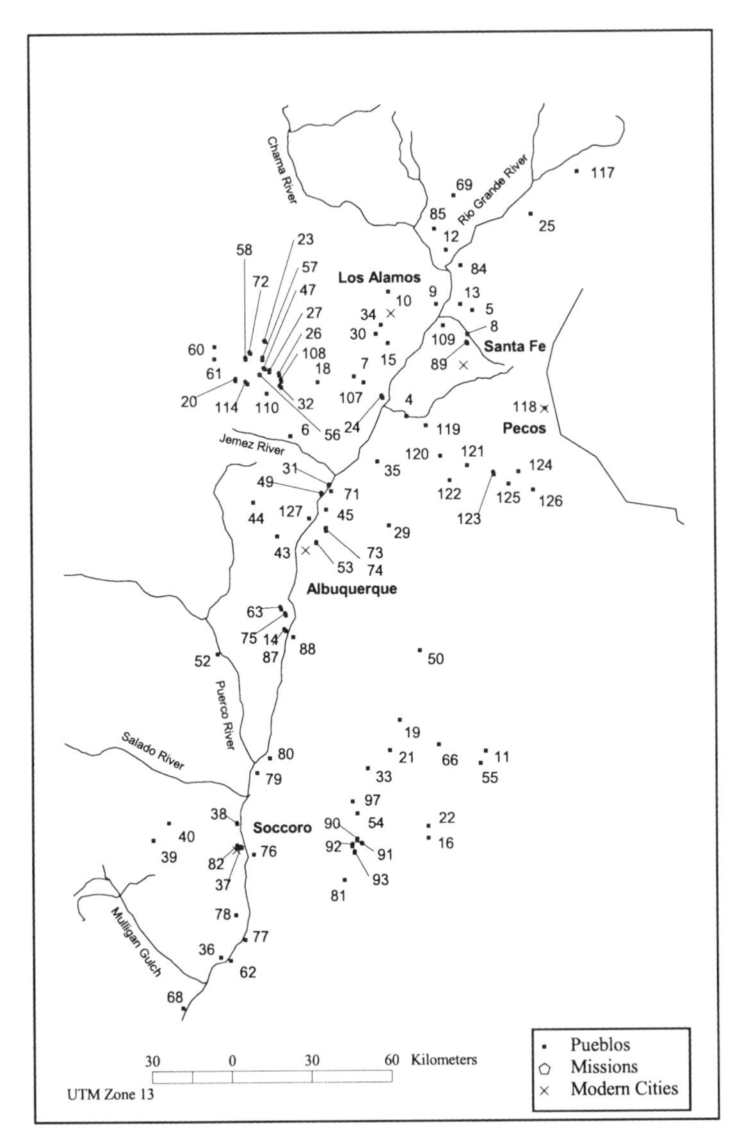

Figure 3.1. Pueblos occupied before Spanish settlement (Period 1). Courtesy Antoinette Wannebo.

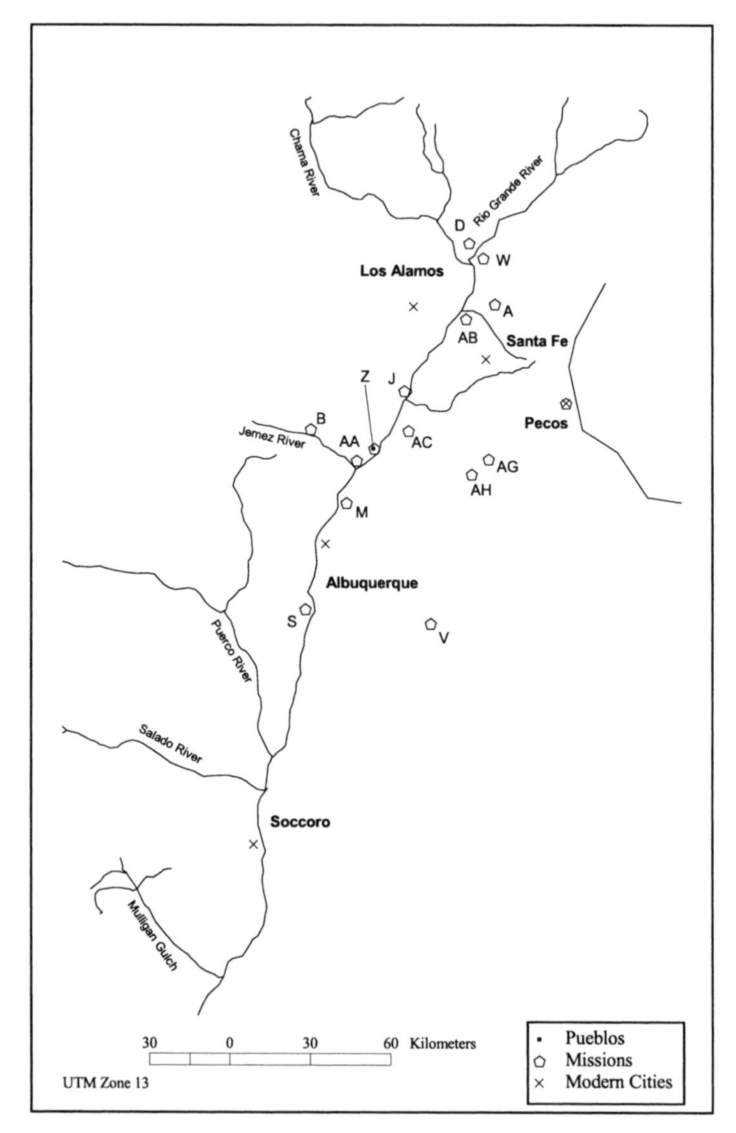

Figure 3.2. Missions begun before 1616. Courtesy Antoinette Wannebo.

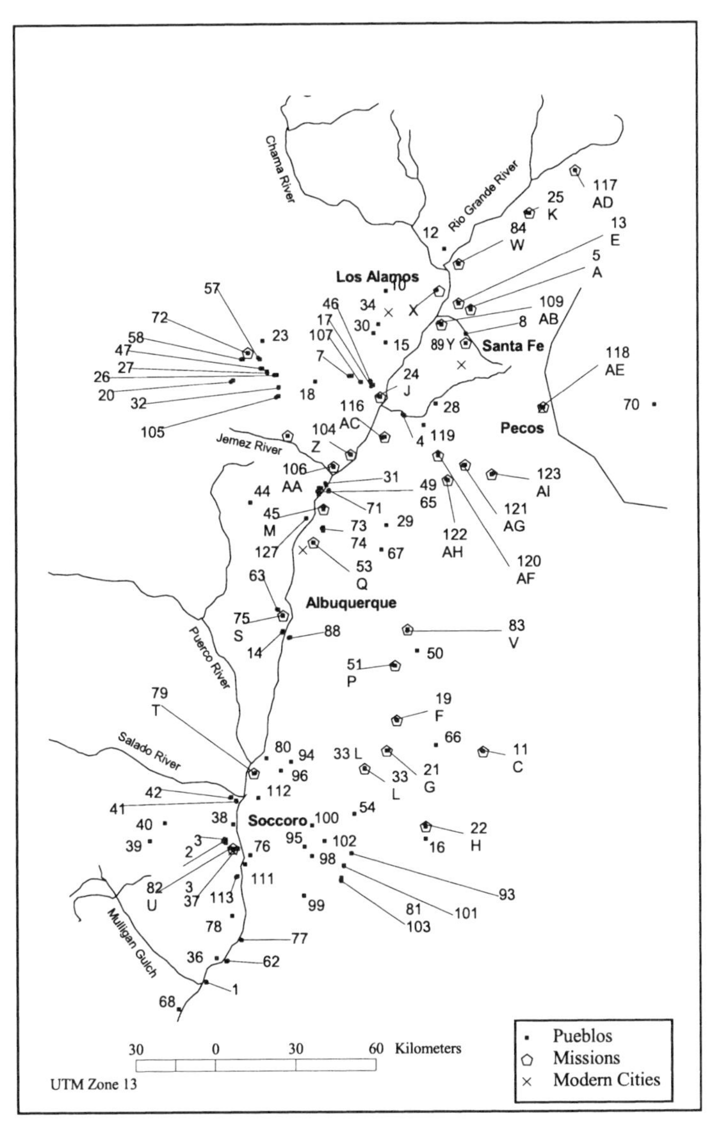

Figure 3.3. Pueblos and missions occupied between 1626 and1650 (Period 2). Courtesy Antoinette Wannebo.

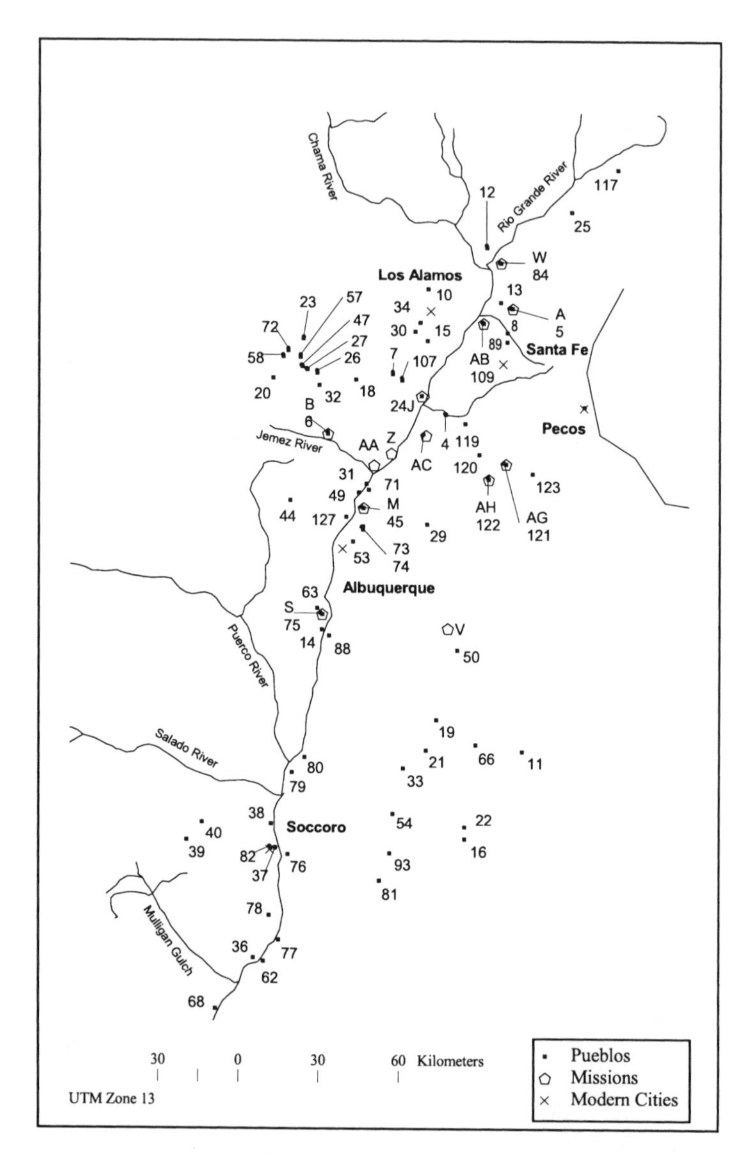

Figure 3.4. Period 1 pueblos and missions still occupied during Period 2. Courtesty Antoinette Wannebo.

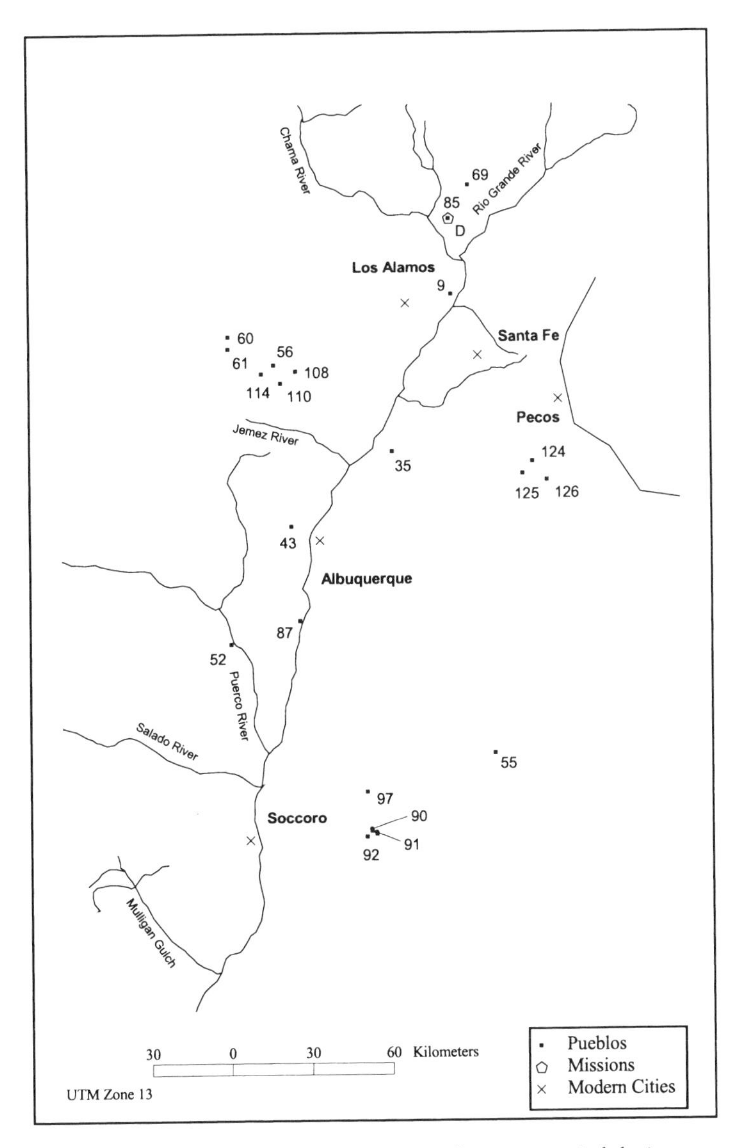

Figure 3.5. Period 1 pueblos and missions no longer occupied during Period 2. Courtesy Antoinette Wannebo.

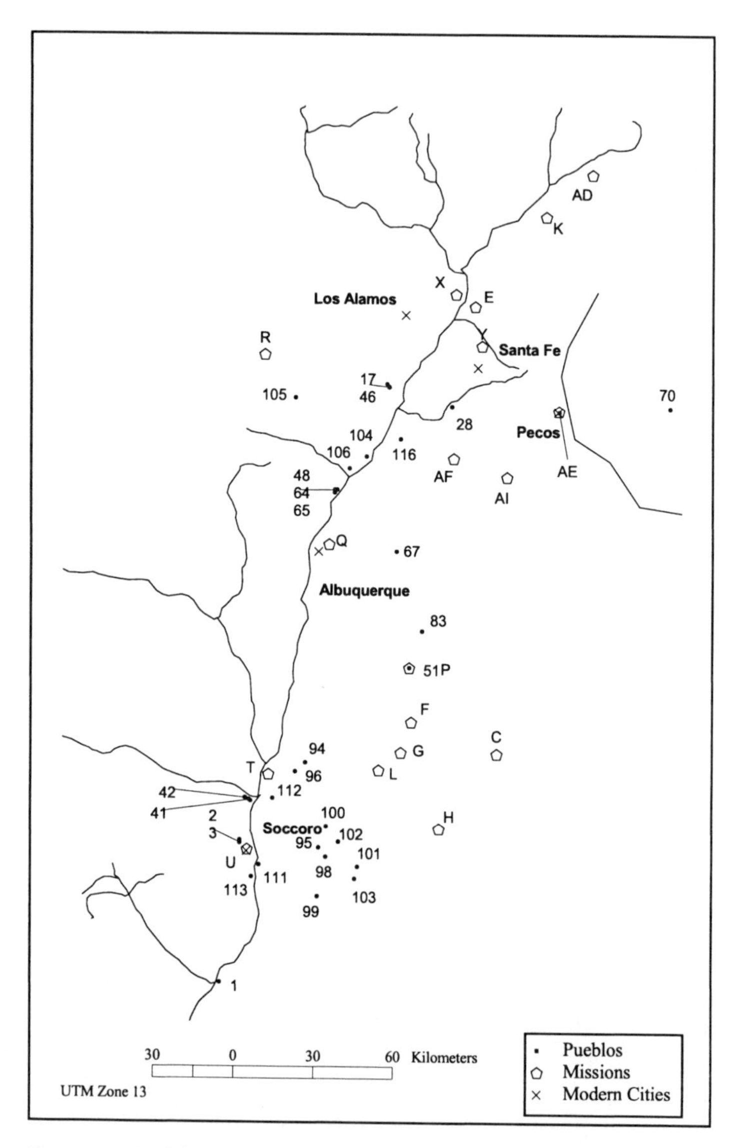

Figure 3.6. Pueblos and missions newly settled during Period 2. Courtesy Antoinette Wannebo.

Table 3.1
Pueblos and Missions in Three Periods

	Period		
Settlement	1	2	3
	Before 1598	1626–1650	1700 and after
Pueblo	93	103	28
Mission	15	32	15

SETTLEMENT CHANGES IN PERIOD 2, 1626–1650

The history of settlement during the second period (as identified through archaeological and documentary information) varies markedly in different parts of the Rio Grande Valley. Two trends are notable: (1) settlement in large sites in the area south of Albuquerque virtually ends shortly after the Pueblo Revolt, and (2) sites located away from the river corridor have a different trajectory of occupation history than those that lie close to the river. Between Periods 1 and 2, settlement changed in three areas outside the Rio Grande corridor: a number of sites in the Jemez Mountains, the Piro area near Socorro, and the Galisteo Basin were no longer occupied during Period 2 (figure 3.5). Many pueblos continued to exist in all three areas, however, and a number of new ones were built, so it is difficult to know whether settlement there simply shifted, or whether substantial population movements or decline occurred. In the Galisteo Basin, the number of missions doubled (two were built and two already existed from the first mission-building phase), whereas almost half of the large basin sites (Pueblos Colorado, She, and Blanco) were no longer occupied, perhaps because their residents had fled from mission presence in that area.

The southern part of the entire Rio Grande corridor includes several peoples, called Piro and Tompiro (for their language groupings), living in part of the region the Spanish called Salinas. In the Piro region around present-day Socorro, occupation of a few large sites ceased in this area (figure 3.5, numbers 90–92) while a number of new small late sites appear to the east of the Rio Grande (figure 3.6, numbers 95, 98–103). Piro sites were typically smaller than those in the northern Rio Grande areas (Earls 1986), and some of these late sites appear to have been situated for defensive purposes, as they are in locations that were not good for farming (Mera 1940). Two large pueblos to the west of the Rio Grande (Magdalena and Bear Mountain, LA 284 and 285, numbers 39, 40) housed approximately one-third of the Piro population during the colonial period when there was no mission (Marshall and Walt 1984; Mera 1940), another example of Pueblo use of locations away from the river, probably to avoid the Spanish presence. In Period 2, 14 pueblos housing an estimated Piro population of 6,000 people in the 1620s were reduced to 4 by the 1670s, at least in part because of the Spanish policy of congregation (Schroeder and Matson 1979:237). Population reduction is another likely explanation, related to the Piro vulnerability to Apache attack and to their ecological situation: they were dependent on annual river flooding from the Rio Grande and experienced a severe drought at the end of the sixteenth century (Schroeder 1965:296). They were also vulnerable to European diseases; being closest to Mexico of all Pueblo peoples and living along the route of travel, they would have been hit early and often by waves of immigrants carrying new pathogens (Ramenofsky 1996).

The southern area had four missions founded in the late 1620s under Benavides's direction; it was not the primary focus of Spanish interest and received attention later than areas along the northern Rio Grande. Benavides reports that he had "baptized the majority and the important persons" before he left in 1630 (Ayer 1900–1901:62). All four missions were apparently still in existence until the 1660s or 1670s, as they are mentioned in various friars' reports (Marshall and Walt 1984), each at one of the *congregación* pueblos remaining: San Luis Obispo de Sevilleta at Seelocu, Nuestra Senora de Socorro at Pilabo, San Antonio at Senecu, and Alamillo about 12 miles north of Pilabo (the ruins of the latter two have not been found; Marshall and Walt 1984).

The area to the east of the Rio Grande, south of Albuquerque and roughly north of the Rio Salado, was called Salinas (or Gallinas) by the Spanish because of the presence of important salt deposits, and was referred to as "Tierras sin agua" (Miera y Pacheco map from 1779, Dominguez 1956). Its residents include more of the "Tompiro" and "Jumano" and the "East Tiwa" (Mera 1940). Benavides (Ayer 1900–1901) reports 14 or 15 pueblos in the 1620s housing 10,000 people, including Chilili (LA 847), Tajique (LA 381), Humanas (Gran Quivira, LA 120), Quarai (LA 95), Abo (LA 97, no. 21), Tabira (LA 51), and Tenabo (LA 200). The problem with taking missionary population accounts at face value, however, is that they may well reflect the friars' desire to impress the Spanish religious hierarchy with their rate of success in conversions. Shortly before the revolt, in 1672, Abo, Chilili, Tajique, and Humanas (Gran Quivira) were abandoned because of drought, famine, and Apache attacks. Other sites in this area, such as Quarai, were also abandoned either permanently or for various periods, which seems to exemplify the same sort of shifting settlement seen elsewhere. Like other Salinas pueblos, Quarai was no longer occupied by the mid-1670s.

Missions in this area were not as secure and long-lasting as those along the Rio Grande. The mission church at Chilili is the only one to have been founded in Period 1, in 1613 (Scholes and Bloom 1944). Abó, Gran Quivira, and Las Humanas all had churches founded around 1629. The churches at Quarai, Nuestra Señora de la Concepción, and San Buenaventura de los Humanos were abandoned early in the 1670s (Ayer 1900–1901:254; Hayes et al. 1981:1). A chapel was begun at Tabira in 1641 but not completed; the date of its abandonment is unknown.

Slightly north of the Salinas region is the area Mera calls Western Tiwa, Schroeder calls Southern Tiwa, and the Spanish called Tiguex, which extends along the Rio Grande as far as modern Bernalillo; it had 15 or 16 pueblos recorded in the 1620s. By 1640–1680 only three or four pueblos remained, a result of Spanish missionary policy and the fear of Apaches (Ayer 1900–1901:253). Isleta (LA 724), Sandia (LA 294), Alameda (LA 421), and Puaray (LA 326) were occupied until about 1680, although the location of Puaray is disputed. Sandia and Isleta exist today, but it is unclear whether they were continuously occupied (Haas and Creamer 1992; Schroeder 1979:244). There do not appear to have been missions in existence at all of these pueblos throughout the colonial period. Two mission churches, San Francisco de Sandia and San Antonio de Isleta, were founded in Period 1, and another at Alameda in Period 2.

Some evidence from site placement in this area indicates a determination to avoid colonial rule. A few, mostly large sites noted by Mera (1940) south of Albuquerque, were built in a location reflecting defensive concerns. LA 489, which dates to the colonial period, is described as "a well-protected communal structure of late occupancy built on an isolated mesa just south of Los Padillas" (Mera 1940:19). This site and a few other Western Tiwa sites listed by Mera (6 or 7 of a total of 41) were unusual in that they were *not* situated along river or stream courses; three others in this category are also late sites, while another (LA 291) was located in what appears to be a defensive position; it is a single-component Glaze E site, used perhaps during the pre-revolt period.

Mera's Keres area on either side of the Rio Grande, with a western extension along the Jemez River (see figure 3.3), is characterized by two land types: high tablelands and the more heavily populated land along streams. Four important pueblos (three of them founded by Period 2) are still in existence today in this area: Santo Domingo (LA 1281), Santa Ana (LA 2049), San Felipe (LA 2047), and Cochití (LA 126). All are located along the river, as are a number of small late structures—LA 7, LA 34, LA 46—as well as Potrero Viejo (LA 84) and LA 295. There is no comprehensive information about periods of occupation for these sites because they are currently occupied, and the occupants are "resentful of investigation" (Mera 1940:26). Limited material is known from Cochití, where pottery from all periods has been recovered (Mera 1940:27).

In spite of this problem, Mera believed that population was reduced significantly sometime during the pre-revolt period as the presence of Glaze E wares indicates 10 large sites were no longer occupied after 1515–1650. The Jemez Mountains area is known to have provided refuge for many who had been involved in the Pueblo Revolt in several large pueblos in elevated areas. Santa Ana and San Felipe were definite refuge sites and have been continuously occupied. Potrero Viejo above La Cañada (Lange [1959]1990:8) was the refuge for people from Cochití, Santo Domingo, San Felipe, Taos, Picuris, and San Marcos (Abbink and Stein 1977: 156). Astialakwa or Guadeloupe Mesa Ruin (LA 1825) has a number of unconnected room blocks, which suggests that construction may have been undertaken quickly, without planning (Elliott 1983). Boletsakwa on San Juan Mesa and Patokwa may also have been used after the revolt, although the former also had an earlier occupation (Elliott 2002). While the Jemez mission remained in existence, some of the Jemez population presumably relocated to these upland sites. Some of this apparent loss of population is undoubtedly a temporary phenomenon, while some is due to a genuine reduction in the population as a result of environmental stress related to drought and epidemic disease. Relocation continued in this area after the revolt. Hopi, for example, was a refuge for people from Tano and Santo Domingo, and Laguna Pueblo was created by migrants from the same two pueblos (Walt 1990).

The Tano-Towa area includes a number of important sites within the Galisteo Basin: one is Galisteo (LA 26), which survived until 1700, while San Lazaro (LA 91), San Cristobal (LA 80), and San Marcos (LA 98) were no longer occupied after the revolt. Paa'ko (LA 162) is an important site to the southeast of Sandia, with two occupations, the second being small and late (Lambert and Rogers 1954). There are also some small late sites that may have been used for refuge. This is the region where, I suggest, the proliferation of missions during Period 2 may have led to local population dispersal.

Archaeological information to the north of these areas is limited. Mera comments mainly on the area close to Taos and Picuris. Modern settlement has been intense there and must have destroyed many sites, while considerable continuity of occupation often makes it inaccessible to archaeologists. The number of occupied pueblos north of modern Los Alamos shows little in the way of a downward trend from Period 1 to Period 2, while some new missions were founded. In Period 3, some pueblos were no longer being used, but the proportional loss is smaller than in most other areas. The pattern of settlement shown in figure 3.7 is restricted to a relatively small area; all sites were located along the Rio Grande or its major tributaries, and almost all were north of Albuquerque.

CHANGES IN PERIOD 3

This is the period that shows the most dramatic changes in settlement. Figure 3.7 shows pueblos and missions that were occupied in 1700, during Period 3 beginning 20 years after the revolt; Figure 3.8 indicates pueblos and missions that continued to be occupied during both Period 2 *and* Period 3. More important, figure 3.9 shows pueblos and missions that had been occupied during Period 2 but were no longer occupied in Period 3; there is only one new pueblo (LA 482), in the Jemez area, known to have been settled in Period 3 (see figure 3.10). In Period 3 the number of occupied pueblos dropped to 28 (table 3.1), with 27 continuing to be used from Period 2 while 75 were no longer occupied and one was newly occupied. The number of missions also dropped to 15, but it was not as marked a reduction as that among pueblos; no new missions were constructed, and 17 of those used in Period 2 were no longer in use in Period 3.

The differences between Periods 2 and 3 are much greater than those between Periods 1 and 2. A large number of pueblos and missions were no longer occupied. Many pueblo sites and missions that were occupied during Period 2 are apparently empty in the third period. The effects of the revolt were particularly marked in the south: settled communities showed a marked decline south of Albuquerque—in the Piro and Tompiro regions—and in the Salinas area. Some pueblos, or parts of them (Senecu, Pilabo, and Alamillo), were reportedly burned by Apaches around

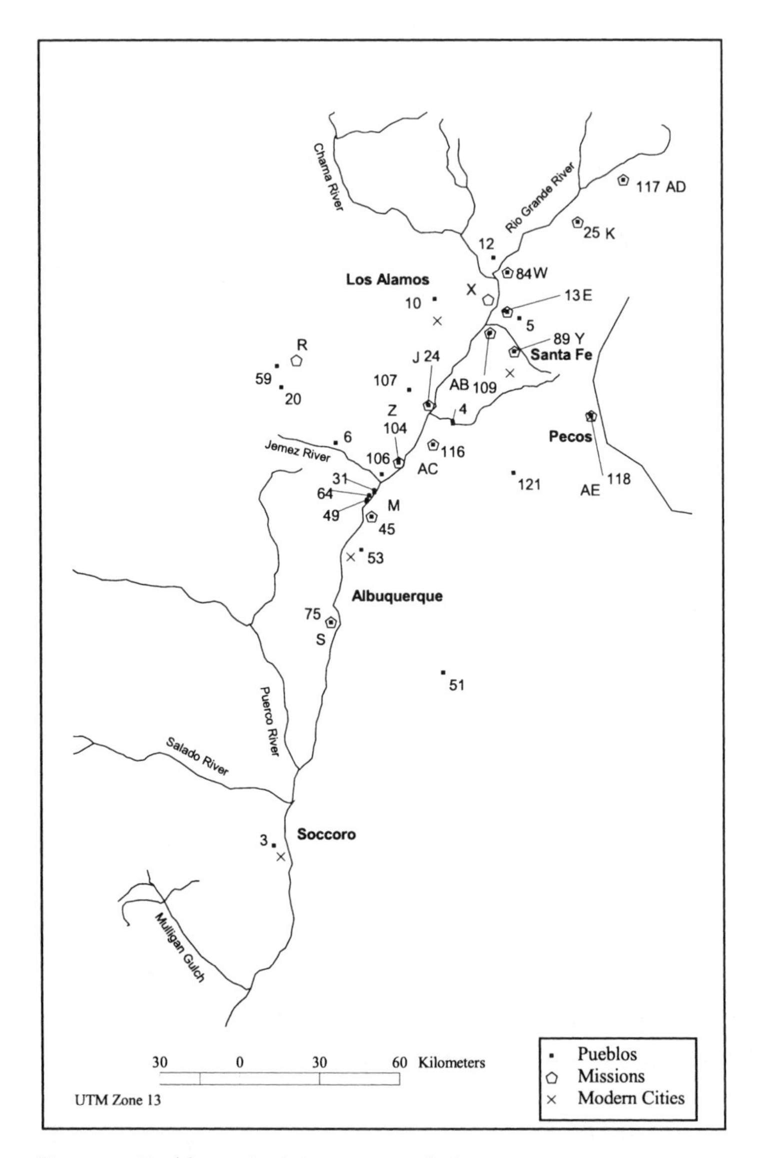

Figure 3.7. Pueblos and missions occupied after 1700 (Period 3). Courtesy Antoinette Wannebo.

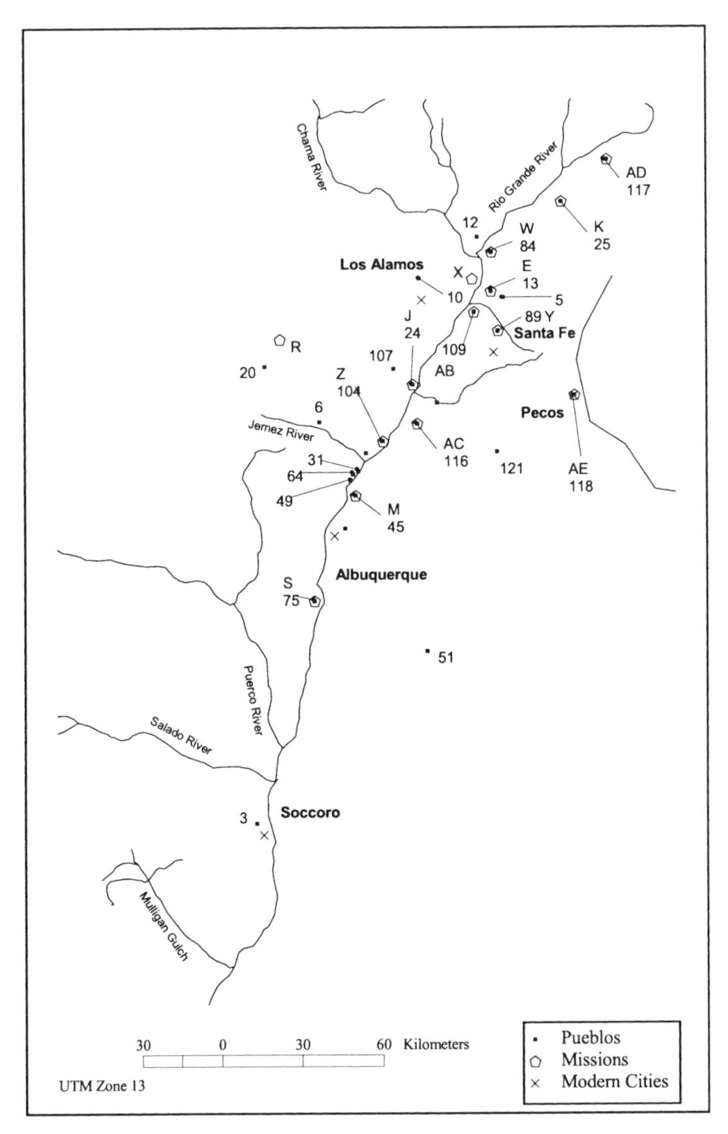

Figure 3.8. Period 2 pueblos and missions still occupied during Period 3. Courtesy Antoinette Wannebo.

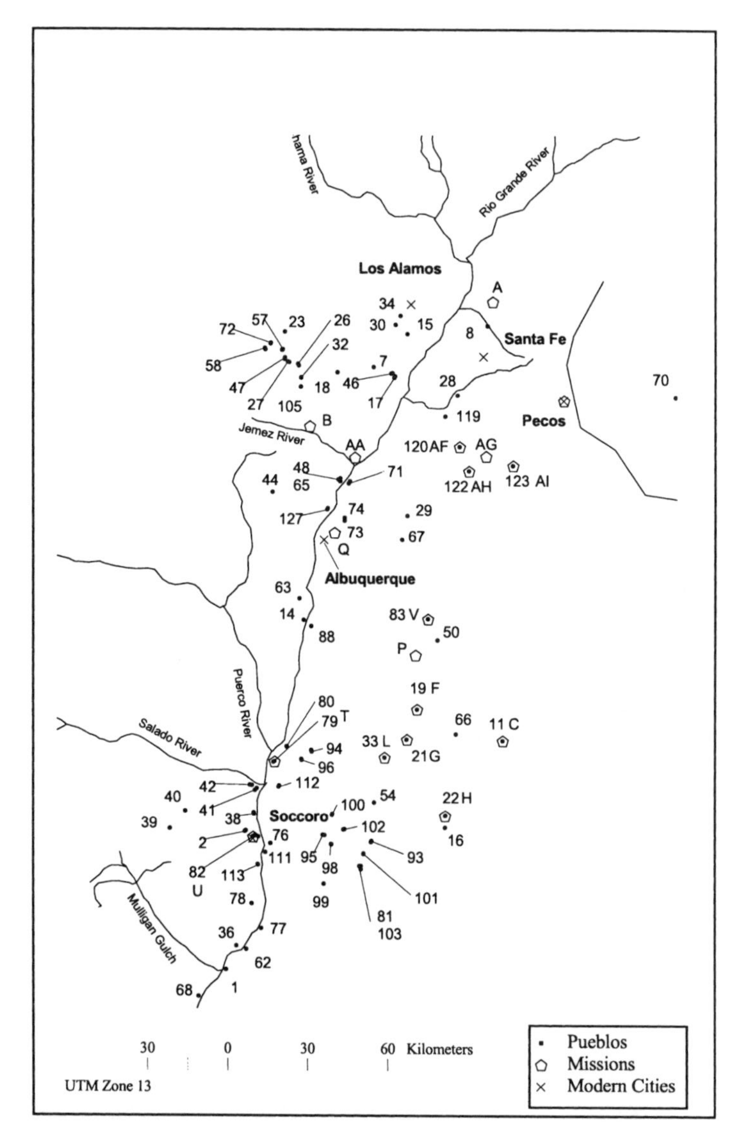

Figure 3.9. Period 2 pueblos and missions no longer occupied during Period 3. Courtesy Antoinette Wannebo.

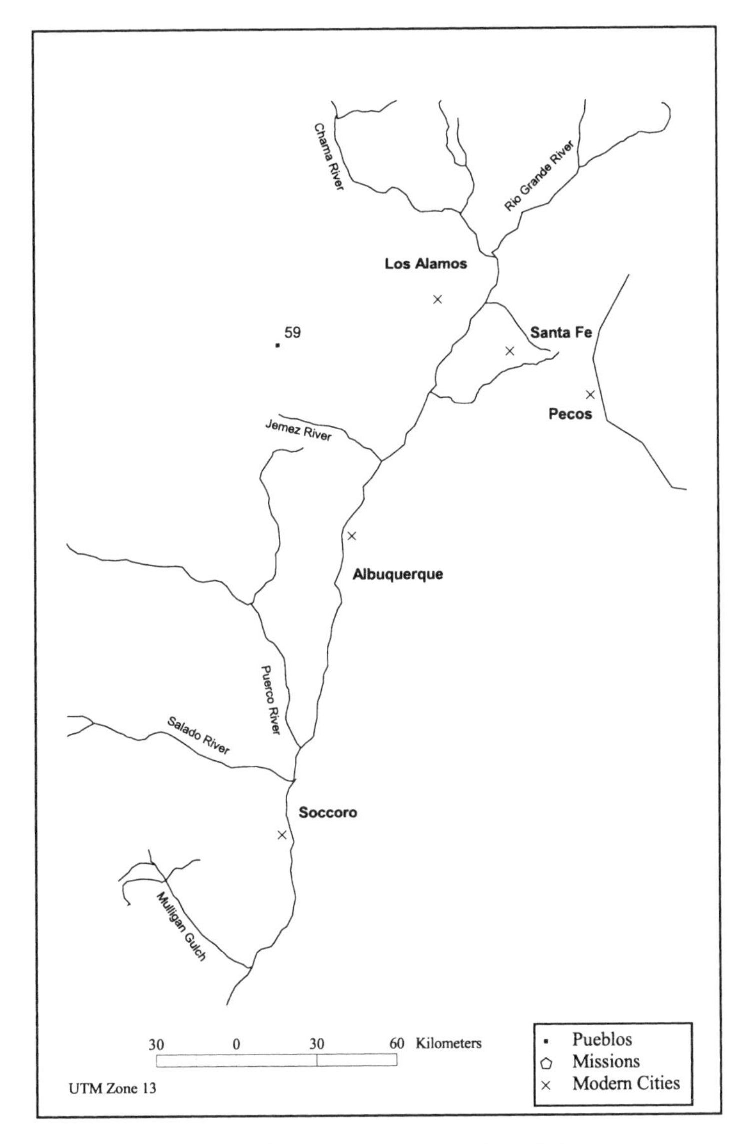

Figure 3.10. Period 2 pueblos and missions newly settled during Period 3. Courtesy Antoinette Wannebo.

1681 (Hallenbeck 1926; Schroeder 1979). Most scholars believe that after the revolt the Piro area was by and large abandoned (Marshall and Walt 1984; Schroeder 1979). Because the Piro lived some distance from the revolt organizers, they were not included in its planning; during the revolt many of them fled south to El Paso with the Spanish (Schroeder 1979:237). However, it seems that not all the Piro chose to go south. In 1696, a Piro living in Taos was reportedly one of the instigators of the rebellion of that year; some residents of both Sevilleta and Pilabo are said to have fled north to Isleta or other pueblos.

The documentary evidence is uneven: a 1695 Spanish map still shows Socorro and Senecu on the west bank of the river, and Alamillo and Sevilleta on the east; it also continues to record the existence of Chilili, Tajique, Quarai, Abó, Humanas, and Tabira. Sevilleta and all of these but Humanas are depicted on Miera y Pacheco's map from 1779. A 1692 census reported by Vargas indicates that Senecu and Socorro still had Hispanic residents, although there were only 2 households in Senecu (consisting of a total of 53 people) and 15 in Socorro (with a total of 128) (Kessell et al. 1995). In 1776, however, Dominguez (a missionary sent to record population and communities) does not discuss the region south of the Rio Salado or the Salinas area, either because no one was living there or because he made an arbitrary decision to ignore them. In any case, it is unlikely that there were many people in the area.

Some efforts to maintain Spanish control after the revolt were reestablished along the Rio Grande south of Albuquerque with the construction of new missions. One was built at Alameda (LA 421) in 1706, and a new church was begun at Isleta in 1710 after Tiguas, Tano, and Jemez peoples settled there (Dominguez 1956:203), the original residents of Isleta and Sandia having left the area for Hopi during the revolt (Ayer 1900–1901). The Sandia church was rebuilt around the same time (Ayer 1900–1901:254; Hallenbeck 1926:11). Later, in 1776, Dominguez (1956:138) records the population of Sandia as 275 non-Spanish speakers, by which he means Indians. In the face of this confusing evidence, it is fair to say that the population in this area was probably relatively unsettled.

SPANISH COMMUNITY TYPES

Spanish settlement types consisted of missions, towns, and *ranchos, haciendas,* or *estancias,* but prior to the revolt there were only missions, one town, and a limited number of estancias (for livestock raising) granted by the king, the ultimate owner of all lands (Simmons 1969:7), to a relatively small number of families not associated with missions. There were also some small farmsteads (ranchos) but their locations were not recorded. Each type of community was located in reference to the resources needed for farming, for defense, and for control of the Indians. In the seventeenth century haciendas were placed to maximize access to good farmland and water, close to Indian settlements where the labor supply granted as part of encomienda was available (D. H. Snow 1992b). These requirements brought them into conflict with the Pueblos, who also had settled in places where water and good land were available. Initially, settlement rules differed *in theory* for priests and settlers. The missionaries (sometimes with garrisons) moved into pueblos, while settlers were supposed to stay at a distance and neither live on nor use Indian land. In reality, the settlers wanted to be close to the conveniences of native goods and services (Deeds 1991); they also wanted to be close to missions. And pueblo lands were much more appealing than other lands to settlers: they had already been cleared, they often had better access to water than other areas, and houses had already been built. Most important, perhaps, even when settlers moved onto what appeared to be empty lands, *tierras baldias,* they were being used by the Pueblos for purposes other than agriculture or settlement: for collecting firewood and wild plants, for hunting game, and for extracting clays, charcoal, thatch; later they were used for pasture (Deeds 1991). We may assume from modern Pueblo practices that they also contained important ritual sites.

There was relatively little nonmission Spanish settlement; only 11 Spanish settlements or estancias are known in the Rio Grande corridor between Socorro and San Juan in the mid–seventeenth century (Ivey 1988:26); 6 were in Rio Abajo (the southern corridor), 4 were located to the south and 2 to the north of Socorro (Marshall and Walt 1984:141). Only a few of the large haciendas created by fiat seem to have been actually settled. They apparently did not survive the revolt and none are known archaeologically. The Spanish were forbidden to live in or have their stock farms near Indian towns (Hackett 1926:85, 89), although this law was not always obeyed and the conflict over resources increased as a result. The indirect impact of Spanish presence came through the introduction of domestic animals, which, as they foraged, trampled vegetation and compressed soils, making it difficult for plants to grow, increasing erosion and water runoff, and creating arroyos (Calloway 1997:14).

After the Pueblo Revolt and into the eighteenth century, a new group of less affluent Spanish/Hispanic immigrants came to the Rio Grande Valley and settled on smaller landholdings, ranchos, or farmsteads, also given through grants, which were scattered and thus not in strict conformity with official Spanish policy (Cordell 1979:115; Simmons 1969:10, 11). Subsistence systems at that time shifted from labor to land exploitation. Settlers rented land, brought sheep, and hired herders to produce wool for the Mexican market (Abbink and Stein 1977:157). This new economic strategy came about in part because of the Bourbon Reforms, but more practically because the Indian labor supply (and population) had decreased while the Hispanic population had increased (Simmons 1969:11).

The only recognizable town for most of the seventeenth century was Santa Fe. After the revolt, as the immigrant population grew, Albuquerque, Santa Cruz de la Cañada, and El Paso de Norte were also settled, Santa Cruz after the Tano were evicted from the river valley (Simmons 1969:11). Throughout New Spain towns were supposed to be laid out on a grid plan, with certain other standardized aspects; however, the New Mexican towns did not conform to the supposed standard. Even Santa Fe had only one street in the late eighteenth century (figure 3.11) (Bustamante 1989:65–78; Simmons 1969:12). The problem was that these towns, based originally on a Roman plan, were not suited to the Southwest setting. Since the major resources of value in the country derived from agriculture, people wanted to be near their fields to protect them from predatory animals and raiding nomadic tribes.

Hispanic villages appeared during the eighteenth century, mostly within the northern Rio Grande area. Midway through the eighteenth century, a series of buffer settlements—Santa Rosa de Lima, Santo Tomas de Abiquiú, San Miguel de Carnué, Rancho de Taos, Las Trampas, San Miguel del Vado, San José de las Huertas, Tomé, Belén, and Ojo Caliente—were established around Santa Fe to protect the capital from marauding groups of Comanches, Navajos, Apaches, and Utes (Brooks 2002:130). These villages granted lands to groups of landless Hispanic settlers and genizaros ("detribalized" individuals who had been captured by nomadic groups and ransomed to work in Hispanic households; see chapter 5). In spite of these new communities, the eighteenth century, as depicted on the Miera y Pacheco map of 1779, shows many areas abandoned, as raiding increased and the frontier shrank (Simmons 1969:17). This situation persisted until late in the eighteenth century, when settlement expanded through a combination of treaties with

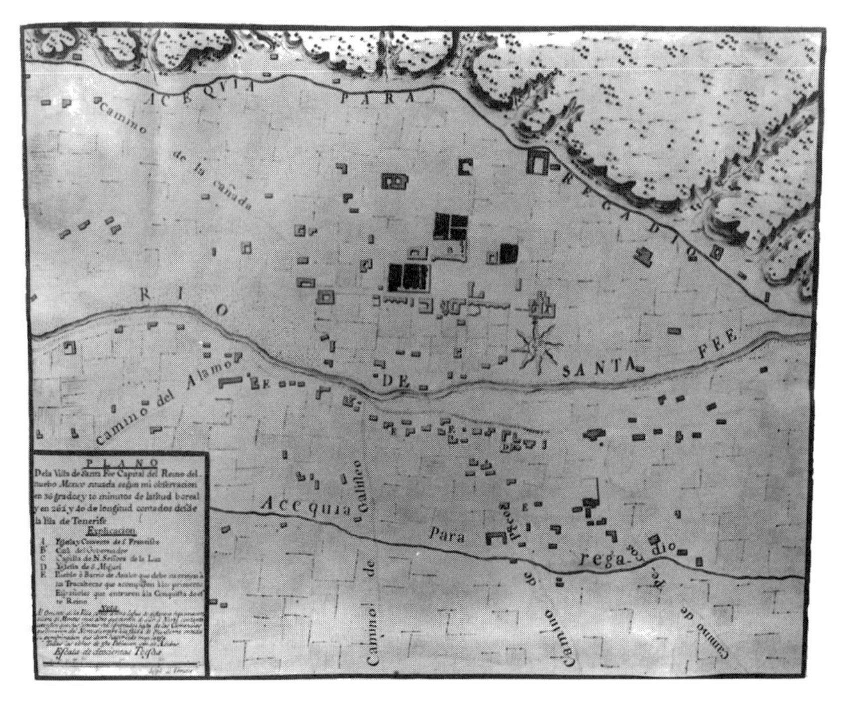

Figure 3.11. Plan of Santa Fe, 1768, quite different in its linear plan from the mandated town plan.

tribal groups (notably the Comanche; Jackson 1998), a smallpox vaccination program, and increased immigration (Frank 1998:37).

LANDSCAPE

The Spanish created an entirely new landscape in New Mexico in the late sixteenth and seventeenth centuries upon invading the territory of native peoples. Their view of land was organized around several concepts, primarily its economic potential but also the manner in which it was owned. They would have perceived land as appropriate for specific activities: farming, preferably along rivers; grazing; and extracting wood and other resources, from upland areas. Cross-cutting these divisions were others that classified territory into municipal lands; common lands surrounding town lots (*ejidos*); pasture lands, also in common; fields, both irrigable and nonirrigable; and private parcels, both in town and in outlying areas designated for farming (Church 1999; Simmons 1969:7). Because water was a vital resource in this dry climate, water rights from the main ditch, the *acequia madre*, were also parceled out, along with joint responsibility for maintaining this facility. There are communities in northern New Mexico today, where these rights are still held and fiercely protected.

The presence of corrals, which were a Spanish innovation associated with the domestic animals they introduced, is associated with the concept of private property, alien to the Pueblos. It has been suggested that the relationships between people and animals are an important aspect of human life (Mullin 1999). In bringing domestic animals–sheep primarily, but also horses, cattle, and large dogs (greyhounds and mastiffs)—the Spanish expressed their view of these animals and the land. Both were subservient to people, and both could be moved, manipulated, and used to express the will of their owners and users. Horses and large dogs were also used as instruments of power and terror against indigenous peoples (Mullin 1999:4). The Pueblos saw animals as part of the natural world, having a place in that world and considerable autonomy, not as creatures that they could control. Through ritual, Pueblo hunters express gratitude to animals they have caught. At least one writer refers to the Spanish "conquest of the landscape, [which w]as a form of violence—this was a war waged with plants, mammals, and microbes" (Taylor and Pease 1994:5) resulting in illness, hunger, destruction of natural resources, and especially the appropriation and redirection of water. The Spanish tried to eliminate indigenous irrigation systems and check dams, as they introduced new crops requiring acequia irrigation.

The Spanish/Hispanic landscape would have been both narrower and more linear than the Pueblo landscape, connecting specific places in New Mexico with one another and with places in Mexico but confining these places to known routes. Their ideas of possession of land and buildings on it are reflected in documents: "I ordered that acts of possession for the holy churches and conventos standing and established in the pueblos of the kingdom of New Mexico be kept, carried out, and fulfilled. The same should be done for sufficient land to plant the crops required for subsistence" (Kessell et al. 1992b:263). The Spanish world was structured by four cardinal directions, the Pueblo by six (adding up and down to north, east, south, and west). The Pueblos also viewed their lands in terms of activities, but included many more categories: the locations of other clans, trading partners and routes to find them, short- or long-term allies, traditional enemies, and historic and sacred places (apart from kivas) would all have been part of the

Pueblo landscape. Subsistence activities went beyond farming to collecting a range of wild resources and the places and times to find them. Both groups inscribed the landscape with their religious beliefs and worldview, including ideas of cause and effect, origins, history, and the afterlife.

ARCHITECTURE

The form of Spanish towns and villages was prescribed. They were meant to be fortified, have rectangular blocks, and one or more rectangular plazas (Simmons 1969:8,12), although they did not always conform to the ideal (see the earlier discussion of Santa Fe). The size of the community was standardized (Cordell 1980:46), as was the spacing between the church and secular buildings (Hackett 1923:187). The town ordinance of 1573 laid out a set of 148 rules for city and political planning; the Spanish believed that if indigenous peoples were settled in towns, they could be better controlled and civilized (Jojola 1997). The Pueblos already lived in aggregated settlements that looked like towns, hence the name assigned by the Spanish. However, the layout of indigenous communities was architecturally distinctive from the Spanish plan, in spite of the fact that both had geometrically ordered, walled, multistory communities with central open spaces. Pueblo settlements varied in size and cohesion; houses were not regularly spaced; and they did not necessarily have a *plaza mayor,* or central place: often there were several plazas, some with kivas. In many instances the structures were contiguous, creating a defensive perimeter similar to the wall that was supposed to protect Spanish towns. Some were composed of unconnected room blocks, while others were apparently planned and built in a coordinated way. Small isolated farm structures were probably used seasonally, whereas most settlement was in year-round communities. Further, Pueblo settlements differed from towns in social ways, as the Pueblo formed socially cohesive communities, structured by kin, clan, and secret societies. Spanish towns, especially immigrant towns, were often composed of unrelated families, hierarchically and occupationally stratified, although some cohesion probably developed from hardships endured together and institutions such as compadrazgo, which united people by fictive kinship ties.

Archaeologists sometimes find it difficult to distinguish Spanish and Pueblo settlements. Each group is known to have occupied settlements created by the other, although it was more common for the Spanish to occupy or remodel part of an empty Indian pueblo than for Pueblo peoples to live in Spanish structures.

The practice probably occurred for pragmatic reasons but could also have been part of the practice of superimposing Spanish structures on indigenous ones to indicate dominance. In terms of architecture, both built rectangular rooms, although Spanish rooms were, on the average, larger and squarer than pueblo rooms (Earls 1986:16; Lambert and Rogers 1954:22; Marshall and Walt 1984:139), with taller and thicker walls, and differently placed and designed doors and windows (Ivey 1988). Construction materials were also similar; the Spanish were familiar with mud-brick architecture, originally from North Africa, and sometimes built mud-brick walls on stone foundations. The Indians, too, used both stone and adobe prior to Spanish contact (see chapter 2). Certain details can be used to identify Spanish or Mexican influence in addition to the grid layout, "elements such as courtyards, portals, and corral enclosures" (Marshall and Walt 1984:139), corner fireplaces, or fireplaces along the wall, and door sills. Spanish homes had benches and more furniture than Pueblo homes (Lambert and Rogers 1954:38). The presence of corrals, whitewashed plaster on walls or floors, and selenite for windows also mark Spanish or Hispanic homes. The use of mold-made adobes, the placement of the hearth, and room size may also indicate Spanish occupation, although none are totally consistent markers. A recent field observation suggests that Spanish houses may be identifiable by a consistent wall thickness of 50 centimeters for one-story buildings (Cordelia Snow, personal communication 2000). Some of these traits were observed at the seventeenth-century household (perhaps the home of Lujàn, the *teniente,* or assistant to the *alcalde mayor,* of Cochití pueblo) at LA 34, in Cochití Springs, and at LA 9138 and LA 9139, both occupied between 1750 and 1800 (Snow 1979:219). It is unclear whether Spanish and Pueblo uses of domestic space were similar. Pueblo rooms typically had a multipurpose rather than single-purpose function. Archaeological analysis of the location of activities has not been conducted but would be useful in differentiating the division of labor and other role distinctions.

The key element in identifying Spanish influence is the presence of churches, chapels, and garrisons, although Spanish churches in New Mexico are quite different from their European antecedents. Some say the difficult environment led the Spanish to choose simpler forms here, but Hanlon (1992) suggests the mission churches represent a fusion of Spanish and indigenous ideas and beliefs about the sacred, possibly because those building the churches were Pueblos. He sees churches as conveying a mixed message, reflecting the arrogance of colonial domination in their scale and placement in the midst of the pueblo, at the same time sharing some attributes of kivas. For example, they were oriented on a north-south axis, closer to the axis within a kiva than to the traditional Christian east-west orientation. In Hanlon's view, Ivey's (1988) analysis of the kivas within patios at Abo and Quarai suggests a desire on the part of the friars to coexist, since evidence shows that those kivas and churches were built at the same time (see the earlier discussion in this chapter for alternative interpretations of this phenomenon).

Settlement in the Northeast

The Dutch and Mohawks followed very distinct land use and settlement patterns, and their interaction, as reflected through this analysis, differed dramatically from the situation in the Southwest. The two groups maintained separate territories throughout the period of Dutch colonial control and after, intersecting primarily at points where trading occurred. The Dutch wanted this separation and enacted laws to protect it, although it was not as complete as desired. A series of maps derived from Snow's (1995) important compendium of Mohawk site information demonstrates their settlement change. While precise locations shifted over time, there was a consistent pattern in that major sites or "castles" were spread through the Mohawk River Valley from east to west. In the sixteenth-century, sites were positioned considerably north of the Mohawk River for the most part (figure 3.12), were just north of the river at the beginning of the seventeenth century (figure 3.13), and then shifted to the southern bank during the period of heavy trade from 1635 to 1646 (figure 3.14), after the Mohawks had driven the Mahicans from the west bank of the Hudson. All of these moves to the north or south stayed within the same approximate east-west space, although the center of gravity appears to have shifted somewhat to the east between 1614 and 1626 (figure 3.13), when trading would have been optimal, and somewhat west during 1635–1646 (figure 3.14), after the first of the large epidemics.

Site location was affected mainly by population change and trade relations. During the seventeenth century, Mohawk population declined dramatically, from less than 8,000 in the 1630s (Van den Bogaert 1988) to some 1,200 in 1677 (in Snow et al. 1996; Greenhalgh 1677:189). In the wake of war, disease, and emigration, the rapid decline continued until only about 500 Mohawks remained in the Mohawk Valley in 1750 (Delage 1991; Guldenzopf 1986:80, 83; Snow 1995:4; see

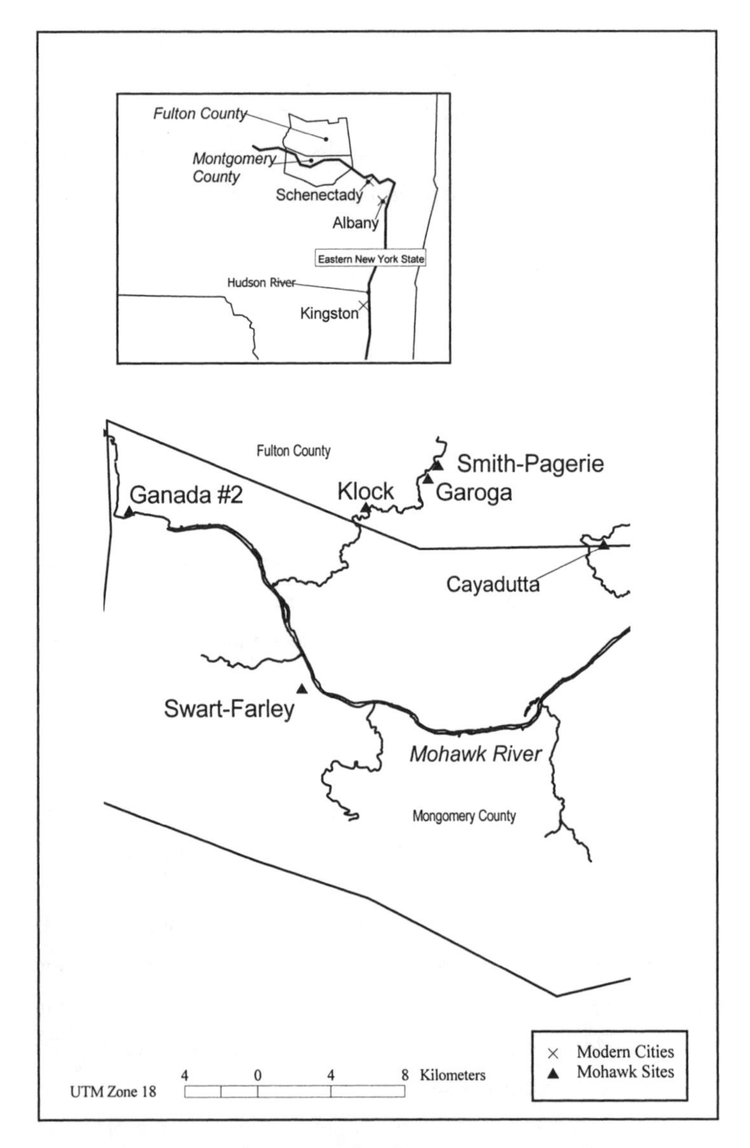

Figure 3.12. Major and minor Mohawk sites, 1525–1580. Courtesy Antoinette Wannebo and Dean Snow.

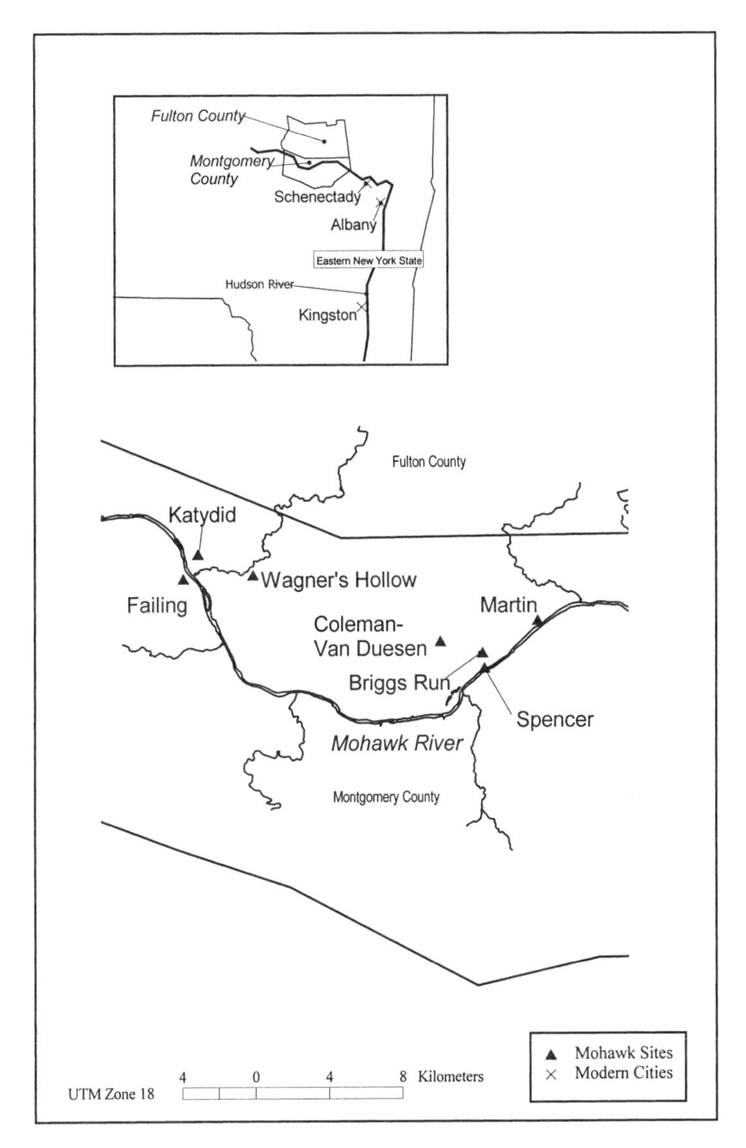

Figure 3.13. Principal Mohawk village sites, 1614–1626. Courtesy Antoinette Wannebo and Dean Snow.

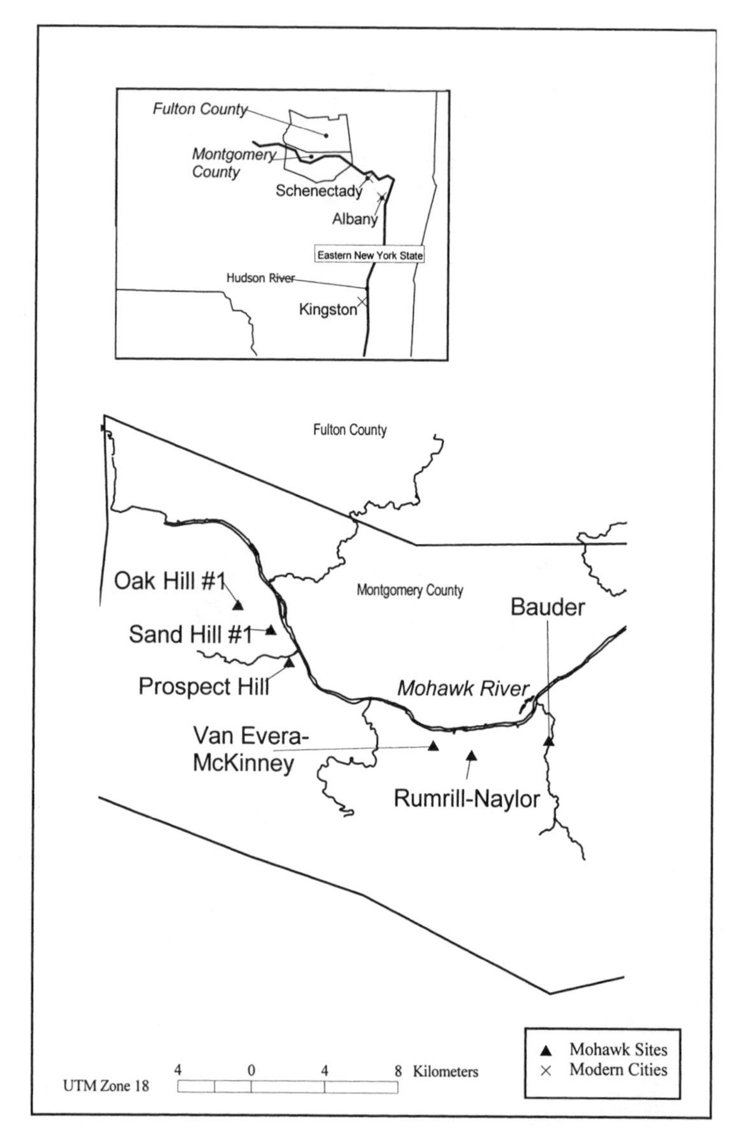

Figure 3.14. Mohawk sites, 1635–1646. Courtesy Antoinette Wannebo and Dean Snow.

also chapter 2 of this volume). The most dramatic change occurs just after the first wave of epidemics in 1634/5. Population estimates based on a comparison of numbers of longhouses and site sizes show a precipitious drop, from 7,740 in 1626–1635 to 2,835 in 1635–1646; there is a concomitant decrease in individual site sizes. "Castles" occupied just prior to 1635 contained up to about 2,000–3,000 people, while later sites held about 700 each (Snow 1995:301). Though population data are always problematic, this appears to be a more radical and faster population decline than in the Rio Grande Valley. Despite these losses, a similar pattern of village spacing persists, with lower, middle, and upper castles until the end of the century (1679–1693), when the population was further reduced and only two large sites remained, a lower and upper castle (Snow 1995:415, 431). This spacing was intended to maintain control of the Mohawk River Valley.

As discussed in chapter 2, the reduction in number of villages was accompanied by a decrease in longhouse size, from a high of 75–80 people per structure in the mid–sixteenth century at Garoga, to 30–40 per structure in the late seventeenth century at Caughnawaga (Snow 1995:435). Another postulated change of the mid–eighteenth century is a different settlement pattern, with the Mohawks living in small "European-style cabins" (Guldenzopf 1986) dispersed around forts built by British administrators. Descriptions of this pattern are based on contemporary observations and have not been documented archaeologically, although a survey of documentary accounts does suggest that beginning around 1715 there were more single-hearth short longhouses than multiple-hearth longhouses (Jordan 2002). Both Snow's work at Caughnawaga and Jordan's research in the Seneca area suggest that the transition was a gradual one and neither as abrupt or complete as others have proposed, particularly for western Iroquois. This alteration in housing and settlement layout is often assumed to imply not only a technological shift in construction methods, but more significantly a change in the cohesion of society centered on the strength of kin ties. The extant evidence, however, suggests that the Mohawks and Iroquois in general maintained the principles of clan and lineage organization even during periods of great stress in the eighteenth century, when many of them relocated to Canada. Changes in housing were undoubtedly influenced by the population decline and perhaps by alterations in settlement placement and subsistence practices (Jordan 2002). Population loss would inevitably have had a major impact on traditional social structure as well, as captives and adoptees were sought to fill in the gaps and clan positions were reorganized.

According to Peter Schuyler and Robert Livingston, reporting in 1700 on Mohawk affairs, two-thirds of the remaining Mohawk population in the Hudson and Mohawk Valleys had emigrated at that time to what is now Canada because they felt that the British were unable to protect them from French attacks. As a result, there were more Mohawk at Jesuit missions in Canada than in the Mohawk Valley. Queen Anne's War of 1702–1713 exacerbated this trend, and in 1711 the British built Fort Hunter at the confluence of Schoharie Creek and the Mohawk River (Guldenzopf 1986:81–83) to provide some protection for the remaining Mohawks. Fort Hunter remained the eastern or lower Mohawk site with the western/upper castle complex built at what is known as Indian Castle (also called Canojoharie, Dekanohage, or Fort Hendrick) (figure 3.15). There have been excavations in the area, both at the site of the home of Joseph Brant, an elite and atypical Mohawk who lived near Fort Hendrick as late as 1777, and at Fort Hunter at the Enders House, but the material is quite limited and comes from contexts that are not well defined. As the Mohawks moved out of the Hudson and Mohawk River Valleys, a number of Europeans—initially Palatine Germans, but also Dutch-Americans and English—moved in and acquired Mohawk land. It may be that the construction of Fort Hunter made the area more appealing for settlement to Europeans as well as the Mohawks, offering them protection from French invasion (Jordan 2002). In their landholding and farming patterns, Europeans settled and farmed a particular piece of land permanently, which meant that the remaining Mohawks were unable to continue their traditional shifting horticulture in that region. Fort Hunter and Indian Castle continued to house a mixture of a few hundred Mohawks (those who had remained and some who returned from Canada), but almost all finally left the area during the American Revolution, having sided with the British during that war (Guldenzopf 1986:88).

Figures 3.12 to 3.15 also show Dutch (and later English) settlements. Whereas the Mohawk sites were all located on the Mohawk River, the European settlements were all located within the Hudson River corridor. Dutch towns were organized in a looser and less cohesive manner than other European colonial ones, lacking New England institutions such as town meetings and collective government (Merwick 1990:196) or the Spanish apparatus of political control. Towns

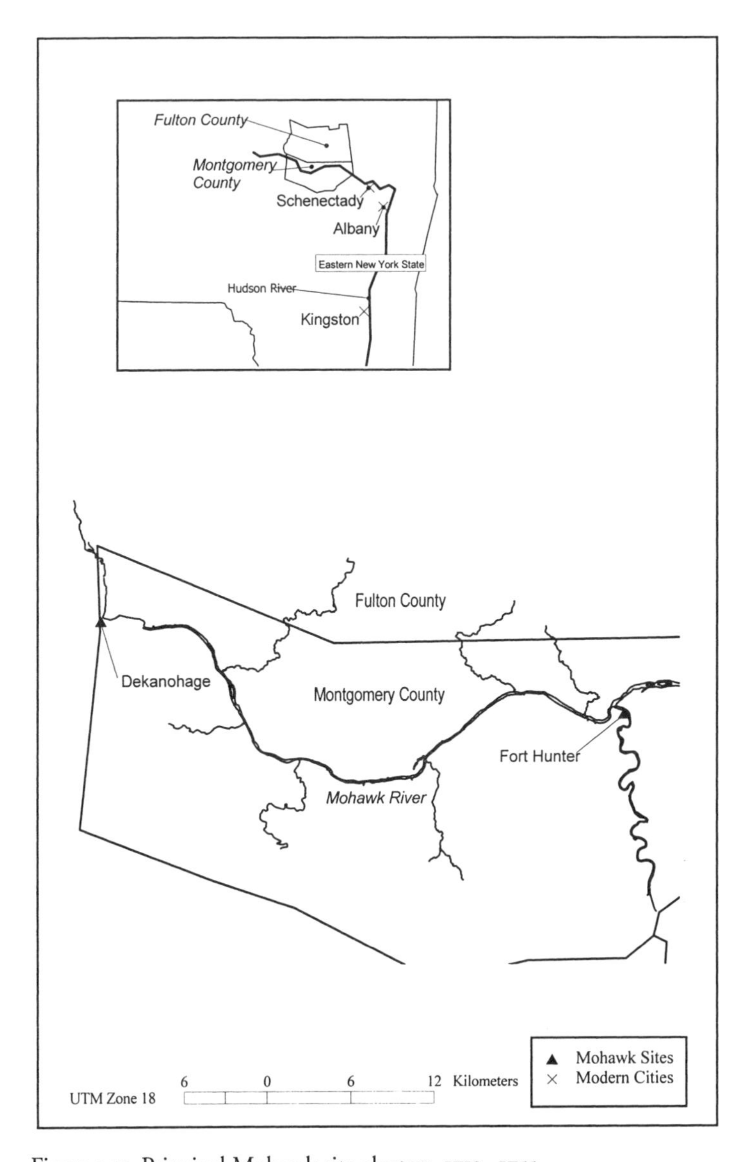

Figure 3.15. Principal Mohawk site clusters, 1712–1755.

were located at both ends of the navigable part of the river to control trade, and although the Dutch were slow to organize towns and villages (Rink 1988b:227–231), a few developed in between. As noted in chapter 2, a series of settlements in the approximate location of today's Albany (Fort Orange, Beverwyck—which became Albany—and Rensselaerswyck) were at the north; New Amsterdam was at the Hudson's mouth; and shortly before the Dutch lost control of the colony, Peter Stuyvesant laid out some new towns for trade: New Amstel on the Delaware River in 1657, Wiltwyck (later called Kingston) in 1658 (Huey 1991), and Schenectady in 1661. After 1657, European immigration increased, and the Indian population rebounded as it recovered from epidemics, but this led to greater conflict between the two groups (Rink 1986: 259). Schenectady was founded when the Mohawks agreed to release the land for it to a group of Beverwyck traders under Van Curler's sponsorship. The Mohawks were motivated in part by the decline in the fur trade (Burke 1991:20), while the Dutch traders wanted to establish a new point of exchange that would be closer to the Mohawks, who would have favored it over Fort Orange and Beverwyck. The arrangement would have provided an advantage to these particular traders over the better-established Fort Orange merchants (Richter 1992:97) and might have reduced the problem of Mohawk carriers being set upon by competing Dutch traders as they neared the fort, each in pursuit of Mohawk furs. But Stuyvesant wanted Schenectady to focus on agricultural production for the colony and refused trade privileges to the investors in the new settlement; consequently Schenectady's economy was based on farming, with the only trade a minor and secretive activity (Burke 1991:20; Richter 1992:98).

Patroonships (see chapter 2) differed from towns in that their populations were less aggregated. Only one patroonship survived long enough to be discussed in some detail. This was Rensselaerswyck, which in 1643 had about 100 people in 25–30 houses built along the Hudson "as each found most convenient" (Father Jogues cited in Arent van Curler's letter to the patroon; Van Laer 1927–1928:17).

Again, in marked contrast to the situation in the Rio Grande River Valley, the Mohawk and Dutch were spatially quite separate, and in general remained in distinct spheres. They met for trade in and around Fort Orange and its successor towns. There were well-defined rules about how both groups should behave, although archaeology and the documentary record (especially the complaints recorded in Fort Orange and Beverwyck court proceedings) make it clear that these laws were often violated, as was true for many of the laws governing other forms of behavior (see Rothschild 1990). In fact, Domine Megapolensis stated in 1644, "They sleep by us, too, in our chambers before our beds" (Huey 1990). During the British period, the community maintained a group of "Little Indian houses" outside the fort for visiting Native Americans bringing furs. In a number of instances, court papers complained that some members of the community were not contributing to their upkeep (Van Laer 1928:2:193). A slightly later reference in 1697 describes Native American fur traders as living in huts "that were falling into disrepair beyond the western wall of the stockade" (Bielinski 1991:4). Colonists were also forbidden to trade outside the town gates or receive beavers there, visit the Indian houses on the pretext of debt, or lodge or entertain Indians overnight (Van Laer 1928:3:340, 461, 498). Other court records noted individuals being fined for having been too close to the Indian houses (Van Laer 1928:2:262) or because the "defendant continually lets his children go to the Indian houses . . . with all sorts of trinkets, knives, paints, etc. to sell to the Indians" (Van Laer 1928:3:473). These comments, as well as Indian pipes and pottery recovered from archaeological assemblages inside Fort Orange (Huey 1988), suggest the presence of Mohawk inside the walls of the fort, regardless of rules to the contrary.

In spite of these exceptions, separation was thought to be important and for the most part was maintained. European traders did not want free interaction between those bringing furs and those acquiring them as it often led to conflict and abuse. Descriptions of traders' representatives chasing Indians in the forest outside of the fort, telling them to go to a specific trader in town, abound (Merwick 1990:90). It is possible that the restrictions promoting separation became increasingly important when furs became scarce. It is also likely that the attempt to maintain separation was due to a feeling of vulnerability on the part of the Dutch and later occupants of Albany; court minutes of August 6, 1677, note: "About 200 Maqua [Mohawk] warriors have come here and are encamped about the city" (Van Laer 1928:2:257). Merwick (1990:95) supports this idea, stating that residents of Albany often expressed anxiety about the woods outside the gates of town.

A mid–eighteenth century observer of Albany life, Anne Grant (1808:1:121–124, 134), speaks of "detached Indians," who lived near the houses of the "more wealthy and benevolent inhabitants" (of Albany) during the summer months. By this time the Mohawks were attempting to maintain their access to European goods despite having few skins for trade by exchanging other products of their labor. The women made handicrafts such as wooden trays, dishes, spoons, shovels, rakes, brooms and baskets, shoes and stockings, which they traded for bread, milk, and other food, while the men smoked sturgeon and eels. At the end of summer these Mohawks rejoined the rest of the group.

LANDSCAPES

In the Northeast, European ideas of settlement and landholding were quite different from those of Native Americans, as Cronon (1983) describes. Towns as well as farms were permanent settlements, clearly bounded and marked. One of the key distinctions pertains to ownership: indigenous peoples held land collectively with possession tied to use, while the Dutch and the British believed in permanent individual ownership accompanied by disposal rights. Colonial settlers argued that Indians made "improper" use of the land, manifested by the lack of permanent settlements, fences, gardens, and animal pens (Seed 1995), to claim it for themselves. This was true in the Southwest as well as the Northeast. A father indignantly notes:

> The Indians . . . are lazy and for the most part idlers and shirkers. Some scarcely plant enough to sustain themselves, while others harvest more than those and squander it on themselves. They trade the goods they customarily use among themselves. When the citizens [Spanish] arrive at their houses wanting to buy goods, they either refuse or sell to them at an excessive price. (Kessell et al. 1992b:285)

Mohawk sites were located in reference to good farmland, defense, and social factors such as clan affiliation. As among the Pueblos, their landscape would have included the places where allies and enemies lived, important travel routes by which to find resources and peoples who mattered, and locations of spiritual and political significance, and they would have existed below ground and in the ether, in a range of time periods including those before and after the present. Their landscape was structured in part by their view of the natural world and their place in it; their perspective did not imply control of that world but viewed their role as participants interacting with other inhabitants in a variety of ways; it was a symbiotic and spiritual relationship, quite alien to the wholesale hunt for beaver (Calloway 1997:15). Christian religion placed God above nature and attached no importance to the relationship between humans and animals; there was only an obligation to God. After God, humans (actually Europeans) were at the top of creation's hierarchy. Indians had a system of frequent ritual practices designed to maintain a balance in the universe and keep spirits content (Calloway 1997:72). A further clash of perspectives between indigenous and European peoples is illustrated by the European idea that animals can belong to an individual and be considered property, which was alien to the Mohawks. When a Mohawk encountered a pig or cow running loose in the forest, he believed that this was an animal like any other that could be hunted.

Perhaps the Mohawk landscape was most dramatically affected by the intensive hunt for beaver, which the Indians themselves conducted. Merchant (in Calloway 1997:15, 20) notes that the decline in beavers and their dams meant that pond levels were not maintained and species such as muskrat and otter were frozen or flooded out. Mink and racoon could not get the frogs, suckers, and snakes on which they normally fed as ponds dried up, becoming marshes and finally meadows. Migratory birds flew north to breed on ponds that could still be found in Maine. In some places, the absence of dams meant faster stream flow and changing fish habitats; it led to flooding and erosion. Other important ecological changes came about as a result of European practices, such as plowing with draft animals and monocrop cultivation rather than the "messy" Indian custom of mixing crops in a single field. Plowing destroys native plants and creates entirely new habitats that support only domesticated species (Cronon 1983), while monocropping leads to soil erosion. As land-clearing proceeds and shade-loving plants die, food chains are altered, animals and birds seek different habitats, and new microorganisms and insects invade the old ones (Calloway 1997:20).

The location of Dutch communities was governed primarily by trade, although farming was the overriding factor for a few settlements, especially the patroonships. Trade required access to water transport, as the seventeenth-century Dutch were particularly aware. Their settlements, no matter where they were in the world, had a similar "look." The Dutch were especially familiar with the landscape perspective of Renaissance painting, in which the observer's viewpoint was the important one. Coming into the harbor of Amsterdam, New Amsterdam or a Dutch colony in the West Indies, travelers would have seen a familiar view. They had a global orientation to trade, and the settlements near today's Albany would have been only a minor part of their worldwide scheme: the Mohawks and other indigenous people would have been similarly insignificant, while the real players would have been other European nations.

Conclusion

The placement of indigenous and European settlements in the two river valleys under consideration indicates a vast difference between Spanish and Dutch goals in settling along the Rio Grande and Hudson Rivers. This settlement affected indigenous landscapes in a variety of ways. The invasion of Pueblo space produced strategies of avoidance and resistance among the Pueblos, and great numbers of settlements ceased to be occupied. In contrast, the Dutch did not wish to live among the Mohawks, but the Mohawks were attracted to Dutch settlements for trade, and the impact on their lives was more insidious because it was less explicitly aimed at control. European colonizers entered Indian lands to create entirely new places, although they attempted to use familiar models to do so. The climate and resources in the Hudson Valley were not as limiting as those in the Rio Grande Valley, but in both cases the clash between indigenous and European constructions of the landscape, and between perceptions of the land and ideas on how best to use it, is dramatically evident.

4

The Flow of Goods and Labor

Colonial interaction in the Rio Grande and Hudson and Mohawk Valleys is elucidated especially well by the analysis of material culture and the degree to which it is shared in each of the two systems. In each case, archaeological data provide support for the degree of connection between the European colonizers and the indigenous residents. In this chapter, I look at similarities in subsistence patterning as reflected in faunal and paleobotanical information. Food is important for economic reasons, but it also serves social and ritual functions. Often the first interactions between groups involve the exchange of foods in ritualized gift-giving. Indigenous foods, also essential to European colonizers for survival, were acquired by controlling native labor. In chapter 5, I examine shared patterns of material culture, visible in artifactual remains. Some of these items—such as pottery—have functional value, as basic requirements for existence. Many of them also convey expressions of identity, and it is important to distinguish between them. When two distinct cultures use similar objects, we need to understand the means by which they were acquired. One of the mechanisms of shared material culture involves exchange.

Anthropologists and others have written extensively on exchange and related subjects (Appadurai 1986; Godelier 1977; Kopytoff 1986; Malinowski 1922; Marx [1867]1976; Mauss 1990; Miller 1987; Munn 1986; Strathern 1988; Thomas 1991).

Some of the important issues are the complex and variable nature of objects and their value, mechanisms of circulation, and the cultural construction or meaning of "giving" an object or one's labor to someone else. Exchange is affected by who does the giving and who the receiving, what is given or received, the perception of the object on both sides, and the expectation of return. The same object may function within the same culture as a gift in some settings and a commodity in others and may move between these states; labor can also be provided as a gift or for hire, and it can be taken without permission through slavery or indentured servitude. The discourse on European-indigenous exchange focuses particularly on gifts and commodities, the distinction between them in various economic systems, and the potential of differing objects to be involved in economic transactions of any sort, which refers to their alienability (Marx [1876]1976; Weiner 1992). Initial colonial transactions may be characterized as gift exchange, although it is unclear whether both parties involved in gift-giving would have understood Mauss's important point—that what appeared to be a gift carried the expectation and the obligation to return something: reciprocity (Munn 1986). When Europeans gave initial gifts it was to establish a favorable climate; they did not understand the network of entailed obligations that their indigenous partners saw, as commodity transactions are quite different and notably are finite.

Commodity-centered economies facilitate the acquisition of goods; colonial extractive settlements were designed to do just that, while gift economies are designed to expand social networks (Strathern 1988:143). If we do not focus on specific objects but on process and the intention behind transactions, it is clear that as contact situations lengthened, more of the exchange in material goods that occurred, especially in the Northeast, would have been closer to commodity exchange than gift exchange. As European demands became better known, context-specific situations developed in which some items came to be produced specifically for exchange and thus began to function as commodities, although they had not previously held this status.[1]

An excellent account of how these concepts applied in real situations appears in Richard White's, *The Middle Ground* (1991), which reveals the complexity gen-

1. Some research has suggested that ceramics were produced in the Prehispanic Southwest as commodities and exchanged in market-like systems (Kohler et al. 2000; Mills 1995b). This interpretation is based on the large quantities being produced above household needs, and above what gift-exchange could have accommodated.

erated by conflicting and disparate economic expectations, specifically those between European and indigenous economic systems. In the systemic conflict between the two sets of cultures White describes, the French use gift-giving to establish peace and good relations, which they saw as a necessary part of the initial interaction period, while the Algonkians and northern Iroquoians thought it was to be a continuing practice. As White explains, the Algonkian interpretation of French behavior—when the French gave the Algonkians less for their furs than they had previously received—was that the French no longer loved them, were being unkind, and were not behaving in paternal fashion.

The Indians' use of the word *besoin,* says White, shows that their concept of need was different from the French meaning. According to White (1991:117, 129), the Algonkians thought that when they acknowledged "need" it implied a moral burden on the French to ameliorate the situation, that being needy should produce sympathy in a partner in an established social relationship. In addition, the fact that the French had certain supplies in large quantities while their partners did not meant to them that the French had an obligation to share these supplies, based on the expectation of generosity. Thus, as their own need became greater and the supplies of beaver declined, they believed that the price per beaver should increase (White 1991:131–132). Actually, this is quite a rational idea in modern Western terms, and perfectly sensible to the Algonkians, but not accepted by French colonial traders, who were facing other economic problems and trying to keep costs down.

Further elucidation of the difficulty in crossing economic systems emerges from White's (1991:114) discussion of credit and loan. The French had observed that if they gave gifts to their indigenous partners in the fall, before the hunting season, they would subsequently receive furs. Traders then began to conceptualize these gifts as loans, or credit advanced, implying a return of a specific amount, but the notion of economic debt of a specific magnitude did not conform to Indian practice. The Euroamerican view of this difference is articulated by La Potherie, a trader, commenting that they (the Huron-Petun and Ottawas)

> [do] not need to go hunting in order to obtain all the comforts of life. When they choose to work, they make canoes of birch bark, which they sell two at three hundred livres each. They get a shirt for two sheets of bark for cabins. The sale of their French strawberries and other fruits produce means for procuring their ornaments,

> which consist of vermillion and glass and porcelain beads. They make a profit on everything. (Cited in White 1991:131)

However, neither "profit" nor "sale" were a part of Huron mentality.

At the outset, there were clearly vast differences between the Dutch and Spanish as colonizers, although in terms of economic systems, both were part of market economies, and they had more in common with each other than either did with the indigenous systems they encountered. The latter can appropriately be characterized as premodern economies in which reciprocal and redistributive exchange were the norms. Such systems take various forms, but they are nevertheless quite different from those exemplifying market exchange. In both case studies, one of the significant impacts of contact was the incorporation of the Native American groups into the global commercial system (Farriss 1984:30), which occurred more rapidly and directly for one than the other.

THE APPROPRIATION OF LABOR

The entire range of concepts that applies to the exchange of material objects pertains as well to forms of human labor, whether directed labor, sex and marriage, or the products of human labor—ultimately the basis of all objects. Modes of production were strikingly different in each of the major parties in these contact situations. Europeans were giving away or trading the products of others' labor; in many cases they were offering commodities that were of low cost and little value to them. Native Americans, in contrast, were providing their own labor or its products, at relatively high cost.

The demand for Indian labor in the Mohawk Valley was less direct than in the Southwest, as it required the production of beaver, although this trade required considerable time and effort and led to a distortion of hunting practices. Women's labor was required to process the skins, but not to provide domestic service as the Dutch maintained a well-defined social distance from the Mohawks, and there is little evidence of sexual services demanded of their women. Dutch documents discuss the proper treatment of Indians in some detail and caution traders against spending too much time with indigenous people and becoming too close to them (Van Laer 1927–1928).

In the Southwest, Pueblos worked for the missions, the governors, and encomenderos, farming and herding, doing construction and other tasks the Spanish defined, but they also labored to produce hides, piñon nuts, and other things as well as present their required twice yearly contributions of textiles (*mantas*) and corn for encomienda tribute. Spanish documents describe their responsibilities in the Rio Grande Valley, although the procedures outlined were often not followed, and labor demands were abusive. Women worked as domestic servants but sexual services were frequently required of them in those settings. It is unclear whether such services were ever provided freely, but it is clear that they were often taken, not offered. Further, the Spanish distorted the traditional gendered division of labor in two ways, altering the normal social structure: first, by requiring men to do "women's work," such as house construction and agriculture (Frank 1998:51), and second, by making tasks more rigidly gendered. Women were the traditional builders. They were especially important in laying adobes, although men were involved in some of the heavier tasks, including getting timbers needed for roofs (Ivey 1988:48). But the Spanish instituted changes and required men to do house construction, which not only altered labor patterns but apparently produced hilarity among the women, reducing male self-esteem (Frank 1998:51; Gutierrez 1991:76). Men were also told not to weave or hunt any more but to herd domestic animals, which often forced them to leave their communities (Frank 1998).

Issues of gender are also relevant in considering the control of labor and the products of labor and services. Many descriptions of colonial contact situations have ignored the element of gender and the variation in economies that adheres to the differences between men and women, often ignoring women's production and assuming that men were the controllers of exchange, and thus of women and their goods (Strathern 1988). I do not focus on gendered products of labor in these case studies, in part because the archaeological data do not allow this kind of analysis, but also because many existing views of work clearly imply a rigidity that is not borne out by detailed analyses; they are stereotypic and narrow. A number of analysts have recently suggested that there was more variability in the way tasks were allocated than has been assumed, with men and women sharing some productive activities, either working on them jointly or performing specific components of them (Lamphere 2000; Mills 2000b; Szuter 2000). The gendering of work was also affected by the location in which it occurred, within the household or outside.

Controlling products of exchange has often been considered a male prerogative in colonial encounters. There were undoubtedly instances of Native American men providing Spanish or Dutch colonists things made or grown by women—agricultural products and pottery are easy examples—but there were probably times when women were the primary dealers in these exchanges, as was true among the Cherokee (Hatley 1993). Pueblo men also exchanged cloth that they wove; Webster (1997:109) notes that if anything served as a medium of exchange in the Precolumbian Southwest, textiles would have served that purpose. Among the Iroquois and the Pueblos prior to contact, women had considerable rights and power in their political economies, and some held positions of ritual significance. It seems reasonable, therefore, to hypothesize that they had some ability to control the products of their own labor (Spielmann 2000).

Subsistence Patterns in the Southwest

The closeness of Spanish and Pueblo peoples is visible in food remains, which are quite similar, although each group had some distinctive characteristics of diet and food use as well. Part of the closeness derives from the Spanish dependence on foods grown by indigenous residents. Oñate's settlers in 1598 brought innovations that they wanted the Pueblos to adopt: farming techniques such as the plow, animal power, and acequia irrigation, along with new fruits, vegetables, and domestic animals. The Pueblos took the ones they wanted, when they could get them (especially sheep), but retained traditional foods and farming methods. Initially there was little change. "Despite the introduction of European innovations, domestic livestock and firearms by early Hispanic expeditions, the pre-existing indigenous adaptive systems remained largely unaffected by Spanish contact" (Abbink and Stein 1977:152).

The food remains of Dutch and Mohawk peoples are not as similar, although the former also depended on the latter, especially at certain times and for certain foods, such as deer and corn. Archaeological data of a faunal and paleoethnobotanical nature and documentary accounts clarify the interaction between the Spanish and the Pueblo peoples in New Mexico for the periods after contact (pre- and post-revolt). I am specifically interested in subsistence practice and change, in the schedule and degree of adoption of European plants and domestic animals by Native Americans, and in the significant reliance on traditional indigenous foods by the Spanish. As subsistence habits changed, the way land and labor were allocated and used would also have changed, as would the perceived landscape (see chapter 3).

Santa Fe farming conditions were apparently similar to those in parts of Spain (New Castile), in that rains came during the same seasons and spring was mild, while summers were extremely hot (Hackett 1937:399). The new crops introduced by the Spanish—such as wheat, chili peppers, a new variety of corn, fruit trees, and melons—appear to have made little impact prior to the revolt, nor were these foods accessible to all; for example, fruits were found mostly in convent gardens (Espinosa 1988:23). Some of these observations about the lack of impact may be weakened by archaeological recovery issues; for example, wheat is hardly ever recovered from archaeological contexts. A number of food items noted in documentary accounts (Scholes 1930), such as chocolate, honey, olive oil, saffron, cinnamon, and sugar, were essential to maintain familiar tastes but would also not leave archaeological traces unless their containers were recovered. Chocolate drinking was a particularly important ritual element of elite Spanish social life in New Mexico and Europe. Vargas, in letters to his family and business agents, mentions sending three cases of fine chocolate to his daughters and brother-in-law, but apparently the ship carrying the chocolate was lost at sea (Kessell et al. 1992b:176), and he was quite upset. In planning his burial, he also suggested paying people in good chocolate (Kessell et al. 1992b:74).

Ultimately, sheep brought the greatest changes in subsistence and the environment (figure 4.1). They survived well in the southwestern setting and provided a steady meat supply, supplemented by cattle, pigs, and chicken, eventually reducing the reliance on hunting. Sheep also provided wool, which replaced cotton in woven goods, initially under Spanish supervision and control and subsequently when the Pueblos got access to them. Horses, mules, and oxen were also introduced, though initially on a limited scale. All of these animals contributed to environmental problems, as their foraging depleted vegetation, increased erosion, and created gullies (Calloway 1997:14), but sheep were the most active agents in this transformation, as they were by far the most numerous of the domestic animals.

Prior to the Pueblo Revolt, most domestic animals were found at the missions and in Spanish domestic settings, where friars, officials, and settlers owned herds of cattle and sheep, which were cared for by Indians on pueblo rangelands and provided the basic foods used by the Spanish, along with wheat and corn. The fa-

Figure 4.1. Sheep wander through a village today, in Lower Nutria, New Mexico. Photograph by author.

thers justified the use of Pueblo lands for cultivation and range, claiming that they provided food to local Indians when needed. Mission Indians also sowed grain and raised some sheep for the poor of each pueblo (Espinosa 1988:22–23). Civic officials gave no such justifications. While Indians were not supposed to have these animals, there is evidence at Quarai of sheep consumption by the Pueblos, and at Gran Quivira both cattle and sheep appear in middens (Spielmann 1991, 1993a, 1993b, 1994a). In most cases they were reserved for Spanish consumption and use (see the next section) and enabled the Spanish to maintain exclusive Spanish control of the production of wool textiles. Inasmuch as animals were capital, they were probably not eaten all that often, except during periods of stress. It is difficult to determine the size of individual herds, although the documentary record provides some hints, mostly preserved only in mission records. In 1595, for example, when Oñate and Ponce de León were competing over who would lead the forces invading New Mexico, Oñate offered to bring 1,000 head of cattle, 3,000 sheep for wool, 1,000 sheep for mutton, 1,000 goats, 100 head of black cattle, 150 colts, and 150 mares (Hackett 1923:227–228), although there is no way of knowing if Oñate, the successful bidder, did as he promised.

To supplement those animals already in the colony, and replace those that died or were eaten, supply trains were supposed to come every three years and bring each friar 10 heifers and 10 sheep (Scholes 1930:105). In 1639, each friar is reported to have had herds ranging between 1,000 and 2,000 sheep in size, while settlers had more than 100 apiece (Earls 1986:69). Friars are known to have been producing cattle for export as well as for subsistence (Ivey 1993; Scholes 1937, cited in Trigg 1999:289), but new shipments were continually needed. One account in 1694 reports the arrival of 500 head of sheep plus some milk cows and oxen at the Santa Ana mission (Espinosa 1988:287). Another statement around the same time notes that 1,400 head of sheep (80 of which had perished) were lost during the unsuccessful 1696 revolt, along with 100 large livestock (Espinosa 1988:254). We can infer that close to 1,400 head of sheep became Pueblo property during this revolt, and many more were undoubtedly taken over by Indians during the 1680 revolt.

The direct impact of this food source on Pueblo subsistence before the revolt seems minimal. No domestic animal remains have been recovered from prerevolt sites, and there is evidence to suggest that the traditional reliance on hunting persisted after the revolt in many places. One friar, Francisco Corbera, who was apparently well regarded by the residents of San Ildefonso, writes of his charges in 1694 that "they go out to hunt just to bring quail and rabbits [figure 4.2] for me to eat, and they bring me buffalo meat" (Espinosa 1988:124), suggesting that the Spanish as well as Pueblos depended on hunted rather than domestic meat at some times, perhaps during periods of scarcity. However, the presence of domestic animals had significant indirect effects. Access to them disrupted trade with the Apache and other nomadic groups who had provided meat in exchange for agricultural produce from the Pueblos. As well, these animals would have competed with native fauna for water and forage in particular econiches. Sheep and goats competed with antelope, while cows and horses drank a great deal of water, reducing the available game nearby (McKusick 1981:64). Grazing also caused environmental degradation, which some believe is indicated by lagomorph indices, as explained later in the chapter. The effects would not have been immediate and would have varied from area to area. In the southern, Piro section of the Rio Grande, a change in vegetation after the revolt is evident in reduced plant diversity and increased grass (Earls 1986:47, 69, 71) and is attributed to the presence of significant numbers of sheep. These conditions may also have contributed to the loss of population in the area at this time and seems to have persisted, since bighorn sheep were no longer found in the Piro area in the nineteenth century (Earls 1986:80).

The colonial period of 1598–1680 also exposed the Pueblos to new forms of agriculture related to the Spanish-introduced complex of plow, metal tilling instruments, and beasts of burden (Abbink and Stein 1977:154; Espinosa 1988:23). It is unlikely that Indians had or wanted access to these technological innovations for their own fields, especially given the seeming difficulty in gaining access to metal tools (see chapter 5). These tools would, however, have been used in mission and other Spanish fields. The missionaries not only wanted the Pueblos to adopt the new farming methods and new foods, but also expected to be fed by them. "The Spanish depended solely on Pueblo agricultural tribute, Apache slaves, and hired servants for survival" (Abbink and Stein 1977:155). The fathers claimed it as their right because they aided the Indians when food was in short supply yet failed to see that Pueblo subsistence crises were created in part by Spanish food demands and the increased population that now had to be fed. The situation is hinted at in a dispute between religious and civil authorities at Las Humanas about the water

Figure 4.2. Desert cottontail *(Sylvilagus audobonii).*

needed by mission livestock and the labor required to obtain water from wells. In 1660, residents of Las Humanas drove 20–30 horses, 20 oxen, and 700 sheep to the mission at Abó owing to the lack of water at Gran Quivira (McKusick 1981: 64). The gravity of the water situation in the Salinas area is reflected in the death of 450 people during 1667 (Ivey 1988:198).

Some documentary information on food donated to Indian people is preserved in mission records (manuscripts provided by James Ivey), especially those from the 1660s–1670s, a period of many droughts. During a major drought in 1669–1672, many missions gave food away from their supplies generated by "the sweat and labor of the minister, aided by the natives" (BNM legajo 1, no. 34, folio 3:6). Distributions were made both to Indians and to Hispanic nonreligious personnel, many of whom were soldiers, living there for protection and excursions against the "infidels." Cultural food preferences are evident in the foods given to each group: the soldiers seem to have preferred wheat (although "wheat" can sometimes mean corn), which was often given in the form of bread and biscuit (BNM legajo 1, no. 34, folio 8:11–12). The Pueblos were almost always given corn and beans. Similarly, beef cattle were given to Native Americans while sheep (mutton and ewes) were for the soldiers. When foods allocated to Pueblos are noted separately, most communities received between about 3 and 30 fanegas a month, while the Hopi communities of Oraibi and Shungopovi received unusually large quantities, up to 83 fanegas a month (1,000 fanegas, or about 1,600 bushels, a year) (BNM legajo 1, no. 34, folios 16–17:22–23). It is not clear why residents of the Hopi pueblos received such large quantities of corn. The same report notes gifts to these two pueblos of up to 1,000 head of animals over a 12-month period, mostly sheep and cattle. These food contributions were not always given willingly; the religious at Las Humanas complained of having to feed their Indian parishioners a great deal of grain in winter (McKusick 1981:64).

The extent to which the expected Pueblo support was forthcoming is reported in letters from friars at each mission in 1694. These documents reveal differences in attitude (and perhaps personality) of the individual missionary as well as what they were given: "I know that if they had more they would give it to me," "they have supported me more than I deserve," and "they have assisted me to the best of their ability" (Espinosa 1988:131, 124, 119). "As for corn, they have sufficient, but it is evident that they do not wish to give me any," and "they have an abundance of corn, beans, and squash, but . . . they bring me 4 tortillas in the morning, four at midday, and four in the evening, and nothing else" (Espinosa 1988:120, 134). Here, too, are justifications for the demand: "They knew very well that it was their obligation to help me with what they had, since I was serving them by administering the holy sacraments" (Espinosa 1988:120).

After the Pueblo Revolt, subsistence practices changed somewhat. Between 1680 and 1692, which were years of independence from Spanish rule, some Pueblos returned to subsistence farming and trade with the Apache (Abbink and Stein 1977:156). However, since the Pueblos had gained control over herds of domestic animals, herding was added to the class of major subsistence tasks. When residents fled to the refuge villages, the animals were taken too, because the Pueblos had learned their value.

Faunal analysis of assemblages from Pueblo and Hispanic sites is potentially a good indicator of interaction between Indian and European peoples and the degree to which new Spanish foods were taken up by the Pueblos or the Pueblos influenced Hispanic culture. Although foodways are important cultural markers, the types of animals eaten are less symbolically loaded than other aspects of food preparation; it is the details of food preparation, sometimes meat cuts or the use of spices in particular combinations, that serve this function. New meats may be prepared in traditional ways and thus not represent significant change to their consumers while signaling meaningful change to archaeological observers. Unfortunately, the faunal data are somewhat problematic in that many of the early reports on Rio Grande Valley sites do not present a detailed enough analysis, sometimes listing species without quantities, for example, and overlooking parts of the skeleton represented or butchering practices. At some sites, the dirt was not screened when it was excavated, and hence large species would be overrepresented. Fortunately, a number of sites from the area flooded by the Cochití Dam project were excavated in the 1970s with rigorous standards, and I will rely in large part on these sites, as well as on several recent reports from the Salinas pueblos.

Faunal Information

Table 4.1 lists the sites incorporated in this analysis, with information on the fauna recovered (presence/absence) and paleobotanical remains. The sites include three early, probably Spanish, structures from the seventeenth century: LA 591, at Kotyiti; LA 20,000; and LA 54,000, in Santa Fe. There are also samples from six pueblos with seventeenth-century components: Teypama (LA 282), San Antonio de Padua (LA 24), Qualacu (LA 757), Paa'ko (LA 162), Quarai (LA 95), and Gran Quivira/Las Humanas (LA 120), as well as a seventeenth-century mission, Abó (LA 97). Five eighteenth-century sites come from the Cochití Dam project: Torreon (LA 6178), a rancho near Pueblo del Encierro (LA 70); houses at LA 9138 and LA 9139; and a room at LA 12161.

Despite considerable variation in percentage composition, diversity, and the presence of particular species at these sites, some trends are evident. Pueblo prerevolt sites showed no evidence of sheep unless they had an associated mission, whereas all early Spanish sites and both Indian and Hispanic eighteenth-century sites did. The bones of wild fauna are found at all sites. There is considerable variation in the proportions of domestic to wild animals. At LA 6178, 23, sheep/goat, 5 horse, and 14 bos (or cow)/bison individuals were found, while only one deer and some rabbit represented wild species. No other domestic or wild fauna serve as such clear markers as sheep, although deer or antelope, or both, are found at all sites, and cow (or bison) is found at many, as are turkey (a pre-Spanish domesticate), fish, various birds, and rabbit (jackrabbit or cottontail). The lagomorph index (Szuter and Bayham 1989), a measure of the ratio of cottontail rabbits *(sylvilagus)* to all rabbits (*sylvilagus* and *lepus,* or jackrabbit), varied widely, from a low of .30 at Qualacu to a high of .89 at Gran Quivira, with intermediate values of .51 at LA 70 and .74 at Quarai. Some analysts believe that this ratio indicates environmental change, specifically land-clearing as a result of agriculture based on econiche preference for the two forms of rabbits. Cottontails preferred bushy settings and thick vegetation, while jackrabbits preferred grass. Thus lower numbers would suggest higher numbers of jackrabbits and more clearing. Not everyone finds this index convincing. Faunal material from Pueblo Colorado, a Salinas Precolumbian site, yielded a lower lagomorph index in thirteenth-century strata (.503) than later, probably fifteenth-century, strata with an index of .648 (Thiel 1998:201). It may be that the lagomorph index reflects varying ecological contexts as much as the degree of clearing from agriculture. Indices such as this and the artiodactyl index (the ratio of large animals such as deer and antelope to lagomorphs) are potentially useful indicators of subsistence in particular deposits, rather than of land clearing. They may also be useful indicators of change over time within the same site. The data analyzed here suggest a wide range in the occurrence of large game animals in deposits, from a very low figure of .05 at Qualacu

Table 4.1

Faunal and Paleobotanical Analysis

Site name and LA number	Date of occupation	Animals, domestic				Animals, wild					Plants				
		Sheep/goat	Cow/bison	Horse	Pig	Deer/ artiodactyl	Rabbit	Birds	Rodents	Fish	Spanish	Indigenous	Source	Lagomorph index	Artiodactyl index
Teypama/Socorro LA 282	1300–1680	x?			x			x	x	x	x	Corn, cheno-am, cacti, squash	Earls 1982	n.a.	
San Antonio de Padua LA 24	17th century		Bison (1)		x			Turkey, x	x	x			Dart 1980	.756	.386
Qualacu LA 757	1350–1650/82					x	x	Turkey, x	x	x			Marshall 1987	.302	.048
Paa'ko LA 162	> 1525–1660/70	x Late		x Late		x Mountain sheep	x	Turkey					Lambert and Rogers 1954	n.a.	
Quarai (Mounds D, E, G 1993 excav.) LA 95	1525–1700	x	Cow?	x		x	x	Turkey, x	x	Turtle		Corn, cheno-am cactus, cleome	Spielmann 1994	.742	.556
Gran Quivira LA 120	1600–1672	x	Cow?			x	x	Turkey chicken		x?	Peach wheat	Corn, cheno-am cacti, bean, cleome	Hayes 1981 Spielmann 1991	.892	n.a.

Abo Mission LA 97	1624–1672	x	Bison		x	x	x	Hawk	x		Grape, plum, peach, melon	Corn, cactus, pumpkin, piñon	Toulouse 1949		
LA 54,000 Santa Fe	17th century Spanish	x	Cow		x						Peach, chili pepper, melon/cucumber	Cheno-am, cactus	Trigg 1999	n.a.	
Kotyiti/Las Majadas LA 591	17th century ranch Spanish	x	Cow?	x		x	x	Hawk		x			Snow and Warren 1969, 1973	n.a.	
LA 20,000	Mid–17th century Spanish	x	Cow			x		Chicken		x	Peach, apricot wheat	Cheno-am, corn	Trigg 1999		
Santa Cruz de Cochiti LA 70	18th century Hispano	x	Cow?			Mountain sheep	x	Turkey others		x		Corn, beans, squash, cheno-am, cactus, nuts	Snow 1976	.508	.141
Torreon LA 6178	18th century Hispano	x	Cow	x		Few	Few	Chicken					Snow 1973	n.a.	
Structures LA 9138	1750–1800 Hispano	x	Few cow/bison				x		x	x	Peach	Cheno-am	Chapman et al. 1977	n.a.	
LA 9139	1750–1800 Hispano	x	Cow?								Peach		Chapman et al. 1977	n.a.	
LA 12161	Early 18th century Hispano	x	Cow?		x?	x	x	Turkey			Peach	x	Chapman et al. 1977	n.a.	

n.a. Not Available

to a high of .56 at Quarai. The variation may often be due to complex factors, however, including excavation procedures. For utmost data confidence, samples should be recovered with the same procedures and analyzed by the same faunal specialists. One other important source of information about subsistence strategies, meat cuts, is not available at the study sites.

At a number of these sites it is difficult to separate components; historic deposits often occur directly on top of Precolumbian ones with no intervening stratigraphy (D. H. Snow, personal communication 1992). And although domestic animal remains are present at all Hispanic and post-revolt Pueblo sites, they are often found in small quantities. Faunal analysis indicates that the bone at a number of these sites is heavily processed and fragmented, which suggests bone-boiling for bone grease. This is not restricted to a single period but extends from the sixteenth century (LA 54147; Vierra 1989) to the late eighteenth to early nineteenth (LA 10114; Binford 1979). The use of metal tools for butchering, seen at LA 6178 (and Hopi Awatovi; Adams 1989), usually indicates a Spanish or Hispanic occupant. Analysis suggests seasonal or gender-specific activities in some cases; at LA 9138, many ollas (for storage), many small animals and fish, with few sheep bones, may indicate expedient eating and brief seasonal use, while LA 12161—with remains from only a single room—is interpreted as having been occupied only by men, owing to a high percentage of ollas, spinning equipment, and bone tools for hide-working (C. Snow 1979:222–223). The location of a community is the largest factor influencing the faunal assemblage: it affects which species were readily available locally and which through trade. Gran Quivira, for example, 45 miles east of the Rio Grande, had an unusually close trading relationship with Plains tribes, which would have made bison quite available to the inhabitants. The faunal report from Hopi Awatovi, a western pueblo, indicates an unusually wide array of imported animals, including pets—greyhound and domestic cat—as well as the usual ones; many of these are found in church kitchen deposits (Adams 1989). It is difficult to know if this finding is the result of atypical archaeological preservation or if Spanish settlers going far to the west of the Rio Grande Valley brought a wider variety of animals, including pets, with them.

Cordelia Snow suggests that some of the Cochití Dam sites reflect the development of an economy in which herding—of sheep, goat, and cattle—was dominant. Since the cultivable land in this area was all owned by Cochití Pueblo and the Spanish were not supposed to live on Pueblo land, she reasons that the Spanish would have had to borrow land or develop another subsistence strategy, in this case herding, using Indian herders, whose labor was required under the encomienda. The owners of the animals did not have to be in residence, and herding required little in the way of architectural construction, as the herders moved frequently. Those sites with corrals and pens may have been used for lambing and shearing. Some farming was also done, but with less success. We know that herding continued as a major source of economic support into the nineteenth century; Snow (1979:217, 19, 25) sees this continuation as an adaptive response to the mixture of cultures in a frontier situation, whereby a new economic system develops and persists after the colonial period ends.

Paleobotanical remains are less often available but reveal a similar situation in which differences between Spanish and Pueblos were greater in the pre-revolt period than in the post-revolt period. This is particularly clear at San Gregorio de Abó, where the mission was excavated and the remains of many Spanish domesticates included peach, two kinds of melons, grape, plum, coriander, and chili pepper. These were found along with indigenous plants, both domestic (corn, beans, and pumpkin) and wild (cholla, prickly pear, juniper, pinon, yucca, pigweed, and wild potato) (Toulouse 1949). The presence of peach remains shortly after contact may be a signal of Spanish/Hispanic identity. They were recovered from five sites besides Abó, four of which were Spanish (LA 20,000 and LA 54,000) or Hispanic (LA 9138 and LA 9139); the other was Gran Quivira, which had a mission. Other plant remains have little diagnostic value, as all sites had corn, many had cotton, and all—even Spanish and Hispanic sites—had wild plants: cactus, nuts, and representatives from the broad class of chenopodium-amaranth. Wheat, a Spanish-introduced domesticate, is only reported from four sites, LA 20,000, LA 54,000, Gran Quivira and Quarai. However, it is rarely recovered in paleobotanical analysis, even where it is known to have been grown—as at Zuni during the nineteenth-century occupation of the farming village of Lower Pescado (Rothschild and Dublin 1995). Fortunately, recent excavations at LA 20,000 (a seventeenth-century estancia) and LA 54,000 (deposits from seventeenth-century Santa Fe) yielded large botanical samples. The latter revealed a particularly wide range of Spanish-introduced plants, including wheat, barley, peas, lentil, watermelon, cantaloupe, and peach (Trigg 1999:158). Without large, well-excavated samples, paleobotanical remains are difficult to use in defining shared subsistence strategies, but they can make an important contribution to one's understanding of varying subsistence strategies.

Subsistence in the Northeast

The region of the country that includes the Hudson and Mohawk Valleys was well supplied with wild plants and a range of edible animals and birds; horticulture was relatively easy; and Mohawk subsistence appears to have been reliable and consistent, at least in comparison with the Southwest. This plenitude is described in occasional accounts of feasts between Native Americans and Europeans, as in the following:

> Dozens of great kettles full of beaten Indian corn, dressed with mincemeat. . . . Here comes [*sic*] two great kettles full of bustards, broiled and salted before the winter, with as many kettles full of ducks, as many [of] turtles [that] was taken in the season by the net. . . . Whilst one was eating, another sort comes, as divers of fish, eels, salmon and carps gives them a new stomach. . . . Nothing is done as yet, for there comes the thickened flour, the oil of bears, venison. (Radisson 1967:74)

The analysis of food remains in faunal assemblages to assess the degree of interaction between Indians and Europeans in this region encounters the same issues pertaining to faunal data. That is to say, the lack of detail is a handicap, although, a number of recent reports have begun to fill in the gaps. Ideally, two kinds of faunal information are needed. First, one needs to know what species were consumed and in what proportions in order to quantify changing subsistence. Second, it is essential to examine the nonsubsistence aspect of animal procurement. Beaver, otter, bear, and deer (figure 4.3) were hunted for trade reasons as well as for subsistence reasons, and frequencies by species as well as butchering methods can provide information on commercial exploitation. In order to evaluate the interaction and impact of each culture on the other, one needs to examine pre- and postcontact settings.

As an example, Jacqueline Crerar (1992) provides an analysis of northern Iroquoian deer (and other mammal) hunting based on quantities of certain species before and after contact periods. She uses beaver frequencies in a range of Precolumbian sites to establish the level of subsistence hunting of that animal (4.7 percent) and is then able to demonstrate the impact of the fur trade on procurement. The Huron average of beaver bone for historic period sites is 11 percent, while Petun Iroquois sites had as much as 29 percent (1992:11). The analysis of the age and sex composition of deer bone at Neutral Iroquois sites suggests that they were not hunting beaver intensively but were able to participate in colonial trade by managing deer herds, first by selective hunting in the sixteenth century, and later on by confining them in pens and controlling their availability for trade. In addition to meat, they exported dressed skins.

Fortunately, recent faunal research has provided data for late Precolumbian through historic period sites. Eleven Mohawk sites have been analyzed or reanalyzed by Junker-Anderson (1986), Kuhn and Funk (2000), Rick (1991), and Socci (1995). Samples from some of these sites are either quite small or contain only small proportions of identifiable bone (table 4.2). Many of the sites rely on excavation reports done when faunal analysis simply provided a species list; few give butchering information or indicate which skeletal parts were recovered. However, even species lists yield interesting information on the kinds of animals consumed and demonstrate remarkable consistency in animal use over a long period, from

Figure 4.3. White-tailed deer *(Odocoileus virginianus).*

late Precolumbian to historic times. There was continuing reliance on deer, beaver, and bear, although their relative frequencies did change over time, with beaver seemingly less important after about 1640. However, some sites have such small sample sizes that it is difficult to assess this situation. It appears that the beaver trade supplemented mainly horticulture and deer hunting, that dogs were domesticated and eaten from the late Precolumbian onward, and that bears were semidomesticated—van den Bogaert reports caged bears being fattened in 1635 (Kuhn and Funk 2000). In general, these reports note that the diversity represented in the assemblages increases from the Precolumbian on to the colonial period (with some decline in the sixteenth and seventeenth centuries as a result of the beaver trade). Although they have not evaluated diversity in reference to sample size, which may affect it (Grayson 1984; Kintigh 1984; Leonard and Jones 1989), the Spearman rank-order correlation coefficient between diversity ranks and sample size ranks (of identified fragments of bone) is not significant for their data (Welkowitz et al. 1971), which suggests that the relationship here is a real one. I focus on four of these sites from the postcontact period that have reasonable sample sizes.

Two important conclusions can be drawn from these data. First, and most important to this project, the appearance of European domesticates came relatively late to the Mohawk. There were no bones from domestic animals at Rumrill-Naylor (Socci 1995) and only two bones (one on the surface and one in the first level) at Jackson-Everson (Junker-Anderson 1986). Whether the absence of this food source represented choice or limited access is not known. When domesticates appear in the eighteenth century at two sites, the Enders House (at Fort Hunter) and Indian Castle, pig is the most frequently occurring animal, in proportions of 30 percent and 24 percent, respectively. Only at the Enders House are domesti-

Table 4.2

Fauna from Four Late Mohawk Valley Sites

Site	Date	Sample size	Identified bone	Deer	Domestic
Enders House (Fort Hunter)	1750/60/80	5,667	474	99	248
Brant House (Indian Castle)	1753–1776	539	246	112	100
Jackson-Everson	1683–1693	2,056	764	74	1–2
Rumrill-Naylor	1624–1640	1,459	81	71	0

cated animals dominant, both in the pre-1760 deposit and that associated with the structure from 1760–1780. Second, the frequency of deer bone shows that it was consistently the single most important species except at the two eighteenth-century sites. At Indian Castle it accounts for only 48 percent, whereas at the other sites examined by Socci (1995:224)—from the fifteenth to the seventeenth century and including Rumrill-Naylor and Jackson-Everson—it ranges from 79 to 96 percent. Indian Castle also had few beaver remains (Socci 222). At most of these sites a wide array of other mammals, birds, and fish were also represented.

Indian Castle would not have represented a "typical" Mohawk site, as it was the home of Joseph Brant, an elite Mohawk whose position was acquired in a non-traditional way: his prestige derived from his relationship to William Johnson, his brother-in-law, rather than through clan membership. His home was unusual in having a full cellar, plastered limestone block walls, and a plank floor; ceramics recovered included Jackfield and white salt-glazed wares, creamwares, delft, and Chinese porcelain, more characteristic of an elite European household than a Native American one. The faunal material here included, in addition to deer and pig, significant proportions of passenger pigeon (14 percent) and cattle (10 percent), as well as sheep, chicken and many wild species. By contrast, the family in a "common Mohawk house" would have lived with dogs, a hog or two, and some chickens and would have used earthenware pottery (Guldenzopf 1986:98).

The Enders House at Schoharie Crossing was located within the original Fort Hunter (Fisher 1992). It had two superimposed components centered on a Mohawk house (built around 1760), one representing pre-house construction deposits and the other associated with the house (1760–1780). The faunal assemblages, quite similar in both, suggest that a consistent subsistence pattern had developed. Pig and deer were the two dominant species, although pig was more common in both components; followed by cattle, bear, beaver, sheep/goat, and a number of other small mammals; birds (including chicken), and some fish (Rick 1991). However, since such a small proportion of the bone assemblage was identifiable (8 percent), it is difficult to draw confident conclusions about diet. Artifacts recovered from the site reveal a mixture of English ceramics and some artifacts more typically associated with Iroquois, such as catlinite and red slate ornaments (Fisher 1992).

There is some documentary evidence that attests to Mohawk and other Iroquois consumption of European imported animals. Court minutes record complaints about the Mohawks killing free-roaming domestic animals, particularly pigs, but also cattle, which the Dutch allowed to live in the woods and scavenge. When a Native American encountered an animal in these settings, he believed it to be wild and thought it "fair game." In other situations, in spite of the fact that Dutch farms were fenced, some animals got loose and ate corn in unfenced Iroquois fields, annoying the Indians and providing all the more reason for killing them (Rink 1988:218; Ruttenber 1971:100). To protect their animals, the Dutch sometimes cut hogs' ears to identify them, branded their cattle and horses, and kept them indoors in winter on fodder. The Senecas, at the western edge of Iroquoia, were reported to have acquired a "vast quantity" of hogs by 1687 (although there is some question as to the truth of this statement), when the French under Denonville attacked. Seneca villages were burned along with cornfields and their stored foods (O'Callaghan 1849/51:1:239, cited in Burke 1991:57). It is unclear exactly how, when, or how many of these animals had been acquired by the Seneca, but these details are less important than the fact that the Seneca were using domestic animals to some extent. The destruction of food was a common military act. In 1666 the Tracy expedition burned Mohawk villages and food resources—described as "enough corn, beans, and squash 'to nourish all Canada for 2 entire years'" on the south side of the Mohawk River (Tooker 1978, cited in Socci 1995:21), another unreliable and undoubtedly distorted figure (D. R. Snow, personal communication 2001). Mohawk villages and food supplies were destroyed again in 1693 (Richter 1992:104, 174).

At a later time, during the Revolutionary War, the Mohawks submitted claims to the British for property losses in a battle in 1777 that destroyed many of their homes and possessions. These accounts mention livestock as well as many things essential for agricultural subsistence. By this late date, some Mohawk individuals were holders of private property and reckoned much of their wealth in terms of European things. They have been described as more prosperous than most European-American farmers in the Mohawk Valley (Fenton and Tooker 1978, cited in Rick 1991). These claims list land, equipment such as plows, barns and houses, animals (often by age or condition, such as "fatning hogs"; Guldenzopf 1986:196), blankets by color, kettles, basins, traps, carpenters' tools, furniture, feather beds, trunks, boards, wagons, suits of clothes, jewelry, guns, and so on. The only indigenous item on these lists was wampum, and it too was part of the European inventory of valuable belongings. While the Mohawks would hardly ask the British to replace anything that was not European, it suggests that their material lives had become dominated by European possessions to some degree.

The evaluation of the impact of European foodways on Native Americans is reflected in the degree to which they had adopted European crops or plants as well as animals. The evidence for this is inconsistent and minimal, consisting of the occasional archaeological analysis of plant remains and some documentary references. The plant remains from the Brant house at Indian Castle did not indicate the use of European domesticates, but rather a reliance on corn, beans, squash, wild fruits, and nuts (Guldenzopf 1986:258). On the other hand, documentary accounts present a slightly different picture. A discussion of the Indian Castle site in 1755 includes a reference to King Hendrick's orchard (Lord 1996:4). A 1769 account of a house and garden at Ahquhaga on the Susquehanna River describes not only domestic animals (cows, pigs, fowl, and horses), and traditional crops (corn, beans, and melon), but also cucumber, potatoes, cabbage, French turnips, salad, parsnips, and apple trees (Smith 1906:66). Some of this apparent difference may simply be due to the difficulty of paleoethnobotanical recovery of evidence of many European vegetables, especially those that do not leave seed or pit remains (typically hardier than leaf or fruit remnants). Because of this, documentary descriptions will always differ from archaeological evidence. The occasional references to Native Americans eating milk and butter, exchanging venison at Fort Orange for these products, will also be invisible archaeologically, unless containers with residues are recovered.

Finally, some documents offer particularly graphic descriptions of foods that were used by Native Americans in times of scarcity or starvation and that are unlikely to be identified archaeologically. Samuel Kirkland's journals describe the consumption of two batches of broth, the second weaker than the first, made from a single set of squirrel bones and bear meat infested with maggots when he was at Kanadesaga in 1765 (Pilkington 1980:29). The captivity narrative of Mary Rowlandson, who was captured by the Narragansett in the late seventeenth century, refers to her captors eating boiled horse feet. "They being wont to eat the flesh first, and when the feet were old and dried and they had nothing else, they could cut off the feet and use them" (Kestler 1990:50). There were days when her only sustenance for the entire day was broth thickened with bark or five grains of corn. As normal fare, the Narragansett also ate bear, horse, and deer, and occasionally pork; boiled ground nuts, parched wheat pancake, samp (corn porridge), and peas (Kestler 1990). The helpless tone of her story notwithstanding, Rowlandson was a resourceful woman and was able to improve her access to food through her needlework skills, trading items such as knitted stockings and shirts with lace edging for various foods.

Dutch Adoption of Indigenous Foods

The other side of the picture of interest here concerns the adoption of Indian food resources by Dutch and British settlers in the Hudson Valley and the Mohawk area. Paul Huey provides important data on Dutch food remains from Fort Orange from 1624–1664, showing a diet dominated by deer and pork. The latter had been imported and raised by the Dutch, along with cattle. Pigs did very well in this setting: De Sille says in 1654 that "children and pigs multiply here rapidly and more than anything else" (Huey 1988:405). Hogs were allowed to roam until fall, when they were rounded up and crammed with corn before being slaughtered, making a "hard and clean" pork, which was stored for winter (Burke 1991:51, 52, 58). When the occasional "wild" swine was brought in by an Indian to sell in town, the bearer had to bring the creature's ears to demonstrate that it was wild (Huey 1967a). Deer were acquired by trade, and one observer noted that, especially in winter, "venison can be obtained that is fat and fine, about 3, 4 or 5 hands of seawan [wampum] for a deer. They would be glad to exchange deer for milk or butter. The meat is fit for smoking or pickling" (Van Laer 1908:35). The fact that deer was an elite food in Europe might have added to its appeal to the Dutch (Huey 1988:241).

Huey suggests that the changing importance of deer to pig as meat sources in Fort Orange between 1624 and 1664 can be monitored by the ratio of teeth of these two animals recovered archaeologically. While this is a sound suggestion, pigs have 44 teeth and deer have 32, so any ratio of pig teeth to deer teeth should be standardized by those numbers (either multiply deer tooth quantities by 1.375 (44/32) or pig teeth by 0.727 (32/44). The sample size (10 teeth) of his earliest, pre-1624 component is too small to allow for much confidence. In that sample he suggests that deer represent 90 percent while 10 percent of the teeth are from pigs, but standardized; there is a ratio of 12:1 rather than 9:1. However, what does emerge from the data is that both species were crucial throughout the Dutch period, and that dependence on deer decreases over time; in the latest deposit, dated to 1657–1664, with a sample of 60 teeth, deer and pig each represent 50 percent (which standardized is a ratio of 1.37 deer to 1 pig) (Huey 1988:70). After 1640, substantial beef remains are found in the assemblages, although beef was less important than pork to the Dutch. Sheep/goat remains are much more limited. It seems likely that a combination of a traditional preference for beef and pork, along with the sensitivity of sheep to severe weather, kept them from being significant in diet. They were important for wool and were kept by Europeans in spite of the presence of wolves, which carried some of them off and made it difficult to keep them (Huey 1967b).

The Dutch, like most immigrants, seem to have preferred to maintain a diet as similar to their traditional one as possible (Rothschild 1990:142) and were not particularly interested in Indian foods. As agriculture was relatively easy in the Hudson Valley, in contrast to the Rio Grande Valley, they were able to grow much of their own produce and meat, but did supplement it with corn, venison, and other indigenous foods, probably prepared in mimicry of traditional Dutch dishes. Corn became particularly significant in the form of *sappaen* or porridge, a Dutch adaptation of an Iroquois cereal dish which added milk to the ground corn and was eaten on a daily basis (Rothschild 1990:162). The Indians also brought and traded fish, crabs, wild fowl, and game, according to DeSille (cited in Fayden 1993:14). Some foods brought in by Native Americans might not have initially appealed to all. Domine Megapolensis is quoted as saying in 1644 that Christians did not like sturgeon, but several faunal assemblages suggest otherwise (Huey 1988:267, 555). Plant foods supplied to the Dutch include squash, maize, beans, tobacco, and wild fruit (Dunn 1994:77).

Archaeological information on European food habits is also available from deposits behind the soldiers' barracks at Crown Point, New York, a fort built in 1759 and burned in 1773 (Huey, personal communication 2001). Not surprisingly, the majority of faunal material indicates domestic mammals, pig, cow, and sheep. What is unusual is the large quantity of fish bone recovered, from 10 species—mainly bullhead, drum, and sunfish. Also identified were a few bird bones from duck and passenger pigeon, and one chicken bone. Rick notes that if the bones represent the consumption of entire animals, the diet would have consisted of 96 percent meat from mammals and 3.6 percent fish (1980:35). Interestingly, in contrast to food remains from many other forts, no deer bone was recovered. Presumably fishing was a recreational activity for soldiers in their free time, but it is somewhat surprising that they did not hunt, unless deer herds were depleted or they felt too endangered to hunt.

Documentary information complements faunal and paleobotanical analysis in providing insight into food practices. A series of inventories on Rensselaerswyck farms from 1632 and 1651 tabulated mares, stallions, milk cows, heifers, and bulls (Van Laer 1908:220–221; 732–740). Pigs were not recorded, perhaps because they were running free and hard to count. A New Amsterdam farm did list the presence of pigs along with other animals in 1632 (Van Laer 1908:192); this may reflect the fact that while pigs did roam in New Amsterdam, they reportedly went home at night (Dickens 1875).

In Anne Grant's reference to plant cultivation in the Albany area prior to the American Revolution, she notes that many vegetables were grown, both "hardy plants" such as cabbages and potatoes, and other items such as celery, asparagus, and salad ingredients in personal gardens; also that each family grew enough Indian corn for family needs, including those of two or three slaves, and feed for horses, pigs, and poultry (Grant 1808:40, 48). They bought other grains and refined flour. On festive occasions, tea, chocolate, cakes, cider, and syllabub (a frothy dessert of cream and liquor) were served (Grant 1808:63). Young Englishmen in the Albany area would undertake trade adventures to provide for a new or prospective wife and family. As provisions they took dried beef and Indian cornmeal, but they also relied on the hospitality of the Indians (Grant 1808:79), a common practice indicating both the continued reliance of Europeans on Native Americans and the persistence of traditional attitudes that allowed them to do so.

Conclusion

The examination of subsistence data shows the real connections between each pair being examined here: namely, they consumed similar foods. In each case, however, certain resources were initially reserved for Europeans and only gradually found their way into Native American diet. Domestic animals and fruit were the main items in this category, along with certain vegetables. In the Southwest, everyone ate corn. Sheep were initially found only at sites with Spanish occupants, where they were kept both for meat and their wool, but after the revolt, the Pueblos had them also. The Mohawks obtained some pigs by killing those animals they found unfenced in the forest. Archaeological data make these situations clear. There are some aspects of diet that are not available through material remains but would have been important. They relate to food preparation and involve meat cuts and the use of spices or other specific items; chocolate played the part for the Spanish that tea did for the British. The Dutch continued to make many traditional dishes in the New World (Fayden 1993; Rothschild 1990), providing familiar tastes and serving as reminders of identity, both social and ethnic.

5

The Exchange of Objects and Identity Construction

Material assemblages present in domestic and other settings provide many clues to the degree of interaction between Native Americans and Europeans and its alterations during the colonial period in the Southwest and Northeast. Both the presence and the absence of certain items may serve as meaningful signals of specific attitudes, either positive or negative, toward the maker of the object. The use of some items expresses identity or aspiration, although there are some instances in which shared material culture does not reflect a shared identity. In particular, I consider the extent to which "borrowing" of the "other's" objects occurred, what kinds of things were borrowed, and what were not. This perspective highlights the real distinction between the two cases more clearly than any other form of analysis. In the Rio Grande Valley, many indigenous items such as pottery and chipped stone tools appear in Hispanic sites after the Pueblo Revolt, and some European things—notably sheep and metal tools—are recovered from Pueblo sites. Even prior to the revolt, however, the Spanish were using the products of indigenous labor, especially pottery. In the Hudson and Mohawk Valleys, the flow of goods went in one direction, with European commodities going to the Mohawks as a mechanism to gain beaver skins.

The relevant questions here concern the meaning of finding goods produced by others. These may be a function of the objects' symbolic and status-related qualities, including the expression of identity, either actual or desired. In both case studies, a mixture of behaviors and reasons was involved. The Mohawks selected European tools and ornaments for their own reasons, both functional and symbolic. The Spanish were making use of indigenous pottery for practical reasons and because many of the women in their households were Indian. However, the pottery was altered in some ways to suit their desires. It is also important to consider the absence of things and whether it reflects lack of access, lack of interest, or refusal to adopt them. The Dutch present the clearest example of the latter, although both Mohawks and Pueblos did not use certain European objects to which they could have had access.

In the two encounters compared here, the differences in use of others' goods is influenced not only by their symbolic qualities but by three other factors: geography, religion, and population. The flow of material up the Hudson River was facilitated by a good harbor in New Amsterdam and water transport up a navigable river. Some ships could sail right from the Netherlands to Fort Orange, although most unloaded in New Amsterdam and transferred their cargoes to smaller boats. For things to reach Santa Fe, after they arrived from Europe by ship, they had to make the 1,600-mile long journey to Mexico City and then up a difficult overland route, the Camino Real, with its 90-mile-long waterless segment, the Jorñada del Muerte. The caravans that brought supplies were subject to frequent raids by Apaches and others. Several breaks in transport were involved in getting goods to the frontier, adding to the time and cost involved (Cooley 1894, cited in Rothschild 1990).

The exchange of goods also depended on the characteristics of those who had emigrated to these new world settlements and the willingness of indigenous peoples to live with the newcomers. Religion provided part of the explanation for the Europeans. Catholicism and the practice of baptism and conversion meant that it was all right for Spanish immigrant men to establish households with Pueblo women; in fact, Isabella encouraged the practice as a way of fostering conversion (Brooks 2002). The Protestant Dutch had neither the inclination, as far as we can tell, nor the approval to do the same. The result of this important difference is what I have called social distance (Rothschild 1996), strongly defined in the Hudson and Mohawk Valleys, but absent in the Rio Grande. No factor was as dominant among Native Americans as religion was to European colonists, but there were differences that affected who was willing to be involved with the strangers.

Single women appear to have been more eager to form relationships with European men than married women (see chapter 1). There are no descriptions of the men who became involved with foreigners. It could have been either the powerful who enhanced their prestige by redistributing European goods or those without power who tried to improve their status by acting as contacts.

The immigrant population arriving in the New World consisted primarily of those who were marginal, poor, or unsuccessful in their homeland. In the Southwest they are called "Spanish," but because there had been a Spanish population in Mexico for about 100 years before the initial colonization effort in New Mexico, there was already a substantial mixing of indigenous, European, and African blood. Most of these immigrants had little access to objects manufactured in Spain, even everyday items such as pottery, although they would presumably have owned some Mexican-made majolicas. They would have had few of the possessions that marked Spanish elite identity, discussed later in the chapter. Because of Pueblo factionalism and other circumstances (in particular, the fact of having been captured by nomads), indigenous women and some men were willing to live in Spanish/Hispanic settlements, notably after the revolt.

The Dutch had difficulty in finding willing colonists, although there were many who wanted to come, trade for a period, get rich, and return home. Few members of the Dutch merchant elite made the journey. However, those colonists who did come had greater access to familiar things than the Spanish did; ceramics, tiles, and pipes are the most notable ones for archaeologists, but other details of domestic life—such as architecture and clothing—were manifestly European. There was little reason for Mohawk women (or men) to live among the Dutch. Any children that resulted from a union of a Mohawk woman and a Dutch man would have been raised among the Mohawk unless something unusual occurred.

The Acquisition of Women's Labor and Services

The most significant mechanism promoting the flow of Pueblo material culture to Hispanic households was the acquisition of women's labor and services, perhaps beginning with sexual services. By contrast, there is little evidence that the labor of Mohawk women was relevant to Dutch domestic life, for reasons discussed shortly. The power that indigenous women had to choose their partners was also an important factor, although it is clearly true that many sexual encounters were not a result of a choice made by Pueblo women. Women's domestic and sexual services were important in three identifiable instances in colonial settings. First, some indigenous men offered their daughters to the newcomers as a way to incorporate the colonizers into their own social system (Axtell 1992), echoing the exchange of women in small-scale societies as controlled by fathers and brothers. Marshall Sahlins records a situation in Hawaii in which a nonroyal daughter was given to a chief in marriage, thereby establishing a kinship link to the chiefly family and enhancing the family's position, while the young woman was then subsequently free to take another husband of her own rank (Thomas 1991).

Two other forms of the demand for women in colonial settings represent entirely different phenomena. Neither appears to be controlled by indigenous men. One was a forceful taking of labor rather than an agreed-upon transaction; it was closer to slavery or indentured labor. The other demonstrates women's agency, and can be characterized as women giving their services as gifts. Sahlins notes that in Hawaii some native women took the initiative in offering themselves to the powerful European newcomers, who were seen as gods when they first appeared (Thomas 1991). European sailors were said to perceive this behavior by women as prostitution, although this is a mischaracterization, as I explain later in the chapter.

It was particularly difficult for Europeans to grasp the concept of matriliny and the power that women had in some traditional societies. This can be seen in the American Southeast in descriptions of the Natchez (Le Page du Pratz [1774]1947), and also among the Cherokee of North Carolina. The English misunderstood both matriliny and the marked gender role divisions among the Cherokee. A trader, Alexander Longe, wrote: "The women rules [sic] the roost and wears the breeches and sometimes will beat their husbands within an inch of their lives" (in Hatley 1993:53). Part of the power women had was a sexual freedom, perhaps related to widespread abortion practices, which at times resulted in sexual contact between traders and Cherokee women, and to women's ability to change marriage partners when they chose to. The consequence of interethnic relations was children of mixed blood, and apparently Cherokee women were much more accepting of these offspring than were the men, who reportedly would not allow them to become warriors. There is also an incident described in which a Cherokee woman warns a Euroamerican woman of an impending raid, suggesting that a gendered (or human) solidarity at times overrode ethnic divisions, at least among women (Hatley 1993:54, 61, 90).

French missionaries' reactions to sexual relationships between single Algonkian women and French traders provides another example of the European perception of the sexuality of indigenous women (White 1991). The missionaries, by and large, understood that women "have the command of their own Bodies and may dispose of their persons as they see fit" (Lahontan in White 1991:63–64). Some Jesuits believed that women were able to induce abortions if they did not want to be pregnant (for fear of interfering with a prestigious marriage); others stated that there was no concern about pregnancy because a woman's family would raise any children she bore (Lahontan in White 1991:63–64), suggesting that the element of shame at having a child out of wedlock was irrelevant. Variability in gender role is suggested by Lahontan's account of "hunting women" who accompanied the men on hunts and were said to be unable to endure "the conjugal yoak," or were too restless to spend winters in the village. Like the sailors mentioned earlier, some missionaries characterized women who formed sexual relationships with traders as prostitutes, but White suggests that the term "prostitute" is inappropriate, for the women did not sell sex acts or solicit "customers" but rather were establishing typical male-female relationships in which their sexual liaisons were linked to a range of other activities.

Historian Ramon Gutiérrez (1991), who examines the colonial period in the Southwest through the lens of marriage and social-sexual relations, finds important differences between cultural systems in the exchange of material things as well as in the offering of services leading to misunderstandings. When Oñate is offered bread, corn, and water at several Pueblos, Gutiérrez (1991:52) comments, "What the Puebloans thought they gave as gifts, the *españoles* thought had been surrendered as tribute." While he offers some insight into the exchange of goods, Gutiérrez (1991:50–51) focuses primarily on sexual contact and exchange, and how this interaction was culturally constructed: he notes an Oñate soldier's description of Pueblo men bringing blankets "to entice with them the Castilian women whom they liked and coveted" and suggests that Spanish soldiers were also sought in the same way, by men and by women; he believes that sanctity and sex were linked among the Pueblo, that men and women "gave their bodies to persons they deemed holy, in order to partake of their supernatural power" and that "Pueblo women cooled the passion of the fierce fire-branding Spanish katsina through intercourse, and by so doing, tried to transform and domesticate the malevolence of these foreign gods." Whether his view is correct or not, it can surely be said that the majority of sexual contact in the colonial Rio Grande area was between Spanish men and Pueblo women, and most of it was *not* sought by the women. There is ample documentation of Spanish abuse of Indian women (Hackett 1937:213, 214, 216, 217, 225). Spanish accounts are mainly silent on the idea of women offering themselves to men, except to make occasional note of Pueblo sexual "bestiality" (sodomy) (Gutiérrez 1991:18, 51) and imply that women as well as men were licentious.

While Gutiérrez's characterization of female sexuality among the Pueblo is rather dramatic, it is a welcome effort as most writers do not consider at all women's agency with regard to sex. However, it is not true that the only bonds between men and women are those of sex, as he seems to suggest: "Through sex women bore the children who would offer them labor and respect in old age. Through sex women incorporated husbands into their maternal households and expected labor and respect from them. Through sex women domesticated the wild and malevolent spirits of nature and transformed them into beneficent household gods" (Gutíerrez 1991:17). Sex is only one of the connections between men and women. It is true that sex may be given as a gift (and also, presumably withheld), but it is better to see it as one of a range of forms of service or kinds of female labor that may be given, taken, bought, or characterized as not available (not alienable in Weiner's [1992] terms). In some settings in North America, as in other parts of the world, women behaved as wives; they cooked, washed, made clothes, and chopped wood for the men with whom they lived and slept (White 1990). So it appears that in some cases, women took charge of their bodies and had relationships with European men that only involved sex, while in others they linked sexual activity to a range of traditional women's activities when they cohabited with foreigners. It is likely that this variability reflected the practices characteristic of their behavior with indigenous men. Most important for this analysis, however, are the material consequences of indigenous women living with European men in the Rio Grande Valley and not living with them in the Hudson and Mohawk Valleys. In the Southwest, this was clearly an important—perhaps the important—mechanism in promoting similar artifact assemblages in Hispanic and Pueblo households. The assemblages themselves reflected cultural "blending" and a new formulation of who people were and how they were to be defined.

Ethnic Identity and Its Recognition

The archaeological study of ethnicity is an important and complex topic. It has been a tenet of both Precolumbian and historical archaeology that group memberships, including ethnicity, will be signaled in the material record (Sackett 1977; Schuyler 1980; Weissner 1983; Wobst 1977), and we would anticipate that foodways, details of architecture, settlement structure, and ceramics and other objects used in households would serve as markers of elective or self-defined ethnic categories; assigned identities would be less likely to be manifest this way. However, this seemingly self-evident concept has often proved difficult to put into operation, in part, perhaps because analysts have focused on parameters of style. Recently it has been suggested that aspects of technology and the sequence of technical choices in pottery manufacturing processes are more reliable than artifact style in marking group boundaries (Chilton 1998; Stark 1998), although no data are available to allow the use of that approach for this project.

Access to certain classes of material and to the ways in which they were used by different peoples is useful in a discussion of ethnicity in these case studies. It is more useful than is style, except for a broad consideration of ceramic styles in the Southwest. The literature on the consumption of goods, although it considers contemporary consumer economies, offers insight into the choices people make, suggesting that they are based on varied factors: material welfare, psychic welfare, or display (Douglas and Isherwood 1996:vii). Much of the discourse on consumption (Bourdieu 1984; Campbell 1987; Miller 1998) downplays "rational" behavior in which people are motivated by economic factors in favor of socially constructed behavior—especially that associated with the marking aspects of consumption rituals, where particular types of objects are essential to connote identity (Douglas and Isherwood 1996:xxii). This approach is vastly different from early evaluations that often assumed European objects were desired because they were recognizably superior. It is easy to recognize some of these behaviors in so-called small-scale societies, where the potlatch or other competitive social institution exists. The concept of appropriate goods for the occasion varies with the individual (in terms of quantity and the kinds of goods offered), and also over time—recent potlatches involve dishtowels (Brenda Shears, personal communication 1991). Display does not merely signify competition, however; Douglas and Isherwood (1996:38) suggest that the role of goods is to stabilize and make visual the categories of culture through their communicative powers based on shared social meanings. Thus, in any setting where celebratory feasting occurs, the presentation of various foods or objects could carry these meanings.

However, there is no simple formula by which goods perform this function. Identity is both self-expressed and assigned. Goods can be used in both modes, by choice and by limiting or denying access to certain resources. Here I focus mainly on self-expressed identities, although this, too, is a complex topic. Individuals possess multiple identities, which they selectively present and negotiate, depending on context, taking an active part in presenting themselves as members of a specific group and using material culture and other means to do so. All of these make simple identity signatures difficult. Another problem is that from the perspective of several hundred years later, we may misunderstand the categories, apply the wrong scale, or not be sufficiently subtle in our analysis to recover the meanings of the time.

The situation in the colonial Southwest is particularly complex because of the number of interacting groups and the fact that these groups shifted and increased in number as new cultural/social identities were created. At the beginning of the sixteenth century, there were Pueblos and Athapaskans living in the Rio Grande Valley. Spanish, Mexican Indians, and a few Africans were added to the mix by the end of the sixteenth century. "Spanish" identity during the first colonial period in New Mexico was claimed by some settlers for themselves even though they had Indian mothers; miscegenation began early in the Spanish New World (Tjarks 1978). During the seventeenth century, new Indian groups (especially the Utes) appeared in the Southwest, and there was considerable spatial mobility as a result of the acquisition of horses. In contrast, there was little possibility of ethnic confusion in the Hudson and Mohawk Valleys, as the Dutch and Mohawks remained quite distinct, physically and genetically.

The Spanish *casta* system was instituted in all of New Spain, including New Mexico, although it was not as rigorously applied in frontier situations as in Mexico and Peru (Bustamante 1989). The casta system was the by-product of a number of factors. It formed part of the colonial system of domination in which legal statuses were identified in an attempt to regulate social interaction, but more important, it served to create groups of people with specific responsibilities and privileges in the political economy. These statuses regulated access to land, provided the basis of taxation, and decreed who was available for labor (Jackson 1999:3–4).

They also determined availability for colonial office—both religious and political—which was reserved almost entirely for Spanish individuals. Basically, it employed racial categories as cognitive labels referring to groups with contrasting positions in the sociopolitical system and the economic organization of production (Seed in Jackson 1999:10). The Spanish believed in the idea of "purity of blood" *(pureza de sangre española)* and created a classification system involving 22 categories (figures 5.1, 5.2) of mixed peoples, depending on the amount of Indian, African, and European blood each had. The system was an attempt to control genetic mixing that was already out of control. It was applied mainly by priests and census takers and was an unworkable system. It was used intermittently, inconsistently, and differently by different individuals. A priest might classify two infants from the same family in dissimilar categories, on the basis of their skin color; this led to negotiation with the parents. The system incorporated social rank as well as skin color, and it must have been clear at the time that it was arbitrary and unworkable, subject to manipulation, allowing some to "be taken for" Spanish (Dominguez 1776, cited in Bustamante 1989:74). Although six racial categories remained in the 1790 census, the system had gone out of use, for all intents and purposes, by the end of the eighteenth century (Jackson 1999), and by the end of the Spanish period, the term "mestizo" was used broadly to mean "mixed" rather than literally to mean half Indian and half Spanish, and the population *was* genetically quite mixed (Bustamante 1991:162), although social differences continued that were validated by perceived physical differences.

The unworkability of the casta system should not be taken to mean that ethnic identity was not significant in New Mexico. During the pre-revolt period, the Spanish would have perceived three groups of people: Spanish (defined by whiteness, eliteness, and a subscription to Spanish ideals), Indian, and mixed or mestizo. Spanish and mestizo would have lived in the same communities. These broad castelike categories would have minimized differences that were highly relevant in Spain, such as place of birth, wealth, and heritage; and while the elite may have recognized the difference between *peninsulares* (those born in Spain) and *criollos* (those born in the New World), for many purposes these differences were not as relevant as the larger ones. After the Pueblo Revolt, there were two major categories of people in European-derived eyes: (1) Indians and (2) a Hispanic identity (Hispano), in which the difference between Spanish and mestizo would have dissolved and which would have included primarily people born in Mexico and in

Typical Eighteenth-Century *Casta* List

NON-CASTAS

1. Español
2. Criollo
3. Other Europeans

CASTAS

1. Español x india = mestizo
2. Español x mestiza = castizo
3. Español x castiza = torna a español
4. Español x negra = mulato
5. Español x mulata = morisco
6. Morisco x española = tornatrás
7. Albino x española = tornatrás
8. Mulato x india = calpamulato
9. Negro x india = lobo
10. Lobo x india = cambijo
11. Calpamulato x india = jivaro
12. Indio x cambija = sambahigo
13. Mulato x mestiza = cuarterón
14. Cuarterón x mestiza = coyote
15. Coyote x morisca = albarazado
16. Albarazado x saltatrás = tente en el aire
17. Mestizo x india = cholo
18. Indio x mulata = chino
19. Español x china = cuarterón de china
20. Negro x india = sambo de indio
21. Negro x mulata = genízaro
22. Cambijo x china = genízaro

Figure 5.1. Diagram of casta system, showing 22 racial categories based on parents' classification.

Figure 5.2. Illustration of *casta:* a coyote has an Indian father and Mestizo mother.

the Southwest who spoke Spanish, identified themselves as Spanish-descended, and had various combinations of Spanish, Indian, and African ancestry.

Although the Hispano category was subdivided in the post-revolt Rio Grande Valley on the basis of rank or class, incorporating skin color and wealth, these distinctions were only operative in some circumstances. There are two lists of immigrants entering New Mexico after the revolt, one in 1693 and one in 1695. The first describes each individual in terms of place of birth (mostly within Mexico, though a few were born in Spain) and physical features (nose and eye shape, hair and skin color, birthmarks, etc.). The descriptions are not obviously racist and do not include ethnic identifications, but it seems that most therein would have been classified as mestizo (Kessell et al. 1995). On the basis of skin described as "swarthy," Bustamante (1991:145) estimates about 40 percent were mestizo. It may be that finer distinctions were less significant when volunteers were needed for resettling. The 1695 list gives more detail and classifies immigrants as "Spaniard, mestizo, mulato, coyote, lobo or castizo." Few of the Spaniards had Spanish origins; most were from Mexico and one from Portugal (Strout 1978).

Another interesting identity was that of *genizaro,* a category apparently in existence from the mid-eighteenth to early nineteenth century, which was not clearly defined but encompassed those who had been captured and ransomed, as well as Pueblos who had left their homes to affiliate with Hispanic households. Some of the latter were women and men expelled from their communities because they had cohabited with Hispanos or others, either because they had been sexually abused (Gutiérrez 1991:155) or chose to do so (Frank 1998:49), and were no longer welcome in their natal group. The term was also used to mean "civilized Indians who were not Pueblo" (Bustamante 1989:73). The majority of genizaros were apparently Spanish-speaking because they had lived in Hispanic households as servants. They were at the lowest end of the casta system but began to acquire land by petitioning the governor. They were placed in communities ringed around Santa Fe, serving to protect it from raiding tribes. The towns include Abiquiú, Belén, San Miguel del Vado, Tomé, Ojo Caliente, Las Trampas, and San José de las Huertas (Carillo 1997; Cordell 1979; Horvath 1979). The genizaros performed well in these communities, gaining some wealth through warfare, and began to intermarry. By the turn of the nineteenth century they were reclassified as castas or españoles (Frank 1998:57). Even at their beginnings these communities were mixed. Some towns labeled as genizaro towns had a relatively small number of genizaro inhabitants (e.g., they made up 25 percent of the population in San Miguel del Vado; Bustamante 1991:157).

The Pueblo would have had their own perception of ethnic differences. Although no documentary records are available, their classification would presumably not have recognized the early-period distinction between Spanish and mestizo, although they would have perceived differences in power and wealth within the category of "Spanish," distinguishing church, government officials, and settlers. The Pueblos were also very aware of differences among themselves, and between themselves and various nomadic groups. These differences would have been amplified by their attitude toward the Spanish and missions, and reshaped after the revolt according to participation and group relocation or stability. For both peoples, an identity of Indian or Spanish would have been relevant when certain kinds of conflicts occurred (the Pueblo Revolt is an obvious example), but as these conflicts subsided, other subdivisions would have appeared within each group. The brief period of Pueblo cooperation during the revolt and its rapid fragmentation into factionalism (Preucel 2002) indicate the strength of smaller units of identity.

Presence and Absence of Materials

While the presence of certain goods may signal ethnic identity, a variety of affiliations, or social structural position, absences are more difficult to interpret. In addition, as noted earlier, both of these may derive from other factors, especially the pragmatic constraints that affect use or change. As an example, the use of local raw materials may persist, not because they are social signals, but because they are easier to get than exotics. Floral and faunal materials were discussed in chapter 4. The absence of sheep in a faunal assemblage, or the lack of botanical evidence of peaches, does not necessarily mean that they were not desired.

Three categories of material are significant here: metal and stone tools, ceramics, and those things that will not be preserved archaeologically but are recorded in documents. First, I briefly consider the meaning of missing things in relation to the concept of resistance. While goods themselves may be neutral (see chapter 4), their adoption and use are not, and subsequent acceptance or rejection of goods may become a political act. The failure to use, or the initial adoption and subsequent relinquishing of European things, may represent resistance to the political domination of the latter (McGuire and Paynter 1991; Miller et al. 1995), although there may be other explanations having to do with archaeological factors such as size of assemblage sample, a loss of access to the materials, or environmental issues. In some ways, I prefer Rogers's (1990) term "rejection" to "resistance"; the latter term implies a monolithic interpretation in which Europeans and their lifeways associated with an object are being resisted. However, the reasons for not adopting—or rejecting—things, as well as for incorporating them, are complex, and we cannot be certain that they are associated with resistance. Resistance may be involved when rejection of objects occurs, but rejection need not always imply resistance.

METAL AND STONE TOOLS

Metal objects and tools were brought by the Spanish and are so scarce during the pre-revolt period that their presence is a good indicator that the structure with which they are associated was occupied by Spanish or mestizo residents. Stone tools were used for many of the same tasks as metal tools; what is interesting is who used which of these, and whether they did so through choice or lack of access to metal. Given the infrequency of supply caravans, we can assume that objects such as guns and metal tools would have been carefully repaired and curated for a long time and thus would be unlikely to appear in archaeological deposits. Oñate's 1595 list of what he would supply when coming to New Mexico includes bellows, iron tools (for farming and construction), and raw iron for making tools, carts, and weapons (Hackett 1923:229). A long list of items from the mission supply service (items *supposed* to be sent to each mission every three years) includes many metal objects: spurs; tools such as knives, scissors, nails, a saw, adze, hoes, augers, and awls; medical instruments; tin plate items necessary for conducting mass; household equipment (spoons, graters, and brass basins); musical instruments—shared among several friars—such as bassoons, clarions, and trumpets (Scholes 1930:100–104). Of course, we do not know the degree to which these intentions were met. There is a plaintive letter from Santa Fe to Mexico in 1639 saying, "No iron has been [sent] since the year 1628. Consequently we are perishing, without a pound of iron or a plough" (Hackett 1937:378).

After the revolt, new settlers were given a plow, an axe, and a hoe as an incentive for migrating to New Mexico (Abbink and Stein 1977:156). A larger supply of European goods (guns, ammunition, tobacco, hatchets, and tin vessels) became somewhat more available during the eighteenth century, at annual fairs in Taos and Chihuahua (Abbink and Stein 1977:159). These items were essential for colonists, but were scarce even late in the eighteenth century (Snow 1979:224). The will of Miguel Romero indicates how valued and highly curated some of these objects were, as they were listed individually. He died at home in 1771, in the settlement of Our Lady of Guadelupe, and his property included two lances, two swords, four old hoes, an ax, an addice, a chisel, a branding iron, and 33 knives (Twitchell 1914: no. 792). A woman from Cochití described as a *coyota* (part español or mestizo and part Indian; Bustamante 1989:74) had six axes, four plowshares or points, an adze, two spades, and two swords (Twitchell 1914: no. 185).

Apparently some metal was being traded to Native Americans as early as the 1580s, during the Espejo expedition (Lange 1990:9), and was welcomed by them. Although occasionally references note that the Indians were paid in hoes, bridles, and spurs for corn (Espinosa 1988:178), evidence of metal at any Pueblo site is rare, because broken tools were reworked rather than disposed of. Knives were reportedly traded to the Pueblos (Hackett 1937, cited in Kessell 1978) and may have served as a surrogate currency, along with cloth (see see the section "Marking Identity"). The Indians apparently took the acquisition of metal into their own hands at times; a report in 1706 by Fray Olvarez notes that the Cochití mission bell could not be rung since the Indians had removed all the clappers for knives and lances (Hackett 1937:375, cited in Lange 1990:10). The Spanish introduced the craft of blacksmithing to the Southwest, and the presence of slag at a number of sites shows that metal tool production was a reality, but raw materials may have been difficult to obtain. Recent excavations at Paa'ko reveal a large smelter and extensive precontact production of copper objects (Lycett, personal communication 2001). Who would have had access to its products is unclear, but this important craft was probably executed under the supervision of missionaries. Other evidence of smelting activity is known from San Marcos (Ramenofsky 2001). There may have been small-scale smelting and the reworking of metal in a number of places that had no continuing supply of metal tools.

ARCHAEOLOGICAL EVIDENCE OF METAL

The recovery of metal objects from archaeological deposits is rare and for the pre-revolt period is restricted to sites that had a mission or Spanish residents. Table 5.1 analyzes a number of well-reported sites from early contact to post-revolt that had reasonable sample sizes. Only presence/absence information is used because assemblages from sites excavated varied in size and were recorded in different ways by different archaeologists; furthermore, only a limited number of identifiable tools or metal fragments were found at the sites. Nails or nail fragments are the most commonly recovered items, and there is an occasional awl, axe, knife, bullet shell, horseshoe, or spur fragment; or a spoon, button, fire tongs, or scissors. Iron projectile points at LA 591 and LA10114 (small domestic sites) suggest indigenous influence on the use of the raw material. Relatively little is known about metalworking in the colonial Southwest; research currently under way on smelting at sites such as Paa'ko and San Marcos may indicate how tools were made and recycled.

Vierra (1989) catalogs metal items recovered from some sixteenth- and seventeenth-century sites. Several of them (Comanche Springs, Las Majadas, Pecos, Quarai, San Gabriel, Santiago, and Tabira) reveal the presence of weaponry, armor, and riding equipment, while three (Comanche Springs, Pecos, and Tabira) also had religious items. Vierra (1989:137) also provides an extensive list of metal items from the Governor's Palace in Santa Fe, including brass candlesticks and other items, a silver galloon, bell fragments, and a piece of a double-barred cross. Through their access to supply caravans, the friars controlled much of the metal used in the Rio Grande Valley, even armor and weapons. All in all, it is evident that metal was hard to get, was intensively reused and heavily curated, and thus is rarely found in archaeological deposits even at Hispanic or Spanish sites. Indirect evidence of the presence of metal tools for butchering may be derived from faunal analysis, even when the tools themselves are not present (e.g., see LA 6178, a Hispanic site; Snow 1979:221). In at least one instance, there is also evidence of metal tools being used for chipped stone production (Moore 1991). Glass in the form of beads or containers is also noted in table 5.1, as is selenite, which was sometimes used for windows but could also have been involved in the manufacture of gypsum plaster.

LITHICS

The ubiquitous presence of stone tools into the eighteenth and nineteenth century at both Pueblo and Spanish/Hispanic sites raises questions about the gendered division of labor as well as ethnic markers. Are they a signal of identity or signify simply a pragmatic choice, given the probable difficulty of getting sufficient metal tools? Do they represent Hispano men learning chipped-stone technology from Indian men or women? Or are they evidence of women making and using stone tools? Since almost all women and many men in New Mexico would have had at least a partial Native American heritage, they would have had the opportunity to observe and perhaps learn chipped stone tool manufacture. Many of the recovered materials are expedient tools, and I suspect that women at least were using them; some men also may have been doing so. The presence of debitage is a clear signal that tools were being produced or modified at that locale. The only sites where debitage is not found are Paa'ko, Abó Mission, and LA 54,000. The reason seems clear in the last two cases: LA 54,000 is a household in Santa Fe, and the mission at Abó is unlikely to have been a lithic production site. But the absence of debitage at Paa'ko is surprising; perhaps it was simply not recorded. Note that ground stone tools such as manos, metates, and comales are present at all sites of all periods, except two small ranches/households, LA 20,000 and LA 9139, which shows that the women grinding corn and making bread were using Native American technology.

The seventeenth-century Pueblo sites appear to have more formal tools and more lithics than the later ones. Table 5.1 shows their presence at Teypama/Socorro, San Antonio de Padua, Paa'ko, and the Salinas pueblos, Gran Quivira and Quarai. The mission at Abó had many tools, probably used by Pueblos working there, although they were not reworking them. The only seventeenth-century site without

Table 5.1
Artifact Analysis: Metal and Stone Tools

Site name and LA number	Dates of occupation	Metal arms/armor	Nails	Beads	Other	Selenite	Glass beads/other	Lithics tools	Ground stone				Source
									Debitage	Metates	Manos	Comales	
Teypama/Socorro LA 282	1300–1680			x				Projectile points	x	x	x		Earls 1982
San Antonio de Padua LA 24	17th century							Projectile points	x	x	x	x?	Dart 1980
Qualacu LA 757	1350–1650/82							Unclear association	x	x	x	x	Marshall 1987
Paa'ko LA 162	> 1525–1660/70	x	x		Awls, rings spoon		x	Axes, knives, projectile points, scrapers		x	x		Lambert and Rogers 1954
Quarai (Mounds D, E, G 1993 excav.) LA 95	1525–1700	x			Ball, wire	x	x	Biface, cores, scraper, hammerst.	x	x	x		Spielmann 1994a
Gran Quivira LA 120	1600–1672	Copper knife		x			x	Projectile points, knives, scrapers, drills	x	x	x	x	Hayes 1981–, x Spielmann 1991
Abo Mission LA 97	1624–1672	x	x			x	x	Blades, choppers, projectile points, axes, scrapers					Toulouse 1949

LA 54,000 Santa Fe	17th century Spanish	Stone gunflints		Decorative hardware		x						Trigg 1999
Kotyiti/Las Majadas LA 591	17th century ranch Spanish	Stone gunflints	x	Iron projectile point, pin	x	x	Biface, scrapers, axe, polishing stone	x	x	x	x	Snow and Warren 1969/73
LA 20,000	Mid–17th century Spanish	x		Awl, buttons	x	x	Projectile points	x			x	Trigg 1999
Santa Cruz de Cochiti LA 70	18th century Hispano	Knife handle, horseshoe	x	Brass pin	x	x	Scrapers, choppers	x	x	x	ceramic	Snow 1976
Torreon LA 6178	18th century Hispano	Stone gunflints				x	Projectile points, drills, scrapers choppers	x	x	x	x	Snow 1973
Sructures LA 9138	1750–1800 Hispano			Fragment of iron religious medal		x		x	x	x		Chapman et al. 1977
LA 9139	1750–1800 Hispano						Few	x				Chapman et al. 1977
LA 12161	early 18th century Hispano	Stone gunflint		Iron, copper, fragment slag		x	Drill, biface	x	x	x	ceramic	Chapman et al. 1977

stone tools was LA 54,000, a residence in Santa Fe. The small ranch site LA 591 and the rural *estancia* LA 20,000 had stone projectile points and debitage (Snow and Warren 1969, 1973; Trigg 1999). The presence of formal tools during this period may be diagnostic, suggesting that the earlier component at Torreon may be Pueblo rather than Spanish, on the basis of the presence of many formal stone tools and the absence of metal. Some of the tools recovered—scrapers and polishing stones especially—could have been used by women, the latter in pottery production. Examples of these were found at Santa Cruz de Cochití (LA 70) and Las Majadas (LA 591). Several eighteenth-century Hispanic house structures—LA 9138, 9139, and 12161—have debitage, which suggests manufacture or reworking; several have cores or bifaces and other tools. Even LA 10114 and LA 13291, Hispanic domestic structures occupied into the nineteenth century (the second is dated at 1850–1900), yield evidence—in the form of debitage, cores, and tools—that stone working was continuing (Snow 1979:226; Binford 1979).

The raw materials used varied greatly, because of either access or selection, ranging from quartzite to obsidian and including chalcedony, chert, basalt, petrified wood, and even chipped glass (at LA 70). An interesting analysis of raw material selection and manufacturing techniques in four Hispanic colonial proveniences at LA 9138 suggests that the toolmakers were unfamiliar with the usage and manufacture of stone tools, and thus that the incentive to use them derived from the probable lack of access to metal tools (Chapman et al. 1977:2:157, 9). In discussing lithic production at eighteenth-century Hispanic sites, Moore (n.d.:195) notes that Spanish-descended New Mexicans would have been somewhat familiar with lithic technology because of the need to produce gunflints and would have used that skill to make a limited number of tools as an inexpensive and necessary substitute for metal tools. Whoever the makers and users of stone tools were, the ubiquity of lithics at Hispanic sites is further evidence of the increasing degree to which material culture was shared in the Southwest.

CERAMICS

Since pottery may indicate social boundaries and might serve to elucidate Spanish-Indian interactions, I now take up the following questions: Who made the pottery used in Spanish and Hispanic households? How did it change during the period of Spanish intrusion into New Mexico? And how were ceramics acquired? A considerable body of research on ceramics indicates that decoration, vessel morphology, and paste and temper analysis are all significant elements marking temporal period and social group. Those studying late Precolumbian and contact period Pueblo ceramics have been interested in the locus and organization of production as well as design (seen through raw material analysis, and the degree of standardization in vessel size and shape [Capone 1996; Mills 1995]) and in the way these factors relate to economic and social networks (Creamer 1996, 2000). Almost all of this research has focused on Pueblo pottery production, but it is relevant to Spanish acquisition of pottery and to changes made in Pueblo pottery to suit Spanish demands.

Following contact, Pueblo people continued to use only Pueblo pottery; there is no evidence that they adopted majolicas or Spanish vessel forms. However, as the Spanish moved into New Mexico and political events unfolded and Pueblo peoples relocated, there was considerable impact on design; in particular, motifs, vessel shapes and sizes, and raw materials changed. As the Galisteo Basin producers of glazewares such as Galisteo, San Marcos, San Lazaro, and Pueblo Blanco dwindled during the late protohistoric period, glazeware production declined. When Galisteo Pueblo was reoccupied after the revolt, limited production resumed for a brief time (Creamer 1996; Warren 1979:192) but then ceased. Tewa painted polychromes, and other types became the common wares used in Rio Grande pueblos, along with plainwares such as Salinas red and Kapo black, which were not culinary pottery. At Kotyiti, a revolt-period refuge village on Potrero Viejo, Pueblo peoples were using locally made late glazewares (Glaze F) and undecorated Salinas redwares; there was also a good deal of nonlocal pottery from Zia, Pecos, the Galisteo Basin pueblos, and northern pueblos (Tewa wares and Kapo), presumably brought by those migrating to the site for safety (Warren 1979:239).

Ceramic analysts have questioned whether glazeware production ended because the basis of identity definition changed or simply because the Spanish took control of sources of lead. At the end of the glazeware period (Glaze F), glaze designs were quite runny. Was the runnyness simply a chemical problem related to a lead shortage (Warren 1979:191)? Was the runnyness used to mask designs, and thus to make an ideological statement (Spielmann and Graves 1998)? Or did glazeware decoration become less meaningful because so much of the production was absorbed by Europeans for whom the designs had no meaning (Creamer 1995)? These are difficult questions that require a detailed, historicized, technical re-analysis of collections of both paste and glaze from sites with and without glazewares to establish their proximity to Spanish settlement. Such a project is beyond the scope of the present work, but a number of other studies have begun to investigate these issues (Capone 1996; Habicht-Mauche et al. 1993; Huntley and Kintigh 2001).

One analysis of the reorganization of post-revolt, intra-Pueblo social life examined ceramic design of whole vessels from the late seventeenth to the mid–nineteenth century (Walt 1990), employing design motifs as an indicator of political affiliation and peoples' movements. Walt believes that glazeware production ceased in reaction to the trauma of colonial domination, that it was not the result of a lead shortage caused by Spanish demand for lead. Using ceramic design attributes visible in small details such as color choices within the design band, paint types, and some design patterns, he identifies a shift in style from three pre-revolt clusters to two post-revolt groupings. The pre-revolt seventeenth-century style is seen in Hawikuh glazewares, used in Zuni and Acoma; the Rio Grande glazewares, used in the valley, except by Northern Tiwa, Tewa, and Jemez villages; and the matte paintwares used by the latter, as well as Tompiro (Walt 1990:187). In the post-revolt eighteenth century, two broad groups emerged and persisted through the nineteenth century, becoming more divergent and subdividing by village (Walt 1990:2). One includes Zuni, Acoma-Laguna, Zia, and Santa Ana; and the other encompasses Cochití, Santo Domingo, and Tewa speakers, The new style groups cut across linguistic groups, uniting in each one some Keresan and some non-Keresan-speakers. Whether or not Walt is correct in his identification of design clusters, we know that there were a lot of post-Revolt spatial rearrangements, which he identifies in some measure on the basis of attitude toward the Spanish. The rearrangements did involve the realignment of groups who had previously spoken the same language (Kroskrity 1993). It is possible that ceramic design could have been used to express new identity for these sociopolitical alignments. In any case the Prehispanic use of ceramics as markers had clearly been interfered with and altered by the end of the seventeenth century, and new styles and decorative techniques developed. It may be more relevant to consider localized identities than broader ethnic ones, with much variation over time and space, as appropriate to the factionalism among Pueblo peoples.

At the very least, ceramics should provide a way to distinguish Spanish or Hispanic households from Indian ones. Deagan's (1983) important research in St. Augustine, a sixteenth-century town in La Florida, reveals the ethnic composition of Spanish households through the analysis of pottery. Spanish women were rarely present in that early colony. In households composed of Spanish men and Indian women, ceramics reflected the presence of both traditions. Majolicas represented the men; these wares were used for serving and presentation, a situation perhaps analogous to the one Anne Yentsch (1987) describes in eighteenth-century Virginia, where the status displayed at the dinner table was that of the man. Deagan (1995:202), in discussing the evolution of Hispanic American culture in the Southeast, finds "conservatism in those socially visible areas associated with male activities" accompanied by "Spanish-Indian acculturation in less visible, female-dominated areas," particularly in the kitchen, where food preparation and storage would have occurred. Since Indian women were part of Hispanic households in the Rio Grande Valley, one would expect to find Indian ceramics at least in the kitchen, while the Spanish influence might be seen in serving vessels, plates, and items used in display to represent the household's identity, whether or not there were Spanish women in the household. Unfortunately, no studies of southwestern households have yet presented data in this form. Ceramics are also found in locations beyond the kitchen as rooms serve multiple functions, and storage—which might occur in all rooms—involves the use of ceramic containers.

Spanish/Hispanic sites in the Southwest are also more problematic than those in the Southeast because there is little pottery that is recognizably Spanish (Snow 1984:96), apart from some small quantities of Spanish and Mexican majolicas and a few fragments of Chinese porcelain. Little imported pottery was brought to, or made it as far as, the Rio Grande Valley, as it was fragile and heavy. Spanish-made majolicas are particularly rare; somewhat more majolica was being manufactured in Mexico, especially in the modern state of Puebla. Because of the technology and organization of labor in pottery production in Spain and in the Spanish colony in Mexico, it had to be manufactured in craft workshops, rather than in households. By the seventeenth century, wheel-made and kiln-fired majolica production was under way (Snow 1984:104). It appears that some late Precolumbian Pueblo peoples were also manufacturing above the level of household need (Mills 1995b; Spielmann and Graves 1998) and exchanging pottery for other goods. Both the Salinas and Galisteo Basin areas reveal evidence of this form of production over a long time span, and the wares produced there were used in many surrounding pueblos.

Most of the ordinary dishes and storage containers in Spanish homes were similar in appearance and technology to Pueblo pottery, and it is safe to assume that pottery was made by local women, mostly Pueblo women, in response to Spanish demands. Evidence of this influence is seen in new vessel forms modified to Spanish taste, such as soup bowls with flat everted rims, candlesticks, chocolate pitchers, and ring-based vessels. Innovations associated with the Spanish also include new decorative motifs, a green glaze thought to be imitative of a Spanish form seen on Iberian storage jars (Creamer 1996), fiber-tempered pottery, and a new technology producing mold-made pots. The Spanish favored micaceous slip on utility wares. It is indigenous to the Southwest at Pueblo sites, and some attribute it to Apache origin (Moore et al. n.d.:299).

Close analysis of Spanish-influenced ceramic design can reveal Pueblo attitudes. At Awatovi, a Hopi pueblo, the differing mission and post-mission motifs reflect Hopi reactions to the friars. During the colonial period, missionaries encouraged the use of Spanish motifs such as flowers, the Maltese cross, and an eight-pointed star and discouraged the practice of burying the dead with ceramics. After the revolt, when the Spanish decided that it was not practical to try to maintain control over the Hopi through missionization, the use of Spanish design elements and forms stopped, and ceramics began to be included again in mortuary ritual (Wade and McChesney 1981:44). New influences on Hopi pottery form and design came from the Tanoan immigrants who moved there after the revolt (Adams 1989).

Carillo (1997) has argued that by the late eighteenth century, as Indian population declined and Hispanic population increased, women in Hispanic villages began to make their own pottery out of necessity, making a blackware that can still be found. The development of Hispanic pottery is a meaningful topic, particularly in reference to the formation of Hispano identity. Genizaro sites seem to be the ideal "laboratory" for such an investigation as they are composed of a mix of people, some of whom began life as Pueblos or members of other indigenous groups; yet in a frontier situation they needed to forge a common identity that was basically Hispano. Some of the early pottery Carillo considers Hispanic comes from the genizaro site of San José de las Huertas and has been described as thick-walled black, sand-tempered wares (Carillo 1997; Ferg 1984). Presumably wares such as this would have been used for cooking and would not have served as an obvious signal of identity. Carillo's discussion of Hispanic pottery suggests that Tewa-produced large vessel forms were used along with Hispanic-produced small vessels and the utility wares that broke most often (Carillo 1997:144). This combination of wares suggests a pragmatic strategy of production and, as well, the possibility that identity was expressed in materials other than ceramics.

Temper characteristics are potentially useful in identifying production location but have only been analyzed at a few sites. Almost no post-revolt Pueblo sites have allowed the archaeological excavation or surface collection of pottery. The situation at many Spanish or Hispanic sites is complex as they have both Pueblo and European components and the mechanisms for acquiring Pueblo ceramics vary greatly. Analysis of temper in some settings is provocative as it suggests some materials may have been used at locations remote from their origins. For example, at Torreon, LA 6178, the local rhyolite tuff temper was not used, but sherds reveal rock-tempering, characteristic of the Galisteo Basin. This leads Warren (1979:192) to suggest that local potters were manufacturing pottery for nonlocal people (Europeans) using imported temper. Again, to be useful in clarifying a complex picture, this tool would have to be applied in a systematic analysis across a wide range of sites.

Distribution mechanisms are equally difficult to discern. Spanish and Hispanic people probably acquired Pueblo pottery by a number of means, first through the well-documented presence of Pueblo women in the households of Spanish men, either as conjugal partners (Barber 1932:73) or, if the men had Spanish or Mexican wives, as servants/slaves. Mexican Indian women may have known how to make pottery, but if this activity were not valued, as Snow (1984) suggests, they may well have adopted Spanish attitudes toward its production. Encomienda requirements included the demand for pottery, and there are accounts of colonists going to Indian villages to get ceramics, through purchase or barter (Snow 1976). Another possibility is that pottery was made commercially by Pueblo women, or perhaps genizaros (Snow 1984:105–106), and marketed to Spanish households. One account describes pottery being brought to Santa Fe in 1694 and exchanged for corn and meat. This was a time when food was scarce, just before the unsuccessful revolt of 1696 (Espinosa 1988:116).

CERAMICS RECOVERED THROUGH ARCHAEOLOGY

The dominant pottery type recovered at Spanish and Hispanic sites was some form of plainware, in many cases Salinas redware, but also polished blackware and micaceous types. Glazewares, especially with late (type F) rims (Kidder 1924), used by Pueblo peoples in the seventeenth century were also found at some of the early Spanish sites such as LA 54147 and the small structure near Santiago Pueblo (LA 326), and some eighteenth-century Hispanic sites. Locally made decorated polychrome Pueblo wares (mostly Tewa, Posuge, Puname, and Ogapoge) were also found, along with some black-on-white wares and some sherds of ceramic types from the western pueblos. Imported ceramics, especially porcelain, have been rare finds in archaeological deposits. Majolica was recovered in small quantities (often two or three sherds from sites where the ceramic sample included more than 10,000 sherds) at Paa'ko; at the Salinas pueblos of Quarai, Gran Quivira, and Qualacu; and at the mission at Abó (table 5.2). It was also found in many of the house sites excavated as part of the Cochití Dam project: Las Majadas (LA 591) and Cochití Springs (LA 34) (Snow 1979:219), which were occupied during the seventeenth century, had two and four majolica types, respectively; Majolicas were also present at Los Ranchos de Santa Cruz de Cochití, occupied by Hispanic settlers at Pueblo del Encierro (LA 70), Torreon (LA 6178), LA 9139, LA 12161, and LA 10114 during the eighteenth century or into the early nineteenth. The quantity of majolica (100 sherds) recovered from Spanish occupations at LA 70 made up 8.5 percent of the assembly of 1,250 historic period sherds, a much larger proportion than at any other contemporary site. Half of these pieces came from one context in a plaza adjacent to a doorway (Snow 1976:E25). Is it unclear whether these sherds all came from one broken vessel, thus skewing the data.

Marking Identity

It is the combined presence of any or several of the following traits, not one characteristic, that indicates a structure had Spanish occupants: majolicas, a Spanish vessel form such as a soup bowl[1] or candlestick, an occasional glass bead, a metate with legs, some forms of metal (especially armor or weapons), and some architectural details such as corner fireplaces (although later these were adopted by Pueblos and Navajos). These objects, along with access to domestic animals, would

1. Barbara Mills informs me (personal communication 2002) that the Rio Grande Pueblos did adopt soup bowl forms, which would thus not be an exclusive marker of Spanish or Hispano households. However, using the complex of traits together, I believe, will distinguish this ethnic identity from a Pueblo one.

have been markers of Spanish and Hispanic households. The predominant array of material culture in Pueblo and Spanish/Hispanic households, however, was shared or similar, and this similarity increased as time progressed. Some sites identified as Hispanic yielded no obviously Hispanic artifacts (glass, metal, porcelain, or majolica), especially in the Rio Abajo area (Marshall and Walt 1984).

This does not mean that Spanish-descended individuals lived undetected among the Pueblo, but it may be difficult for archaeologists to perceive the differences. Cordell (1979:115) notes: "The ceramics found on seventeenth and eighteenth century Hispanic sites are predominantly the same as those reported for contemporary Indian communities, while materials used in house construction were represented by local resources almost entirely." I suggest that the shared material culture after the revolt marks the existence of a common economic domain in which Pueblo and Hispanic people participated. The domain was defined by a difficult environment, one in which it was necessary to maintain agriculture in the face of limited water, protect domestic animals, and guard against marauding nomadic raiders. Two separate categories of people occupied this domain, although the boundaries were somewhat blurred. Each was relatively undifferentiated in terms of social hierarchy. Hispanos had a small, hereditary elite population, while Pueblo populations had no hereditary elite; their elite consisted of ritual leaders. Each population may have perceived itself as superior to the other. In spite of this common domain and similar material culture, however, Pueblo and Hispanic residents would have been entirely clear as to the ethnicity of community residents. Identities would have been apparent from traits that are not archaeologically accessible, such as religion, language, hairstyle, and clothing. Father Dominguez in his 1776 census and survey seems to have relied primarily on language (1956). A study of the Arizona Tewa by Paul Kroskrity (1993) suggests an example of language serving as a device to maintain an ethnic identity. These Tewa, who migrated to the Hopi first mesa in 1696, after the second Pueblo revolt failed, have maintained their language and kept it for themselves, so that no Hopi speak Arizona Tewa, while the latter all speak Hopi. He also suggests that linguistic analysis, particularly the number of Spanish words borrowed, and whether they are conjugated or not, is a mirror of adaptation or resistance (Kroskrity 1993).

Another set of markers serving to delineate the Spanish/Hispano population is depicted in descriptions of the possessions that some of the first Spanish settlers in New Mexico brought with them. These would have been important symbols of

Table 5.2
Artifact Analysis: Ceramics

Site name and LA number	Dates of occupation	Number of sherds	Majolicas Spanish/ Mexican	Soup bowls	Ring-base	Other forms	Porcelain	Predominant Pueblo decorated wares	Pueblo plainwares	Source
Teypama/Socorro LA 282	1300–1680	6,663		x		x		San Lazaro, Agua Fria, Espinosa	Corona plain, obliterated corrugated	Earls 1982
San Antonio de Padua LA 24	17th century		x					Glaze E, F, Puaray, Kotyiti	Striated, indented corrugated	Dart 1980
Qualacu LA 757	1350–1650/82	3,232	x					Glaze E, F, mostly on surface		Marshall 1987
Paa'ko LA 162	> 1525–1660/70	> 14,000	x	x				Glazewares A, D, E, F, Santa Fe black/white	Plain	Lambert and Rogers 1954
Quarai Mounds D, E, G 1993 excav. LA 95	1525–1700	> 6,600	x	x		Cup, bell		Glaze E, E/F, F	Salinas red, corrugated, smudged	Spielmann 1994
Gran Quivira LA 120	1600–1672	> 78,000		x				Glaze E, F, Kotyiti Chupadero & Tabira or black/white	Salinas red	Spielmann 1991 Hayes 1981

Abo Mission LA 97	1624–1672	n.a.	x	x	x	Candlestick	x	Glaze E, F, Tewa polychrome, Posuge, Puname, Hopi, Zuni, Tabira	Salinas red, striated, smoothed	Toulouse 1949
LA 54,000 Santa Fe	17th century Spanish	15,000	x			Green glaze				Trigg 1999
Kotyiti/las Majadas LA 591	17th century ranch	> 9,000	x	x	x	Green glaze		Kotyiti, Pecos, Tewa	Saninas red, plain, micaceous	Snow and Warren 1969/73
LA 20,000	Mid-17th century Spanish	3,523	x							Trigg 1999
Santa Cruz de Cochiti LA 70	18th century	1,200	(8% of total)					Tewa, Ogapoge, Rio Abajo, black/white	Micaceous	Snow 1976
Torreon LA 6178	18th century Hispano	> 900 rims		x				Tewa, Ogapoge, Glaze red, Glaze yellow, Glaze F	Salinas red, plain, micaceous, Kapo black	Snow 1973
Structures LA 9138	1750–1800	580						Puaray, Puname, Ogapoge	Smeared, plain polished black,	Chapman et al. 1977
LA 9139	1750–1800	1,250						Puname, mineral polychromes	Plain micaceous	Chapman et al. 1977
LA 12161	Early 18th century Hispano	328		x	x			Kotyiti, Glaze F, carbon polychromes	Salinas red, plain polished, micaceous	Chapman et al. 1977

their elite status in Spain and Mexico: Italian velvet, Chinese silk and satin clothing, Spanish leather and other things worn in Mexico, lace cuffs, satin hats, fancy slippers, and tortoiseshell combs, a pearl headdress. Occasional gilt buttons and other traces of these belongings have been found in excavations at the Palace of the Governors (C. Snow 1993:70), but most would have perished and not be recoverable archaeologically. These elaborate items were not restricted to women. Churches were equipped with beautiful cloth, carved *retablos,* and many objects of precious metals that came from Spain. Vargas's will (in 1704) reveals the possession of silver vessels, jewels, fancy clothing, saddles, pistols, and a gold cane; and the list of Captain Alonso de Quesada's equipment when leaving for New Mexico in 1598 describes his suits, boots and shoes, bedding, armor, and household possessions in elaborate detail. He took with him: 4 suits, 1 of purple velvet with a short cloak, 1 trimmed with silver braid; 4 hats, 2 expensive and 2 plain; doublets of silk and linen, 10 linen shirts, linen breeches; 4 saddles; a fine coat of mail and other armor; a bed, bedspread of green cloth, 4 sheets, and 4 pillows; 10 pairs of cordovan shoes and 6 pair calfskin; 3 pair boots; and many other items, including 3 servants, 4 cavalry horses and 12 ordinary horses, tools, horseshoes, and 100 cakes of soap (Snow 1993:134).

The differences between elite individuals and ordinary folk are also seen in these accounts. A soldier's belongings in 1598 included two suits, a sword and gun, two pairs of boots and four of shoes, a suit of mail, and six horses (Snow 1993:135). A mestizo's possessions are listed as a well-worn doublet, two cotton shirts (one worn out), one pair cordovan leather shoes, an antelope-skin muffler, a cotton pillow and coarse mattress, a bar of soap, a catechism book, and some medicinal herbs (Knaut 1995:138–139). A woman described as a "poor" widow, in spite of the fact that she owned land—near Albuquerque and very valuable today—had only a few petticoats and coral bracelets (Simmons 1991: 110–112). While sumptuary laws existed to prevent certain groups from consuming specific goods, such as luxury textiles (Jackson 1999: 4), these laws would seem to have been unnecessary, as the goods were not available on New Mexico's frontier, and the number of situations in which they could be used must have been small. They became less relevant in the post-revolt period. However, fabrics needed for ordinary clothing—wool, baize, and linen—make up a major part of a list of goods received by migrants to New Mexico in 1693 (Kessell et al. 1995:249–252).

Bernard Cohn (1996:141) provides particularly rich detail on the importance and complexity of cloth and clothing and how it "made visual the categories of culture" in nineteenth- and twentieth-century India. He describes Gandhi's use of home-made cloth as a symbol and form of resistance, the restriction of access to various elements of British dress, and a particularly interesting example of how a low-caste group of Indian women used clothing to circumvent and destabilize cultural categories, appearing to accede to Christian missionaries' attempt to have women dress more modestly but adopting an article of clothing similar in appearance to that worn by upper-caste (Nair) women, irritating the latter considerably. Clothing is a particularly effective class of goods used to convey social meaning, and even though it is not likely to be preserved in archaeological assemblages, it may be depicted or often incites comment. Cloth was very important in the Pueblo world. Some of it was woven in kivas, and Webster thinks that some textile products, such as dance costumes and mantas for brides, might fit Weiner's description of inalienable objects (Webster 1997:34, 211). Weaving was an important activity in the colonial context. The extraction of woven goods for encomienda tribute and by missions led to a major labor drain. Oñate is known at one point early in the settlement of New Mexico to have extracted some 2,000 cotton mantas up to 1½ yards in length and width (Webster 1997:144). Spanish demand for both cotton and woolen woven and knitted products was continual, and a workshop for cloth production *(obraje)* was established in Santa Fe (Webster 1997:141). Cloth itself has been identified as a form of currency in the colonial period (Trigg 1999:191; Webster 1997:109) in relation to its role in encomienda.

Initially, Spanish and Pueblo peoples would have looked quite different from one another; those differences would have persisted for women, but men's dress came to look more similar. We know that Spanish and Hispanic men tended to put aside traditional garb (often quite impractical) in favor of deerskin garments, which were not only more appropriate for local conditions but also more available (Simmons 1991:3), and that the friars tried to get Pueblo men to wear fitted pants (Webster 1997:536), although it is unclear how successful they were. In spite of these rather superficial similarities and materials, the two clothing types would have looked distinctly different and still served to signal identity.

Deagan's (1995) description of a Spanish woman as the ultimate status good in the Southeast may also be relevant in the Southwest, although there were fewer of them in New Mexico than in La Florida. Documents describe ways in which the Spanish adopted many aspects of Pueblo material life, but there were undoubtedly other belongings in homes, such as beds and bedding, that were not as visible or status-bearing as clothing but that were linked to Spanish/Hispanic identity.

It was as important to the Pueblo to express their identities as it was to Spanish and Hispanic residents; moreover, the retention of a Pueblo identity was a deliberate act. The Spanish were quite amenable to Indians' becoming mestizo, if they were willing to adopt language, dress, hairstyle, and religion (Jackson 1999:11). A Pueblo person who did so would presumably have given up rights to traditional land ownership, and it is hard to see the clear advantage to becoming mestizo, although there surely were instances of individuals finding Spanish/Hispanic life more appealing than Pueblo life. The situation was different for Pueblo women than men. The former had easier access to Spanish customs and language, as they worked in Hispanic households as servants. However, working in a household often had other consequences. If a servant woman were impregnated by the man of the house, she might not have been able to go back to her family. Women in colonial settings have different choices and restrictions than men do, and the fluidity and cross-cutting of gender, class, and ethnicity make identities difficult to disentangle.

Material Culture Similarities in the Northeast

The situation in the Hudson and Mohawk River Valleys was very different from that of the Southwest. The reciprocal adoption of European things by indigenous people and indigenous things by Europeans did not occur in the Northeast. The situation in this region was very unbalanced or unidirectional in that many European objects were taken into Indian lives whereas the Dutch used almost no Mohawk artifacts. This derives in large part from practices inherent to the fur trade, in which the Dutch used trade goods to motivate indigenous people to hunt beaver. However, while some Europeans in the Northeast made use of Native American technology—canoes and snowshoes, for example—the Dutch did not, another manifestation of the social distance they expressed. The only items they consistently desired from the Mohawk were furs and food—venison and corn primarily—although they are known to have adopted one Iroquois artifact, a deerskin bag that they called *notas,* which may have been used to carry wampum (figure 5.3).

Archaeology reveals the presence of a few Indian things—wampum, ceramics,

Figure 5.3. *Notas* bag, the only Mohawk-made object known to have been used by the Dutch.

and Native American pipes—in Dutch houses, but these objects indicate trade or visiting Mohawk and are not a signal of Dutch use (Huey 1988:251). The analysis of archaeological assemblages in Dutch homes in Fort Orange demonstrates the social distance quite clearly, as it shows no Indian artifacts save these. Huey (1984:73) says that there was a strong and rapid transfer of the entire Dutch material culture to the New World, with delft tiles and dishes, traditional cooking wares and *roemers* (glassware) all in use. During the colonial period, the English showed greater interest in natives and their technology, but as curiosities to be collected for museums or put on display in England. There is no evidence that indigenous objects were adopted in European homes. Several prominent Mohawk described as "kings" of the five nations made a voyage to London in 1710 with two British military leaders: Tejonihokarawa (Hendrick), Sagayonguaroughton (Brant), Cenelitonoro (John), and a Mahican, Elowohkaom (Nicholas) (Richter 1992:227, 368). Their portraits were painted by a famous artist, and they met the Queen and attended many plays and other entertainments.

Mohawk Use of European Goods

The Mohawk incorporated many imported objects into their daily lives, but a number of observers have assumed that in adopting European things indigenous people immediately perceived the technological superiority of European goods, that they took everything offered them, and that once they had used an item, they were completely dependent on continued access to it.

> At the end of the seventeenth century most of Iroquoia had an absolute dependence on articles of European invention and manufacture. Once the axes, knives, kettles, shovels, guns, cloth and many other articles became common everyday utilities and necessities, there was no turning back to flint tools and points, stone pipes and axes, clay cooking vessels and bone awls. (Rumrill 1985:1)

This perception is incorrect, as the Iroquois and others clearly selected the items that they preferred, often adapting them for their own purposes, which might differ from European usage, and redefining their meaning. Axtell (1988, 1992) and Bradley (1987), among others, note some of these variable uses: wearing a metal axe-head as an ornament, or cutting up a copper kettle to make projectile points or for inlay on traditional carvings, are examples. What is significant is the agency expressed by the Mohawk, individually and collectively, in determining what they wished to use and how they wished to use it.

Although the first European trade goods appeared north and west of the Mohawk among the Huron in Ontario in the mid–sixteenth century, Mohawk access to them was limited until the first third of the seventeenth century, when the Dutch settled in the Hudson Valley. Several classes of European objects were acquired and used by the Mohawk: they were interested in ornaments, tools—especially those made of metal such as knives and axes—and cloth "duffel," while their attitude toward guns was a bit more complex, as I explain shortly. They also incorporated a set of objects with symbolic value and power, such as glass beads and wampum—the latter had quite different significance to Europeans and indigenous peoples. One European good that was received with mixed feelings was liquor, as relatively early indigenous leaders recognized its disabling qualities and requested—unsuccessfully—that traders not provide it to their fellows.

While the exchange that occurred between Iroquois and Dutch (subsequently English partners) is described as the fur *trade,* initially the Indians would have perceived it as a different form of exchange more characteristic of reciprocal and redistributive forms (see chapter 3). Bradley (1987:66) suggests that the Onondaga treated early European goods—copper, iron, and glass—as if they were similar to traditional nonsubsistence items—such as native copper, walrus ivory, marine shell, and exotic lithics—that were exchanged in a long-distance trade network in prestige items among and between Native American groups just prior to contact in the sixteenth century. He believes the Onondaga were flexible in adapting to innovation; to them, European objects were just another set of exotic elements to be integrated in traditional ways (Bradley 1987:4), through traditional mechanisms of exchange. Eventually, however, the exchange of furs for European commodities became trade and was controlled by both parties in a two-way process. Europeans adjusted their imports in favor of those items that would "sell" best, as demand became specific. Axes and knives were desired as practical items; they had an important military role because many Mohawk enemies such as the Huron had received them from the French, and they were an economic asset that could be used in trade to establish intraregional ties and prestige.

Europeans would not have understood the meanings of things adopted by Native Americans, especially if choices were made for symbolic rather than practical reasons. Duffel cloth was another of the more desirable items. Initially red was favored, but soon grey, blue, or—best of all—black was demanded to reduce visibility while hunting (De Roever 1996:78). Quinn (1979:512) notes, "Almost all metal objects might at first prove disposable, but later objects might be made to suit Amerindian requirements, for example, copper cut into holed gorgets for hanging round Indian necks and beads searched for from Italy or specially manufactured in the Netherlands to fit demand." The size and color of glass beads were an important factor (Merrill 1989, cited in Crerar 1992:25), white, red, and black being favored because they corresponded to preexisting aspects of Iroquois cosmology. These items were similar to traditionally used materials such as crystal and native copper. In accepting European things, the Iroquois were selecting objects that already had meaning within their own cosmological system. Hamell (1983) has written eloquently on the ideological significance of certain substances and qualities to northeastern indigenous peoples that reflected valued qualities of lightness and brightness. As an example, light was life, knowledge, mind, and Greatest Being, and any material (such as shell, crystals, copper) or color (white or the blue of the sky) acquired the properties of these things. The same qualities would have governed the kinds of trade goods that were desired or valued because of their ability to reflect light, for example, making copper, mirrors, white wampum, and glass beads of certain colors especially valuable.

Changes occurred in trade relationships, as exemplified by the Mohawk-Dutch interaction, which became special and particularly effective once the Mohawk had displaced the Mahican (Burke 1991:27). The Dutch got the furs they wanted; the Mohawk, after axes and knives, wanted cloth, guns, and other metal tools (Burke 1991:26). Goods and clothing were relatively straightforward, but providing guns to indigenous people was not so straightforward. The Dutch may have originally armed the Mohawk in order to help fight the French, but as early as 1639 they tried to get the sale of guns to the Mohawk outlawed. However, by this time the Mohawk were repairing their own guns and making their own shot from lead they acquired at Fort Orange (Snow 1995). By the 1660s, any privileged access to guns the Iroquois had disappeared, as all Indians were equally well armed (Richter 1992: 98–99). The question of the utility of guns is an interesting one. Some authors maintain that indigenous people lacked the technology to maintain and repair weapons, yielding a declining demand for them, citing as evidence the frequent requests for smiths who could fix guns (Ray 1974:73, 81; Ruttenber [1872] 1971:

132). However, it is unlikely that the interest in guns declined, even though they would have had limited utility in some settings because they were slow to reload and most hunters probably had better aim and were more effective with a bow and arrow, at least initially. Their value in warfare would have been obvious, for display purposes and in open areas, and Native Americans came to rely on them to some degree. In the early eighteenth century, Ohio Indians had reportedly used guns with shortened and darkened barrels and relied on their bow and arrow skills as dusk approached and the light faded (McConnell 1992:36).

Regardless of the items being exchanged, the social aspects of trade were important, and traders—for the most part apparently men—were in powerful positions. The operation of the clan and lineage system meant that redistribution, rather than the accumulation of wealth, was the means of achieving prestige. Some items were accumulated personally, such as gifts made by Europeans to individual Native Americans, especially medals or items of European clothing. Mary Jemison, an eighteenth-century woman captured by the Seneca, who chose to remain with them and married two Seneca husbands, reported that British commissioners gave several members of her group suits of clothes, brass kettles, guns with powder and lead, tomahawks, scalping knives, and pieces of gold to ensure the help of the Iroquois in subduing those who had rebelled against the king (Kestler 1990:132). Presumably some of these items might have been kept by the recipient and should be seen as inalienable objects (Weiner 1992). It is unclear whether access to trade increased prestige or whether existing prestige or rank was a criterion defining who was in a position to trade; both are possible. Iroquois ideas of rank involved power but did not include personal wealth; European traders were interested in power primarily as a way to amass individual capital. It seems as though a Middle Ground (Sensu White 1991) would have been a basic requirement for long-term encounters.

Another important object in both Iroquois and European lives was wampum, although its meaning strongly differed in each culture. The Dutch recognized that wampum was valuable to Native Americans quite early in their interactions, but they mistook the reason for its significance and treated it as currency. The Dutch used it in bartering for furs, as a medium of exchange by which other values were established, or in one case, a ransom for a chief was set at 140 fathoms of seewan or wampum (Ceci 1977:183). A fathom was a string about 6 feet long (Cantwell and Wall 2001:134). There was some variability in setting equivalent values. An article in the *New York Times* in 1895 reports on bread and drink prices in stivers (a Dutch coin), beavers, and wampum in the late 1650s: "A can of French wine could be had for 22 beaver skins, 36 strings of wampum or 18 stivers; a gill of brandy for 7 beavers, 10 strings of wampum, or 5 stivers; an 8 lb. loaf of wheat bread for 10 beavers, 14 strings of wampum, or 8 stivers" (Rosendale 1895).

However, these were Dutch values; it is unclear how the Mohawk would have set values, and it is likely that they would not have been consistent but situational. While the Dutch and the English treated wampum as a medium of exchange—money—particularly important when other forms of currency such as coins were in short supply, indigenous peoples did not view shell beads as currency. Native Americans valued wampum for its symbolically significant qualities such as those Hamell (1983) describes. They wove it into belts or headbands and considered it the most important element in a number of interactions such as condolence rituals or agreements between groups. Dean Snow (1994:98) supplies a list of situations in which wampum was essential: to wipe away tears, replace the sun, dispel the insanity of grief, and satisfy the relatives of a murdered kinsman. William Johnson, who settled close to Albany among the Mohawk in the 1730s as a trader, was one of a small number of Europeans who do seem to have understood the meaning and purposes of wampum belts. Johnson's accounts of his activities and observations fill 13 published volumes, one of which provides a list of expenses submitted to New York's governor in 1746 for reimbursement. It mentions belts of wampum or strands of wampum that he gave away for specific purposes: to condole deaths, to wipe the tears of a grieving parent, to call a group to war, to open the mouths of an Indian group so they might speak freely, and to insist on the steadfastness of Indian partners when a delay of action had occurred (Martien 1996:94, 98). While he submitted each item given in terms of its value in British currency, it appears that he gave the items as gifts and lists some things as "treats." As his papers indicate, he understood that the wampum belts or strands served as contracts: "It is obvious to all who are the least acquainted with Indian affairs, that they regard no message or invitation, be it of what consequence it will, unless attended or confirmed by strings or belts of wampum, which they look upon as we our *letters, or rather bonds* (Martien 1996:92). The Covenant Chain, which is referred to frequently and which established the bond between Dutch and Iroquois (perhaps as early as 1613; Martien 1996) was renewed periodically and represented by belts and strings of wampum. The Iroquois were not interested in beads per se, but only in strung beads or wampum belts, which they perceived as creating meaningful bonds and promises between those individuals or groups who exchanged them.

Both the Dutch and the English attempted to increase the supply of wampum as a means of getting a larger share of furs, and during contact times, they encouraged (or even forced; Rubertone 1989) coastal tribal people to mass-produce wampum. Peter Kalm, a traveler to this area in 1749 who kept a highly detailed journal, suggested it was being manufactured in Albany by Europeans; this would have been a labor-intensive task requiring great patience to grind and drill shell and manufacture the small beads. Wampum continued to be manufactured into the eighteenth century because it was still being used for the western fur trade (Martien 1996:91, 131).

The different views of wampum provide one of the clearest examples of misperceptions in contact situations. Manipulating the manufacture of wampum was an expression of the market system, and the English, and Dutch as well, saw all the transactions between them and the Iroquois as sales. As Martien explains, "There . . . is the fatal misunderstanding: in that double sense of 'bonds,' where the very symbols that marked and kept the agreement—the beaver, the beads, even the handshake, our original five-and-ten—were convertible to money, and as good as ready cash. The promise was for sale" (Martien 1996:98). Wampum's significance is noted in the oral tradition of the founding of the League of the Iroquois, which was recorded on paper in the early twentieth century (Snow 1994: 59). There are many accounts of how specific arrangements of symbols on belts conveyed particular historic events. The Hiawatha Belt (figure 5.4), once stored in the vaults of the New York State Museum in Albany but now repatriated to the Onondaga Nation, is described as a symbolic map of the Great Law of Peace and represents the formation of the Haudenosaunee:

> The first of the squares on the left represents the Mohawk Nation and its territory, the second square on the left and near the heart represents the Oneida Nation and its territory and the white heart in the middle represents the Onondaga Nation and its territory. It also means that the heart of the Five Nations is single in its loyalty to the Great Peace. . . . Further it means that the authority is given to advance the

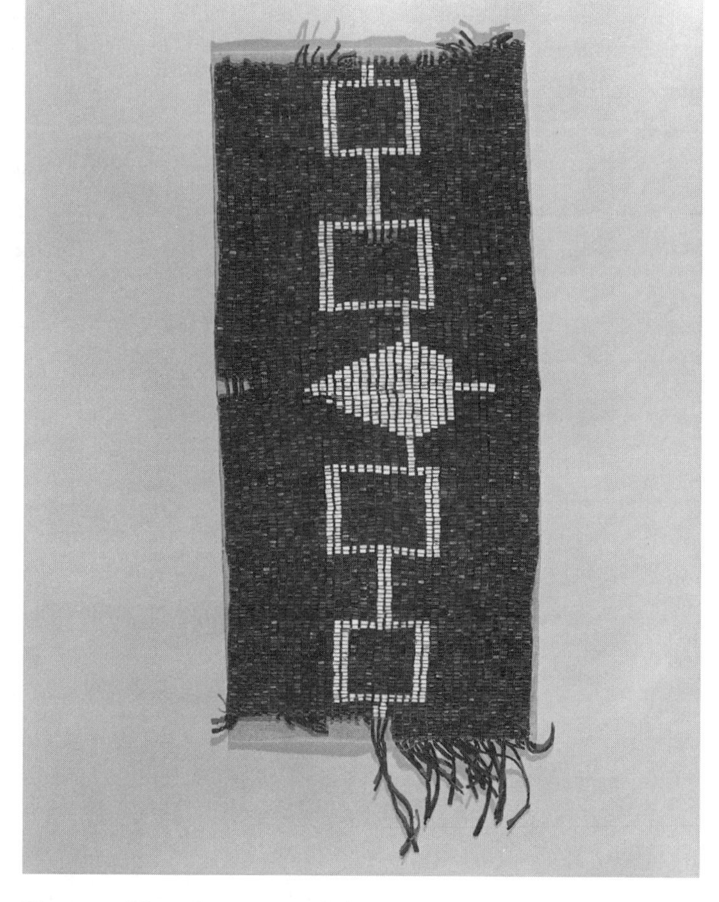

Figure 5.4. Hiawatha wampum belt.

> cause of peace whereby hostile nations out of the League shall cease warfare. The white square to the right of the heart represents the Cayuga Nation and its territory and the fourth and last square represents the Seneca Nation and its territory.
>
> White here symbolizes that no evil or jealous thought shall creep into the minds of the chiefs while in council under the Great Peace. White, the emblem of peace, love, charity, and equity surrounds and guards the Five Nations. (Martien 1996:109)

The Great Law of Peace, which is still in effect, was transcribed by Arthur C. Parker from the words originally stated by the prophet Dekanawida. It suggests that purple represents "the dark and bloody ground" that the northeastern woodlands had become prior to the Great Peace, and would again become with the arrival of the Europeans (Martien 1996:110).

After the fur trade dried up, the Mohawks were in a difficult position. They had become accustomed to using some European goods and tried to maintain their access to them by several strategies (through trade in other items, gifts, and their labor; see chapter 4). Ultimately, however, they traded their land to Europeans, who moved onto it for farming (Schrire and Merwick 1991). European land use meant permanent possession, which interfered with the Iroquioan practice of shifting horticulture. As noted in chapter 3, European interpretation of land transactions differed from that of the Indians, who believed that they were "selling" permission to live there, rather than exclusive use or ownership, and that this permission was a necessary part of forming an alliance with Europeans (Delage 1991:127).

ANALYSIS OF MOHAWK SITES

The analysis of relative frequencies of trade and indigenous goods in archaeological sites was made possible by Dean Snow's major compilation of data from known Mohawk sites. I examine objects found in Mohawk sites from five periods between the sixteenth and late seventeenth centuries when there was direct contact: 1580–1614, 1614–1626, 1635–1646, 1646–1666, and 1666–1675. Unfortunately, the eighteenth-century sites are more difficult to analyze; few sites have been excavated, the samples are small (often derived from collectors), and the contexts are not well defined, so components are likely to be mixed. I employ data from the Seneca Townley-Read site, dating from 1715–1754 (Jordan 2002), as a substitute for the eighteenth century. Although the Senecas had different interactions with Europeans, being more distant from the Hudson and the Dutch, and were incorporated in direct trade later than the Mohawks, by this period they were closely involved with European trade networks. Because of the difficulties inherent in using assemblages of differing sizes from sites excavated and recorded in different ways by different archaeologists, I did not attempt to quantify materials but simply looked at the presence or absence of certain items over time. I classified objects as either indigenous or European, and then as having subsistence utility or serving social or ritual functions. I should note that these were all domestic sites; mortuary data would probably tell a somewhat different story but are not generally available for the Mohawks. The analysis demonstrates a number of points, two of which are particularly clear. First, the frequency of many categories of European objects gradually increased until 1635–1646; subsequently, the presence of all varieties decreased (table 5.3) as fewer furs were available to trade. This is the period when population declined and both artifact sample sizes and artifact diversity from sites decreased (Snow 1995). Second, even though European objects of many types equivalent to Native American ones were added to the material inventory, the Mohawks continued to manufacture and use their own tools and ornaments throughout the period in question, although their formal tools were produced in declining frequencies.

Glass beads are the most common and frequent type of European object recovered, although brass or copper beads and other jewelry are found throughout all periods as well. White ball clay (kaolin) pipes are adopted in the third period and continue in use throughout the time examined. Other European items in the social-ritual class are most frequent in the years between 1614 and 1646. Items used in subsistence display a similar pattern: the interval between 1614 and 1646 shows many more European subsistence-related items than the periods before. The frequency of subsistence-related types then declines somewhat, but it is unclear whether this is a meaningful decrease or a consequence of reduced population, site size, and assemblage size. At Townley-Read, the eighteenth-century Seneca site, iron tools continue in use, even though more of them are being included in mortuary disposal than in domestic contexts (Kurt Jordan, personal communication 2001). European goods still in common use are items such as nails, awls, axes, projectile points, and knives; these persist through most periods. European gunflints are found in all periods after 1635–1646 as guns became more common.

Native American objects show a different pattern, although here, too, some items persist and the number of object types in later periods decreases (table 5.3). Shell beads and jewelry, animal canines, quartz crystals, and indigenous ceramic pipes continue in use throughout all or most periods. These objects were used in ritually and socially expressive ways, so it is not surprising that they would persist. White ball clay pipes probably had different fucntions than did traditional pipes; it seems, however, that shell beads (apart from wampum) and glass beads were both worn during the same periods.

In the subsistence category, stone-working continues to occur at the Mohawk sites, as indicated by the presence of cores and flakes in most assemblages. Knives, scrapers, and projectile points persist throughout all periods, even when European tools were being used, although we do not know the relative proportions of each tool type in use. Stone woodworking equipment (axes, celts, and whetstones) go out of use, replaced by metal tools. Stone hoes are no longer found after the first period (1580–1614) and bone artifacts are also replaced by metal. A whole range of indigenous utilitarian objects is found in periods one and two, but the number of subsistence-related tool types declines abruptly in period three, and then more slowly after that. Those tools still in use from 1666 onward are mostly expedient tools. A fine-grained analysis of lithics recovered from the Jackson-Everson site (1666–1680) suggests that the tools still in use at that site were primarily for scraping (Cushman 1983). The decline in food-processing equipment (pestles and metates) is interesting, especially in contrast to the Southwest, where indigenous grinding tools were present in all households. Iroquois and Pueblo cuisine were different, with the former relying more on a stewed corn ("mush") than on tortillas or similar products. It may also be that cooking in metal pots or kettles, which were traded to the Iroquois but are not represented in assemblages (except in fragments), required less grinding of grains than cooking in ceramic vessels. The prevalence of metal pots represents a distinct difference with the Southwest where metal pots were scarce and presumably owned only by Spanish and Hispanic families.

Following Rogers's logic (1990), I suggest that the reduced use of native utilitarian items in the third period is directly attributable to the ample supply of beaver and consequent availability of European goods and reflects the process he describes as "addition." However, the continued production and use of traditional tool types is clearly maintained in spite of good trading conditions; "replacement" does not occur across the board, although it is more frequent with some kinds of materials or tool types. Smaller assemblages of European objects at later sites may reflect declining population and less archaeological examination of the period, but it may also reflect resistance to colonial control, increased curation, and reworking of European materials, or all of these influences; it is difficult to interpret the *absence* of items in an assemblage. Whereas such analyses are complex, the continuing manufacture of traditional ornaments and ritually important items is a clear indication of selection. There was no blanket acceptance of foreign goods and associated replacement of indigenous parallel items in those aspects of material life that would have had particular cultural and social meaning. European-made

Table 5.3
Mohawk and Seneca Site Inventories

	Mohawk					Seneca
	1580–1614	1614–26	1635–46	1646–66	1666–79	1715–74
Native American social and ritual objects						
Shell beads	x	x	x	x	x	x
Shell jewelry	x	x		x	x	
Ceramic jewelry	x	x				
Stone beads	x	x				
Animal canines	x	x	x	x	x	
Quartz crystals	x	x	x	x	x	
Wampum			x	x		x
Red ochre			x			
Yellow ochre			x			
Galena			x			
Mica			x			
Red pipestone beads						x
Paint pot/concretion	x	x		x		x
Bone comb						
Bone jewelry		x		x		
Gaming stones	x					
Turtle carapace	x		x			
Ceramic pipe	x	x	x	x	x	x
Stone pipe			x			x
Stone tamper	x	x				
Bone effigy	x					
Antler comb		x				
Slate tablet		x				
Ceramic effigy				x		
Native American subsistence-related objects						
Ceramics	x	x	x	x	x	
Stone biface	x	x	x		x	
Stone point	x	x	x	x	x	
Stone scraper	x	x	x	x	x	
Stone drill	x	x		x		
Stone sinker	x		x		x	
Stone celt	x	x				
Stone axe		x				
Stone cup		x				
Whetstone	x	x				
Hammerstone	x		x			
Anvil	x	x				x

Table 5.3 continued

	Mohawk					Seneca
	1580–1614	1614–26	1635–46	1646–66	1666–79	1715–74
Muller	x	x	x			
Pestle	x			x		
Metate			x			
Stone hoe	x					
Straightener/Spoke shave		x	x	x		
Bown awl	x	x		x		
Bone punch	x	x				
Bone needle	x	x				
Bone harpoon	x	x				
Bone pin		x				
Bone flaker		x				
Shuttle		x				
Bone knife				x		
Core	x	x	x	x		
Flakes	x	x	x	x	x	x
Local gunflint			x	x		
Pyrites	x	x				
Strike-a-Light		x				
European social and ritual objects						
Glass beads	x	x	x	x	x	x
Copper beads	x	x				
Brass beads	x	x	x			x
Other glass			x			
Copper jewelry	x	x				
Bells					x	
Brass jewelry	x	x	x	x		x
Tinklers		x	x			
Coils		x	x			
Buckle		x				
Iron ring		x	x			
Metal ring				x	x	
Tubes		x				
Religious medal/ring						
Metal pipe		x				x
Lead objects/effigy		x	x			
White ball clay			x	x	x	x
Pewter			x			
Silver			x			

Continued on next page

Table 5.3 continued

	Mohawk					Seneca
	1580–1614	1614–26	1635–46	1646–66	1666–79	1715–74
European subsistence-related objects						
Iron axe	x	x	x		x	
Iron knife	x	x	x	x		
Iron nail	x	x	x	x	x	x
Iron awl		x	x	x		x?
Iron chisel		x				
Iron pick	x					
Iron rod			x			x
Iron fishhook			x			
Iron lock				x		
Iron hoe		x			x	
Iron scraper					x	x
Iron sword		x				
Iron gouge		x				
Iron kettle part		x				
Copper point	x		x			
Brass point	x	x	x			x
Brass kettle part	x	x		x		x
Copper saw		x				
Copper knife		x				
Brass thimble			x			
Gun part			x			
Musket ball		x				
Lead shot		x	x			x
Lead pig			x		x	
Lead sprue			x			
Lead strip				x		
European gunflint			x	x	x	x
European ceramic		x	x			x
Prunt			x			

Source: Snow 1995; Jordan 2002

tools were accepted, although some indigenous tools were retained, especially multipurpose items such as knives, and tools such as scrapers that had no easy equivalent in imported items. Expedient stone tools continued to be used. The use of bone as a raw material for tools declines after the second period, probably replaced by iron for awls. This analysis can only be seen as suggestive, since a number of unresolved issues affects assemblage composition. One of these is assemblage size—which is particularly relevant for its effect on variety or diversity. Other factors include site function, pothunting and other collecting biases, and postdeposition site disturbances. The potential impact of these elements complicates interpretations but does not negate the conclusions suggested here, namely, that Mohawks adopted European ornaments and tools in accordance with their own needs. At first, when trading was going well, they used many more European goods, although they still relied on their own ornaments, pipes, and other ritually important items, as well as certain kinds of tools. In later periods they continued this pattern, replacing certain indigenous classes of material (e.g., bone) with metal, but may have had reduced access to European commodities.

SENECA MORTUARY DATA

A similar examination of material recovered from Seneca mortuary sites offers a significant comparison, except that these are mortuary not domestic sites, and the location of the Senecas as keepers of the western door meant that they had less contact with Europeans than the Mohawks. Three large sites from the Rochester Museum of Science collections date from the late sixteenth to mid–seventeenth centuries: Adams, dated at 1575–1585; Dutch Hollow, from 1605–1620; and Power House, occupied from 1640–1655. The meaning of finding objects in graves is quite different from retrieving them from domestic deposits, at least in terms of purposefulness and perceived utility in the afterlife, but mortuary sites are subject to the same kinds of assemblage problems as domestic ones, especially pothunting, postdeposition disturbance, and uneven retrieval of information.

While the time period for the Seneca sites is shorter than for the Mohawk ones, the trends seen during the comparable period are similar. The use of European subsistence-related and social and religious items increases over time. Because of a lag in the recovery of European material from Seneca sites, there are few items from the first two periods, but in Power House, dated from 1640, both social/religious and utilitarian items increase substantially, as they do in Mohawk sites during the period between 1614 and 1626, probably as a reflection of the Mohawk geographical position and closer location to European traders. At the same time, there is no major decrease in the use of Native American social/religious objects, while subsistence-related items begin to decline in certain activities. Those tools used in woodworking (celts and chisels) and stoneworking (hammerstones and choppers) are not present at the Power House site, but stone projectile points and knives and a range of other bone tools persist. Abrading, polishing, and grinding continue to require aboriginal tools. As table 5.4 suggests, many new European objects are added by 1640, some of which make use of European raw materials (iron and brass) for traditional objects such as projectile points. With the exception of a lag in gaining access to European goods, the pattern seen in Seneca and Mohawk inventories is similar. In both settings, and in both domestic and mortuary contexts, indigenous items, especially those with social and ritual functions, continued to persist in importance even when European things were available, while certain tools were replaced by similar ones made of European materials.

A more quantitatively precise analysis of the Seneca sites is possible because they were analyzed by the same group of individuals at the Rochester Museum and Science Center, with Charles Wray the initial analyst and Martha Sempowski and Lorraine Saunders continuing the task after Wray's death. For this analysis, I have classified objects into the categories used by Rogers (1990), which represent specific tasks or activities. Again, using the same three sites—Adams, Dutch Hollow, and Power House (table 5.5)—we see that Native American tools used for certain functional activities (perforating, knapping, scraping, cutting, and chopping) decline over time in mortuary analyses, to varying degrees. Other task-oriented activities (smoothing, grinding, abrading, and containing) continue to be reflected in Native American artifacts and increase a bit. Native American objects associated with social and ritual activities (smoking, worshiping, and wearing ornaments) increase over time, the last of these substantially, while less traditional equipment used for painting appears.

European tools associated with piercing, fastening, cutting, and containing increase drastically in mortuary context over this time span, while those related to chopping, perforating, and joining increase slightly. Smoking and religious equipment become more significant in both Native American and European artifacts; the latter is represented by Jesuit crosses and rings, although they are rarely recovered. Objects of personal adornment maintain consistently high numbers, except for an interesting reduction in Native American items at Dutch Hollow that corresponds to a sharp increase in European items at that site. The increase in the mortuary inclusion of both Native American and European jewelry in graves suggests a change in burial custom, and it seems likely that the increase in the burial of pots (especially European ones) implies a similar process. It is only in equipment related to cutting and piercing activities that imported tools seem to replace indigenous ones. If more of the Seneca burials had been identified as to sex, it might have been possible to determine whether any of these changes in artifact use were related to gendered activities.

In addition, interesting information on the use of significant European goods that would not be recovered archaeologically is reported in documents. Clothing, dress, and the decoration of the body can be highly significant material elements, capable of expressing social statements at varying scales. Captivity narratives provide one example. Mary White Rowlandson, an English woman who lived for several months among a group of Nipmuck, Narragansett, and Wampanoag who had captured her in Massachussetts in 1676, reports her distress on seeing "a company of Indians to us, near 30, all on horseback. My heart skipped within me thinking that they had been Englishmen at the first sight of them, for they were dressed in English apparel with hats, white neckcloths, and sashes about their waists, and ribbons upon their shoulders" (Kestler 1990:49). Her account also details the use of Holland lace from a pillowcase for an Indian child's shirt and describes her master and his wife, dressed for a dance:

> He was dressed in his Holland shirt, with great laces sewed at the tail of it; he had his silver buttons, his white stockings, his garters were hung round with shillings, and he had girdles of wampum upon his head and shoulders. . . . She [his wife] had a Kersey coat; and covered with girdles of wampum from the loins upward, her arms from her elbows to her hand were covered with bracelets. . . . She had fine red stockings and white shoes, her hair powdered and face painted red, that was always before black. (Kestler 1990:58)

This description of two Narragansetts in the seventeenth century suggests that they had taken objects valued by Europeans (British in this case) for conspicuous display in a ritual performance, although it is worth noting that they were also wearing wampum and face paint. In conjunction with the previous description of

Table 5.4
Seneca Mortuary Site Inventories

	Adams 1575–1585	Dutch Hollow 1605–1620	Power House 1640–1655
Native American subsistence-related objects			
Ceramics	x	x	x
Stone core		x	
Stone point	x		x
Stone knife	x	x	x
Stone scraper	x		
Stone celt	x	x	
Stone chisel	x		
Maul	x		
Hammerstones	x		
Chopper	x		
Polishing stones		x	x
Grinding stones		x	x
Sandstone abrader			x
Graver	x		x
Antler flaker		x	x
Beaver incisor	x	x	
Bone point			x
Bone awl	x	x	x
Bone fish hook	x	x	x
Bone chisel			x
Local gunflint	x		
Native American social and ritual objects			
Shell beads	x		x
Shell jewelry	x		
Stone jewelry	x	x	x
Animal teeth/claws	x	x	
Wampum	x	x	
Red ochre	x	x	x
Yellow ochre		x	
Paint mortar		x	
Bone comb		x	x

Table 5.4 continued

	Adams 1575–1585	Dutch Hollow 1605–1620	Power House 1640–1655
Bone jewelry		x	x
Turtle carapace	x	x	x
Ceramic pipe		x	
Bone effigy		x	x
Antler pendant		x	
Bone whistle			x
European subsistence-related objects			
Metal axe			x
Iron knife	x	x	x
Iron point			x
Iron spike	x		
Iron celt			x
Iron scraper			x
Metal fish hook			x
Metal awl	x	x	x
Brass point			x
Brass kettle			x
Gun parts			x
Bone knife handle			?
European gunflint			x
European social and ritual objects			
Glass beads	x	x	x
Copper beads	x		
Brass beads	x	x	x
Glass buttons			x
Brass jewelry	x	x	x
Bells		x	x
Tinkler/rattle			x
Iron ring			x
Iron bangle			x
Jesuit ring			x
European pipe			

Sources: Wray et al. 1987; Sempowski and Saunders 2001.

Table 5.5
Seneca Mortuary Sites, Rogers Analysis of Artifact Classes

Sites	Adams (2)		Dutch Hollow (2)		Power House	
No. burials	160		173		229	
Date	1575–1585		1605–1620		1640–1655	
Native American						
Pierce	15	0.09	26	0.15	14	0.06
Perforate	25	0.16	1	0.01	16	0.07
Pound	3	0.02	1	0.01	0	0.00
Knapp	16	0.10	4	0.02	10	0.04
Scrape	8	0.05	7	0.04	0	0.00
Smooth	0	0.00	1	0.01	5	0.02
Grind	1	0.01	9	0.05	4	0.02
Cut	8	0.05	1	0.01	2	0.01
Chop	10	0.06	0	0.00	1	0.00
Abrade	3	0.02	8	0.05	9	0.04
Contain	56	0.35	85	0.49	87	0.38
Paint	26	0.16	26	0.15	16	0.07
Smoke	4	0.03	14	0.08	21	0.09
Worship	6	0.04	14	0.08	20	0.09
Opa*	74	0.46	43	0.25	169	0.74
Game	0	0.00	10	0.06	2	0.01
European						
Pierce	1	0.01	4	0.02	43	0.19
Perforate	1	0.01	5	0.03	12	0.05
Join	2	0.01	0	0.00	7	0.03
Fasten	0	0.00	0	0.00	18	0.08
Cut	1	0.01	14	0.08	49	0.21
Chop	1	0.01	16	0.09	21	0.09
Contain	2	0.01	10	0.06	64	0.28
Smoke	0	0.00	3	0.02	10	0.04
Worship	0	0.00	0	0.00	3	0.01
Opa*	71	0.44	127	0.73	124	0.54

opa = object of personal adornment

Sources: Wray et al. 1987; Sempowski and Saunders 2001.

a group of Indians who appeared at a distance to be English because of their clothing, it is evident that indigenous people were appropriating for their own use some European things that they found particularly significant. They were not masquerading as British but were accepting some elements of British dress because it fit their own ideas of symbolic meaning. Note the colors mentioned (red, white, black) and the use of silver; white lace and ribbons would also have had analogues (deerskin fringe, bone beads, wampum) in their own semiotic system. Stern (1998) provides an interesting example from 1690 of Pueblos wearing Spanish clothing while hunting buffalo in order to fool the Utes into leaving them alone.

Figure 5.5. Sir John Caldwell, holding "tomahawk" and wearing elements of Native American clothing (headdress, jewelry, leggings, and moccasins).

Many European colonists are known to have worn items of indigenous apparel, although it is hard to know how common the practice was. An eighteenth-century portrait of a British officer, Sir John Caldwell (see figure 5.5), shows him wearing "an Indian headdress, breechcloth, leggings and moccasins, and Indian jewelry in his nose and ears" (Calloway 1997). A portrait is a posed setting; one can imagine Caldwell using the occasion to show off his acquisitions. It does not imply that this was his regular apparel. The same volume has a portrait of Hendrick (figure 5.6) (Tejonihokarawa, misidentified as Theyanoguin; Dean Snow,

Figure 5.6. Hendrick or Tejonihokawara (misidentified as Theyanoguin), with English hat, coat, waistcoat, and shirt given to him by King George II, in London.

personal communication 2001) painted in 1710 on his visit to London. He has facial tattoos and is holding a string of wampum but wears English clothing. In this case I suspect the outfit was probably meant to incorporate him, and by extension, the Iroquois into the British universe. A recent paper by Loren (2000) examines ethnic "cross-dressing" in the American Southeast, especially Louisiana, and the ways in which practices of dress contested orthodox codes of status, particularly among Europeans. Portraits by European artists such as George Catlin, Charles Bird King, Karl Bodmer, and the photographer, Edward Curtis, often display important Indians wearing a mixture of indigenous and European clothing. A group of fascinating Plains Indian drawings (the ledger drawings) of their own and European subjects depict the same mixture. It has been suggested than Native Americans assumed items of European apparel to indicate their ability to act as go-betweens or mediators in contact situations (Loren 2000). In any case, what may be most significant for this study is that the Dutch did not apparently assume any items of Iroquois attire.

Social and Sexual Distance

The social distance maintained by the Dutch between themselves and the Indians is expressed in a number of ways: the spatial separation between settlements of Dutch and indigenous peoples, the absence of attempts to convert them or incorporate them into "civilized" society, or even learn to speak with them, and, what I focus on here, the limited sexual contact between Dutch men and Iroquois women.

The Mohawk may have derived an unintended benefit from the lack of proselytizing. The Huron commented that the Dutch "have preserved the Iroquois by allowing them to live in their own fashion, just as the black Gowns have ruined the Hurons by preaching the faith to them" (Thwaites 1959:43:291). There were some conversions. The Jesuits report baptizing 3,000 Iroquois (not just Mohawk) between 1668 and 1679 (Richter 1992:116), but close to half of these (1,200) died right after baptism and presumably represent "death-bed" conversions. An Anglican missionary, John Ogilvie (later assigned "to the Negro congregation at Trinity Church"; Hamilton 1961:331) came to the Mohawk in the 1750s and reported some success. He baptized 41 men and 37 women during the 10 years he spent with the Mohawk, although by this time only a few of them were left in the area.

In many colonial situations, interaction between invader and invaded was not limited to the exchange of objects. Sexual and social intercourse characteristically took place between the two groups, especially because the colonists were often, especially in the early days, predominantly men. This interaction was marked by the same misperceptions of who "the other" was and what he or she wanted as other intercultural transactions, including trade. Characteristically, however, a range of sexual interactions occurred, from rape to consensual sex, to marriage and other conjugal arrangements. What was different in the Dutch New Netherlands was the relative absence of this kind of interaction, except among a few individuals who were regularly "in the woods," such as Van Curler, and are known to have fathered children by Mohawk women.

Documentary information offers hints as to the extent of sexual contact. DeVries in 1643 says, they "gave us their daughters to sleep with by whom we begot children" (cited in Ceci 1977:190), and a comment published in the *Documentary History of the State of New York* reports that while married women were unwilling to sleep with Dutch men, the single ones were very friendly (Dunn 1994:78; O'Callaghan 1849–1851:3:41). There is little evidence that Dutch men expressed extensive sexual interest in Indian women. Undoubtedly some sexual contact occurred between Dutch and Mohawk, but very few marriages or households were established. Only two Dutch men are recorded as having fathered half-Indian children: Cornelius Van Slyck had four or five (three sons and one or two daughters) and Arent Van Curler had one daughter. Both had been appointed as emissaries to the Mohawk and thus had frequent contact with them. Van Curler was extremely close to the Mohawk, as noted in several comments by them, and by his employer (Van Rensselaer) in letters admonishing him "not to mix with the heathen or savage women" or stating "I hear you spend too much time in the woods" (Van Laer 1908:29, 442). Identifying half-Dutch children is complicated by the fact that they would likely have been raised as Mohawk and thus their birth may not have been noted. One of the known half-Dutch children was either cast out by her maternal Mohawk kin, or left them when she became a practicing Christian. Van Slyck's daughter Hilletie married a Dutchman, Daniel van Olinda, and moved to Schenectady in 1680 (Richter 1992:107), which was for a period of time a frontier-like community, attractive to "half-breeds" and Europeans returned by their Indian captors (Burke 1991:150).

Possible explanations for the lack of sexual contact could be either that an ample supply of Dutch women came to the New World from the beginning of the colony or that Calvinist doctrine viewed such connections as abhorrent, but neither can be demonstrated. In comparison with the American Southwest, the climate in the Hudson Valley was better for European women, and the trip was shorter, but it was a while before Dutch women wanted to emigrate and settle there. There was one European woman in Albany in 1623 (O'Callaghan 1849–1851:3:50), while the ratio of women to men among the 174 immigrants to Rensselaerswyck between 1630 and 1644 was low. There were 102 single men, 2 single women, 16 wives, and 51 "dependents," which may have included other wives as well as children and minors. The ratio ranges from an extreme of 1:26 in 1637 to 1:3 (in 1643–1644), but all the women who came during this period were married except two. From 1644 to 1657, the trend shifted from mostly single men to mostly families (Rink 1986:146, 159), with 438 men, 228 women, and 397 children making the trip to New Netherland (O'Callaghan 1849–1851:3:52–63). The ratios are lower, ranging from 1:4.25 to 1:1.1, with almost half of this group of women single. Still in 1654, De Sille (1920:101) wrote back to the Netherlands complaining of the lack of women. While fewer women than men were arriving, some of the children grew up to be wives, and many women were widowed and remarried, so that the initial shortage was alleviated to some degree.

Calvinist doctrine may not have favored intermarriage, as suggested by the disapproval expressed in letters to specific colonists and general instructions as to how colonists should behave that warn of such connections. However, these religious prohibitions did not prevent Dutch immigrants to Batavia, under the sponsorship of the East India Company, from forming extensive and long-term relationships with indigenous women there, apparently with VOC endorsement. Examination of Dutch behavior there is very enlightening. The colony was established in 1595 and was much more successful than New Netherland, lasting for 200 years. It was a trading post, centered on the spice trade (pepper, nutmeg, cloves, cinnamon, and mace), and on tea, silk, cotton, and dyes. Plant products, unlike furs, were renewable. It was also a much stronger magnet for emigrants: 126,000 Dutch went to Batavia during the period of New Netherland's existence (Bruijn et al. 1987:144), in comparison with about 9,000 who went to the New World. Asia may have been perceived as a better place to develop wealth. The men who went to both places were probably somewhat similar, described as "ne'er do wells" (Rink 1986:159), or rough around the edges, but clearly not successful at home. It is more difficult to get a sense of numbers of women migrants; sometimes they were not tabulated. When the ship *Verenigde Provincien* left Wielinger for Batavia in 1652, it made an unplanned stop in the Canary Islands "to get rid of some women who had been surprised by the sudden departure" (Bruijn et al. 1987:109). On another voyage, two children were born during the passage in 1659 (Bruijn et al. 1987:131). In 1670–1671, ships carried 33 free male burghers and 84 women and 91 children, many or most of whom were presumably family members (Bruijn et al. 1987:147). However, the stream of emigrant families soon dried up, and very few European women made the trip.

The women who were willing to go to the East originally were socially marginal individuals, such as poor orphans or those described as the dregs of society (Abeyasekere 1987:14; Taylor 1983:12–13). Company officials could bring their wives, but after some years of problems, the VOC began to discourage European women, telling them that the tropical sun was fatal to them (Abeyasekere 1987:14). The real problem for the company was that middle-class Dutch women wanted to go home as soon as their husbands had accumulated some wealth—a practice that was quite disruptive to the colonial enterprise. For ordinary employees, the company began to encourage bachelorhood, limited marriage to Asian women, or the taking of "concubines," women with whom they lived but were not married to (Abeyasekere 1987:20; Blusse 1986: 81; Taylor 1983:14, 16, 45), as long as they were Christian (i.e., baptized) and free. Local women had fewer health problems with the climate and the company did not want men to repatriate; if a man was married to an Asian women, he was not allowed to repatriate while his family lived (Blusse 1986:173; Taylor 1983:29). Thus, many VOC servants started "real" families in Batavia (Bruijn et al. 1987:147). The colonial administrators saw marriage as an expedient means to good relations with native people and a way to create "a harmonious climate in which colonial exploitation could take place" (Bagley 1973:40).

A complex multiethnic culture developed in which mestizo men could become soldiers, and the women soldiers' wives. They were, of course, lower in status than European men, with or without Dutch wives, and were less educated than the Dutch, as there were no clergy or schools for them (Taylor 1983:xix, xx, 8, 45, 76). Other ethnic groups in the colony included a substantial Chinese population that farmed, and Mardijkers, who were almost as elite as the Dutch, spoke Portuguese, and were Christian; many of them were descended from Indian slaves from the Portuguese colony at Goa (Blusse 1986:165; Taylor 1983:47). The Dutch are described as tolerant of color differences, especially in contrast to the English in India (Bagley 1973:66).

In this setting, class and ethnicity intersected, and status was expressed by a number of important material symbols (Taylor 1983:50, 59, 62–68). Sumptuary laws offer strong support of the symbolic importance of certain kinds of clothing and body adornment items in many colonial contexts. Specific things, such as parasols, carriages, and gold ornaments, were reserved for the use of the elite, and were not to be used by the colonized, even if through marriage or concubinage they had access to them. Interestingly, these were usually quite visible things, such as parasols and carriages, gold buttons and buckles on men's clothing, pearls and the uses of certain fabrics for women, and the number of slaves that could appear in public with a member of the household (Taylor 1983:57). The ethnic intersection extended beyond the Asian appropriation of symbols of European prestige. Dutch men adopted Asian furniture, domestic arrangements, language, and slave practices, while Asians took up European religion, dress, names, manners, and occupations (Taylor 1983:50, 61). Customs acquired in mixed households reflected gendered aspects of culture in particular, so that European traits were allocated to men's domain and public spheres and Asian customs to domestic and women's spheres.

The absence of social distance in Jacatra (Jakarta) meant that race and class intersected, as they did in the southwestern United States, and in both cases race played a somewhat subordinate role to class. In the nineteenth century, after the VOC was extinct, its policy was reversed: Dutch women were brought in and interracial marriage was banned, for another set of historically contingent reasons (Stoler 1992). Regardless of the fascinating mutability of Dutch policy, this account demonstrates that social distance in New Netherland was not likely to have been defined for reasons of Calvinism, racist ideas, or qualities inherent to Dutch character. The Dutch colony in South Africa at the Cape of Good Hope offers another example of Dutch behavior with indigenous women. It was more similar to the Mohawk situation than the Indonesian one in the infrequent interbreeding occurring there, although some Khoikhoi women did bear Dutch children. There, too, the leadership of the colony brought their wives, and it has been suggested that interaction with indigenous people was limited as the colonial outpost's primary function was to provide meat for ship crews as they stopped at the Cape on the way to and from the East (Hall 1997:230; Schrire 1995:66).

Several factors may be responsible for the social distance maintained between Mohawk and Dutch. One is the Dutch view that the Mohawk were savages (wilden), which would have led to the perception of them as too much "the other." This would not have been their perception of indigenous peoples in the East; Asians were from a state society and were politically complex, stratified, and more familiar (Rothschild 1996). European men may have also found Asian women, with their lighter skins, more acceptable. And there may have been a certain fear of the Mohawk, whose behavior in war was described vividly by many Europeans; this fear is visible in the design of Dutch New World settlements, with their walls and fortifications. A second factor was the priority placed on trade above all, and the concern about competition among traders. Since most settlers were drawn by the opportunity to trade, the Dutch laws designed to regulate trade, forbidding colonists to establish personal relationships with Indians so that all would have equal access, were taken seriously. However, a third important factor lies in the limited incentive for Mohawk women to become involved in liaisons with Dutch men, which, owing to the power and the political roles of significance they held in their own society, was less than would be true for women in many other groups. Dean Snow (1994:121) comments that Iroquois women were less available to or interested in marriages with French traders than Algonkian women were because of their significance in their own culture and also because they were at home in their villages while the men were involved in political negotiation with Europeans. Batavian indigenous society, in common with more complex sociopolitical systems, disempowered women, who might, therefore, find marriage to a European appealing.

Conclusion

Material culture—both shared and unique—sheds light on identity construction in the two very different contact situations under consideration in this volume. The relevant circumstances of the two settings include environmental differences, which affect the ease of access to European goods and the conditions of settlement, and attitudes toward cohabitation between indigenous women and European men.

The analysis of stone and metal tools and ceramics in the Southwest reveals a flexible and evolving situation, with the use of these items shifting during the colonial period. Pueblo and Spanish households are more readily distinguished prior to the revolt than after it, while Hispano and Pueblo inhabitants share many components of their material culture in response to a common set of circumstances. Ceramics do not readily function as identity markers in this region since Spanish and Hispanic settlers relied primarily on Pueblo ceramics and had only small quantities of majolica. Identity would have been clear through cultural traits such as language and through clothing. Genetically, there was a considerable amount of overlap between groups.

In the Northeast, the identities of inhabitants is never in doubt, owing to the social distance maintained between Mohawk and Dutch. Indian artifacts are rare in Dutch sites. European goods are common at Mohawk and Seneca sites, and although they are frequent, they are not adopted uniformly. The Mohawks continued to use their own tools and ornaments but adopted European ones that fit their own needs. They kept important social and ritual items in use; some of these are analogous to "inalienable possessions" in that their users would not replace them with European objects. While Weiner (1992; see also Mills 2001) uses the phrase to refer to items not available for exchange, I think the same principle can apply to those objects that were too important to stop using or to replace with a European analogue. Despite their striking differences, both settings provided considerable room for individual agency, and women, in particular, were crucial in defining identities—their own and others'—and futures.

6

Understanding Complexity

This book began with a paradox and a question. The Spanish went to New Mexico with the intention of gaining mineral wealth by controlling the labor, the bodies, and also the souls of Pueblo people. The Dutch had a simpler and seemingly more benign agenda, namely, to make a profit on the beaver trade. Why then are there no Mohawks remaining in the Mohawk River Valley while the Pueblo peoples are still present? In answering this question I have relied on a great deal of historical detail as background and have considered two very different approaches in order to explain the end result: one concentrates on cultural-philosophical factors, the other on material-economic ones, which are best manifest in archaeological data. The first takes into account differences between Catholicism and Protestantism and variations between the Mohawks and the Pueblos in social structure and accessibility. The role played by women in the two settings is crucial. The second uses the role of goods to monitor interaction between peoples. It focuses on geography (the Hudson River's accessibility as a trade corridor), the economic orientation of the Dutch as a mercantile capitalist and urban nation, in contrast to the medieval perspective of the Spanish; and the resulting material flows—notably of European goods—that entered each indigenous area. In each case, the interactions between the two societies, indigenous and European, reveal the ways in which each party attempted to control the situation, the areas in which each was successful, and those in which they were not.

These cases represent two different forms of colonialism and associated repression, one quite explicit and the other more subtle. In the Southwest, the Spanish goals for the Pueblos amounted to cultural annihilation, which failed to occur and which paradoxically may have produced the kind of resistance that led to survival. The other system kept indigenous people in a separate "nonhuman" box, interacting with them only for purposes of trade, with the trade involving unsustainable resources (Sider 1986).

The Pueblos and the Spanish

The differences between the Spanish and the Dutch were vast and had a great deal to do with final outcomes. Pueblo-Mohawk differences were also important, but perhaps less extreme. Catholicism required a rigorous control of indigenous peoples encountered in colonial adventures. Much of this control had as its main purpose the exploitation of labor and the extraction of a range of services, including sexual ones, from colonial subjects. This control was justified as a means to securing the salvation of souls. Ironically, these demands had two repercussions that fostered the preservation of Pueblo society, although Pueblo retention of much of their land played an important role as well. First, these demands strengthened resistance to religious control and motivated Pueblos to maintain their ritual despite the insistence on conversion. Second, they helped create an intermediate society, in which most of the women were Indian (from Mexico and various southwestern groups). The men (and some women) of this society claimed a Spanish identity, often asserting direct descent from Spain although almost all of their mothers were born in the New World, as the Spanish had been in North America for a century before the first settlement in New Mexico. The mestizo culture was the foundation of Hispanic culture, melding a variety of defined racial/ethnic categories. It incorporated material elements from both cultural ancestors and is visible in archaeological deposits combining Pueblo-made pottery and stone tools with Spanish objects of metal and small amounts of majolica. Hispanic diet similarly fused Indian corn and Spanish-imported sheep.

The Hispanic culture developed in the eighteenth century after the successful

Pueblo Revolt, when Spanish-descended immigrants began coming to New Mexico in greater numbers and Pueblo population had been reduced by European-borne disease. It included a range of immigrants who combined sheep-herding with farming and settled on small tracts of land, as well as genizaros captured by nomads and ransomed by the Spanish, and Indian women who had been sexually abused by Spanish men and could not go back to their own villages. The creation of this mixed culture acted to mutually define both Pueblo and Hispanic lifeways. Neither had a great advantage in the economy of the Southwest. The formal political power of the state was retained by men who claimed "purer" Spanish ancestry and sometimes had whiter skin. However, the two cultures, as well as other nomadic groups, were part of the same overall sphere, isolated from both Mexico and Spain in an environmentally difficult and agriculturally challenging setting. The Pueblos retained much of their land and continued to live in settlements that were architecturally similar to ancestral forms. They continued to practice traditional religious rituals, although Catholicism had entered their lives as well. They maintained their languages while learning others and maintained many aspects of their sociopolitical organization.

The continued persistence of Pueblo culture was due to the relatively equal power that accrued to both Spanish and Pueblos in spite of the initial Spanish attempts to dominate local peoples. Sheep farming offered a new form of subsistence, and the decimation of Pueblos by smallpox and other epidemic diseases made room for immigrants. The Spanish were unable to achieve control, found little of real extractive value, and modified their goals to conform to the reality of the situation. Their continued interest in the New Mexico colony was driven by their need to protect the territory from the encroachment of other European colonizers, rather than its economic success. Those who came after the Pueblo Revolt had relatively modest plans, aware that the expectations of the first wave of settlers had been unfulfilled. They adapted their material lives to incorporate locally available resources, while introducing some innovations more broadly—metal tools, horses, sheep, and fruit trees. Over time the two cultures became more similar in the details of material culture, although they differed in important ways. The survival of the Pueblos was based on their own power and Spanish failure to control the situation; the development of the Hispanic culture offered another cultural option for disenfranchised indigenous peoples and relates as well to the adaptability of women who were able to combine elements of two cultures, maintaining attributes of Indian culture and incorporating them in Hispanic domestic lives. Seeking sexual services, Spanish and Hispanic men often acquired domestic ones as well. In acquiring the labor of indigenous women, Hispanic men acquired their material culture.

The Mohawks and the Dutch

Neither the Dutch nor the Mohawks had reason or occasion to want to live in a mixed society. Since the Dutch did not typically take Mohawks or other women as servants, slaves, or captives, there were no Indian women who could not return to their homes because they were shamed; as well, Iroquois women had important and powerful roles in their own societies. Protestantism did not promote conversion, their urban backgrounds made the Dutch want to live in towns, there was no incentive to live among the Mohawks, and their focus on trade actually worked against intimacy with the Mohawks as the Dutch feared that some individuals would gain unequal access to furs. They clearly desired a distant relationship with the Mohawks, compartmentalized so that their only contact was in trade and some political negotiations. Since the Dutch were not socially distant from indigenous women in Batavia and in other colonies, I suggest that it was not a religious requirement but a pragmatic orientation that led to the development of codes of behavior designed for the specific setting and conditions.

The beaver trade had a number of significant, unanticipated—and devastating—impacts on the Iroquois as a whole, but perhaps it was felt most among the Mohawks as those who were closest to and most involved with the Dutch. The location and characteristics of the Hudson River made the interior of what is today New York State accessible. It allowed the Dutch the opportunity to control a rich fur-bearing region, and they took immediate advantage, extracting well over a hundred thousand skins in the relatively brief period of their colonial control. In order to get these furs, they provided large quantities of European goods to the Mohawks. Although there was no immediate wholesale adoption of these goods, and the Mohawk did not use them in identical ways to the Dutch, the advantages of metal for cutting and piercing, and cloth for clothing manufacture became clear relatively quickly. Other trade goods—such as glass beads and materials of specific colors and qualities—were appealing to Native Americans because they fit into existing symbolic systems. The Mohawks became involved in the world economy but in a marginal role determined by the Dutch. As the beaver supply shrank, their ability to achieve their goals was reduced and they became impoverished and marginal members of this economy. Their own subsistence and settlement pattern had been negatively affected by the quest for furs, ultimately in devastating proportions.

The Dutch did not set out to co-opt the Mohawks and impoverish them, but in classifying the Mohawks as providers of a commodity, they had no particular concern for them. The period of formal Dutch control of the colony was brief, and the impact of disease and poverty had not yet reached its peak when it ended in 1664. The Mohawks did well in trade, extending their search for furs to other areas and peoples, and they successfully negotiated political relations with the Dutch, but as war and disease diminished their population, their social structure was affected. Many of the Mohawks left the Mohawk Valley beginning early in the eighteenth century, with the few relatively affluent ones remaining finally leaving after the American Revolution because they had allied themselves with the British. They sold their land; it was their last valuable resource. Their move to Canada was an adaptive success in perpetuating their culture, but in some sense they had no choice, both for political reasons and because they could not maintain their way of life in the Hudson and Mohawk Valleys.

The Importance of Goods and Their Exchange

Throughout this work I have stressed the significance of material manifestations of interaction as the way to understand the process of colonial entanglements, the degree of interdependence, and the formation of identities. The difference between the two pairs that are described here is seen in the flows of goods and labor between them, and is expressed in archaeological terms through settlement pattern and landscape, through subsistence information, and in artifact assemblages. In the Southwest, Pueblo labor and services were appropriated and in "exchange" the Spanish offered/imposed Christianity. A limited Spanish dominance appears in the pre-revolt period in the exclusive control of some resources (such as sheep) and better access to metal by Spanish settlers. After the revolt, the Pueblos obtained sheep, which became economically important but also contributed to environmental degradation. They also gained more access to metal tools, although metal was such a scarce commodity that Hispanos as well as Pueblos used stone tools in addition to metal ones.

The post-revolt period was marked by greater acceptance of Pueblo religious practices by the friars, demonstrating the failure of Spanish colonial power. The location of refuge settlements is also a marker of events just prior to and after the revolt, as is the movement of peoples seen in changing ceramic styles. The early decline in site numbers may derive from the Spanish policy of consolidation, but even prior to the revolt some Pueblos moved to smaller sites that may have served for refuge in less accessible locations than the Rio Grande Valley. The later and striking decline in numbers of sites is a reflection of population loss due to disease and emigration to the western pueblos. The continued maintenance of the New Mexico colony was driven by the need to protect Spanish territory.

The similarity in material culture between Pueblo and Spanish sites reflects the degree to which they were involved in a single overarching economic and cultural sphere, mediated in large part by women. This should not be taken to mean that there were no differences between Hispanic and Pueblo peoples, or that there was no social hierarchy. Certain goods that were not shared (elaborate clothing of silk and lace, precious metal objects, both sacred and profane, for the Spanish; symbols of office and ritually crucial objects for the Pueblos) would not appear in archaeological assemblages and would not have been used in daily life but represented cultural capital in Bourdieu's (1984) sense. It was possession and knowledge of these things rather than frequent use that mattered and validated the status of their holders. Some of these would have been the most significant and inalienable objects in both cultures and would have been the meaningful markers that "stabilized and made visual the categories of culture" (Douglas and Isherwood 1996) in the Southwest. Language was also essential in defining identities. Spanish was both a marker of Hispanic culture and a reflection of attempted hegemony. The retention of indigenous languages became a form of resistance as well as an identity marker.

Again, the contrast between the Rio Grande Valley and the Hudson Valley offers a way to clarify each context. The distance between Mohawks and Dutch is clearly seen in settlement location and structure, in the early presence of fortifications (which the Dutch maintained although the Iroquois stopped living in stockaded villages before Dutch settlement). The social distance and lack of integration between Dutch and Mohawk societies is seen in the one-way flow of manufactured goods. New Netherland Dutch archaeological assemblages include delft plates and tiles, Dutch cooking pots, white clay pipes made in the Netherlands, and almost no Mohawk objects. Mohawk assemblages include copper and brass objects and ornaments, many glass beads, and iron tools. The return flow included Indian foods eaten in Dutch households, although they were prepared in Dutch ways, and beaver skins.

The forms of exchange that occurred in these two regions of North America differed to some degree, although gift exchange was characteristic of both settings, especially in the early stage; in the beaver trade, commodities were offered on both sides, by Mohawk and Dutch people, "commodities" being taken to mean something alienable, produced for exchange with the intention of receiving something in return (Appadurai 1986). The acquisition of pottery by the Spanish from Pueblo or genizaro women also may have involved commodity production—it was certainly that during the post-revolt phase of contact, and perhaps even before contact protohistoric Pueblo women may have been making pottery as a commodity (Mills 1995b). It is the moment of exchange that defines whether something is a commodity or a gift (Appadurai 1986), and both goods and people can function in either capacity, at different times. Genizaros represent an excellent example of individuals who were first defined in a commodified state (having been ransomed by Spanish individuals and working for them), were subsequently released and un-commodified, but were landless. They were ideal candidates to settle in the buffer settlements constructed around Santa Fe in the eighteenth century to protect the capital. Their reputed talent as soldiers got them land, and sometimes they acquired wealth as booty from fighting (Quintana and Kayser 1980).

The demand for and provision of services conformed to the same kinds of economic exchange that pertained to objects. For the most part, labor was extracted directly from Pueblo peoples by the Spanish and was indirectly acquired from the Mohawks through the incentive of trade goods that became desirable. One of the interesting differences between these contexts concerns the appropriation of women's domestic and sexual labor. The Dutch used this labor little if at all, while Spanish and Hispanic men made great use of it. In both parts of North America there is documentary evidence suggesting that women sometimes offered these services of their own volition, while in the Southwest in particular there is ample evidence of their forced extraction. Men were also required to perform labor, in the fields, in military service or other capacities, or indirectly by hunting beaver. In the Mohawk Valley I suspect that the apparent reluctance of Dutch men to exploit indigenous women's sexual services was matched by a lack of interest on the part of Mohawk women, although it may be that they had fewer opportunities to meet Dutch men than was true for Algonkian women (Snow 1994), who were sometimes willing to have a relationship with a European—either sexual or one that linked a range of women's activities together. If a Mohawk woman had had such a liaison, she would have kept as her own any children from that union.

Misperceptions and Identities

In both of these colonial examples, and in many others, there are striking examples of each society misunderstanding the other's intentions. Whether it was the difference between the offering of food as a gift, which was taken as tribute, or the implications of the "sale" of land, often meant as the sale of use rights but taken to include rights of disposal, these were crucial to the ultimate outcomes of colonial encounters in these and other case studies. Differences in dress and sometimes in attitudes toward sex on the part of indigenous women and men were also misinterpreted and taken as a sign of sexual availability, which suited colonial men's wishes.

A number of archaeologically visible elements are important monitors of all colonial relationships. Land use and the control of land are critical to the interaction and to an understanding of it. Land use is reflected in the variant landscapes that may exist within a single terrain. The connections between peoples are better understood through the congruities of these landscapes than through the concepts of boundaries and frontiers, which are limited and too concrete. A landscape view is more nuanced and allows for changing and multidimensional understandings and the complexity of cultural interactions in colonial settings. The landscape itself is made of layers of mind and memory as much as rock and dirt (Schama 1995:6). It is remarkable that even in the Rio Grande Valley, with the Spanish living among the Pueblos, the Pueblo landscape was theirs alone in many ways and remained private, with secret places. The Mohawks also retained control of their landscape as few Dutch wanted to enter it. The Pueblos retained much of their land, however, whereas the Mohawks ultimately gave theirs up and had to leave the Mohawk Valley, demonstrating at a very basic level the different outcomes of the situations being compared.

The contrast in identity formation and expression is another crucial element in this comparison. Ethnogenesis did not develop in the interaction between the Dutch and Mohawks, but it did in the interaction between the Spanish and Pueblos in the Southwest. The Spanish policy of control from within, with concomitant sexual intimacy, was responsible for the creation of a new people, the Hispanic people, with a unique identity. Though genetically a mixture of Spanish and Indian (including indigenous members of Mexican and New Mexican groups), socially they considered themselves separate from indigenous peoples. The notion of clearly manifest, stable ethnicities is not appropriate in situations like the Rio Grande Valley. Initially, the Spanish-defined castas represented an attempt to create racial identifications, but the system was impractical and unworkable. The establishment of the Hispanic culture took considerable time and ultimately reflected both Hispanic and indigenous ancestors. It also developed in opposition to Pueblo culture, and each was constructed to some degree, in contrast to the other.

Finding material signals of ethnic identities is easy in the Mohawk Valley for there is little chance of confusing Dutch and Mohawk sites because of the clear social distance between the peoples involved. Hispanic material culture, however, is a true mixture of both antecedents, with stone tools in use through at least the middle of the nineteenth century. The development of Hispanic pottery, thought to have occurred in the eighteenth century (Carillo 1997), may not have served as a meaningful identity marker. In some sense the lack of marking of Hispanic culture relates to the difficulty in gaining access to European goods, but there were items and practices in use that made identities clear, even though these are not as accessible through archaeology. Subsistence practices were rather similar in both settings because many basic foods themselves are unmarked, although control of domestic animals was reserved for Europeans through at least the early stages of interaction. Even though goods are neutral and their uses social (Douglas and Isherwood 1996), not all goods necessarily serve as social markers. We may, however, use similarities in assemblages as indicators of proximity and the interconnectedness of people. From this perspective, peoples living in the Rio Grande Valley were closely associated, regardless of their stated identity. The Dutch and the Mohawks were clearly connected, but in a different, less mutually dependent way. In both settings, identities would have been clear to all parties. Hispanic identity was less clearly marked because of limited access to European goods, but also because the Hispanos had indigenous ancestors. Mohawks retained clear expression of their own identity, even with the adoption of many European goods, selected to suit Mohawk needs. At the same time, the Mohawks retained their objects of traditional significance.

As this project has demonstrated, archaeological data can depict the interactions and forms of interconnections between peoples in colonial settings. In the past, as in the present, material aspects of peoples' lives convey important information about social situations. The use of spatial information, the analysis of food remains, and examination of utilitarian objects underline the dramatic differences between the two cases studies examined here. Interpreting all these forms requires a historicized knowledge of the culture and its context, especially in complex situations such as those described. It is also crucial to evaluate gendered control of various forms of goods. While much existing research has examined the material manifestations of identity, unmarked forms of material culture, such as foods or certain types of casual tools—often ignored in material culture studies—may produce highly significant knowledge about connections between peoples.

Appendix

The maps of changing settlement locations were created by Antoinette Wannebo of the Goddard Institute of Space Science using ARCINFO but necessarily rely on the work of a number of other scholars who have compiled the placement of sites. For the Mohawk area, I was fortunate to have access to a set of maps created by Dean Snow (1995), which he generously provided for me in electronic format.

Mapping the Southwest was much more complex at various periods of pueblo and Spanish history. I have compiled information from several major sources: Mera's *Population Changes in the Rio Grande Glaze-Paint Area* (1940); Schroeder's article from the *Handbook of North American Indians,* vol. 9, *Pueblos Abandoned in Historic Times* (1979); an article by Jonathan Haas and Winifred Creamer (Vierra 1992); and Marshall and Walt's (1984) Rio Abajo study. The map in figure 3.12 shows the areas covered by some of these researchers. Supplementary information comes from Mark Lycett's (1995) dissertation and a paper by Elinore Barrett (1997), published by the University of New Mexico. I have also consulted the well-organized site files of the State of New Mexico, which are an invaluable resource. Data on missions were taken from France Scholes and Lansing Bloom (1944, 1945), Benavides's memorial of 1630 (Ayer 1900–1901), and Dominguez's review of missions in existence in 1776 (1956).

Scholars who produced these major studies have not provided equal coverage for the area of concern to this project. Haas and Creamer discuss only the northern Rio Grande area, and Marshall and Walt cover only a narrow strip along the Rio Grande south of where the Rio Salado joins the Rio Grande. Some subareas are discussed only by Mera and Schroeder, or only by one of them. As well, their information sources vary. Mera makes use primarily of the archaeological information available at that time, while Schroeder relies on Spanish expedition descriptions of where the pueblos were as well as archaeological site data. Haas and Creamer and Marshall and Walt both have more current site file information. There is one additional issue of concern, namely, that sites are more reliably documented for the northern Rio Grande area (Rio Arriba [and Medio]—than the southern—Rio Abajo), which means that I have somewhat less confidence in the data from the latter area. These areas differ in several respects: topography and climate are obvious factors, but more significantly for this project, they differ in the survival of pueblo peoples after the revolt, as many fewer intact pueblos remained in the southern Rio Grande Valley than the northern for reasons discussed in chapter 2.

The data from these different sources also cover time periods that vary somewhat. Haas and Creamer use data that span the longest interval, beginning in 1450 and continuing in some cases to the present, but their article provides the most precise dating of all those scholars examining this area, as they have been systematically collecting stratigraphically ordered ceramic samples, trying to link them with dates derived from dendrochronology and using seriation to understand the relationship among Mera's types. Marshall and Walt's (1984:138) chronological scheme involves a period called "colonial," which dates from 1541 and the initial Spanish contact, to the late 1670s and the revolt, when the large Piro pueblos were abandoned. They use ceramic types to date sites (E and F glazes, local Escondido glaze, Polvadera and Lemitar polychrome wares, Spanish vessel forms and majolica) and architectural clues (large square rooms in grid patterns, adobe construction on stone footings, and chapel or church and compound block structures (Marshall and Walt 1984:139).

Site dating is a significant issue for the production of these maps. Unfortunately, the dating for most of the Pueblo sites is quite imprecise and is based largely on Mera's ceramic scheme (modifying Kidder's original chronology based on rim shape) for glazewares, in which they were divided into Glazes A through

F. He assigned dates to this scheme, using surface collections from a number of sites but never confirmed the dates with stratigraphic excavation or seriation. He used the glazewares to establish periods (his Periods 4 and 5 are 1515–1650 and 1650–1700, respectively), but I prefer to use his data to provide a rough, rather than a precise, framework. A number of later archaeologists have considered his dates and modified them, but most agree with the approximate beginning dates and especially with their order of manufacture (Warren and Snow 1976; Spielmann 1991; Earls 1982). I have selected those sites from his compendium that are from period 5, with only glaze F pottery. Occasionally I have included sites that he dates to periods 4 and 5, that have E and F glazes. However, discussion of the specific period for the manufacture of Glaze F can be found in the literature; Mera assigns it to 1650–1700, but independent confirmation from some contexts dated by tree rings indicates that Glaze F is associated with a seventeenth-century occupation, in the northern Rio Grande, although it may be the first half of the seventeenth century rather than the second (Creamer et al. 1994). Cordell and Earls (1984) think it was first made prior to 1580 or 1600, while at Pueblo del Encierro it seems to have been introduced between 1550 and 1575, and David Snow suggests that at Gran Quivira it was contemporary with glaze E wares (in Spielmann 1992: 109, 110). Most scholars seem to believe that the glazes were ordered correctly by Mera in terms of early to late manufacture and thus may be usable for relative dating. When a number of different glaze types are present, however, the most reliable indicator of period of occupation is represented by the latest glaze type. Glaze A, in particular, seems to have been manufactured over the entire glazeware period, making it less useful as a temporal marker. The question of why certain types, once established, apparently continue to be made is an interesting one that is beyond the scope of this work. There may be functional or social reasons for this situation, but it is worthy of focused consideration.

To ensure that the maps shown here are as accurate as possible, I located sites, when possible, on the basis of information from at least two sources. This represents my effort to compensate for imprecision in dating, and to be somewhat cautious. I discuss sites from south to north and refer to the linguistic/ethnic areas used by Mera, Schroeder, and others (and by the Spanish initially), although observers vary in the ways they group people, on the basis of different interpretations of similarities in linguistic data and material culture. My interest is not in classifying pueblos into these groups, but in locating them on the ground, and much of the discussion of site location relies on these groupings, which share, to some degree, similar histories and distinctive behavior.

The maps themselves are chronologically structured. Figure 3.1 shows pueblos recorded as existing at 1590, just prior to Spanish entry, taken as pre-Spanish occupation. Figure 3.2 shows the area where the Spanish concentrated their early efforts in 10 missions begun by approximately 1616 (Scholes and Bloom 1944:335). Figure 3.3 shows those pueblos in existence during a somewhat arbitrarily defined period during the first period of Spanish occupation of the Southwest, between 1626 and 1650, and missions that were in existence during the same period; and figure 3.7 shows those pueblos that seem to continue after the revolt and reoccupation (around 1700) and missions in existence after the revolt. Figures 3.4 to 3.6 and 3.8 to 3.10 are designed to show changes between occupation periods. Figures 3.4 and 3.8 indicate those pueblos and missions that have continued to be occupied from the previous period; figures 3.5 and 3.9 show pueblos and missions no longer occupied that had been in use during the previous period; and figures 3.6 and 3.10 indicate pueblos and missions newly settled during the period in question.

Bibliography

Abbink, Emily K., and John R. Stein

1977 An Historical Perspective on Adaptive Systems in the Middle Rio Grande. In *Archaeological Investigations in Cochiti Reservoir, New Mexico,* vol. 1, edited by Jan V. Biella and Richard C. Chapman, pp. 151–171. National Park Service, Albuquerque, N.M.

Abeyasekere, Susan

1987 *Jakarta: A History.* Oxford University Press, New York.

Adams, Charles E.

1989 Passive Resistance: Hopi Responses to Spanish Contact and Conquest. In *Columbian Consequences,* vol. 1, edited by David Hurst Thomas, pp. 77–91. Smithsonian Institution Press, Washington, D.C.

1991 *The Origin and Development of the Pueblo Katsina Cult.* University of Tucson, Tucson, Ariz.

1996 The Pueblo III–Pueblo IV Transition in the Hopi Area, Arizona. In *The Prehistoric Pueblo World, AD 1150–1350,* edited by Michael A. Adler, pp. 48–58. University of Arizona Press, Tucson.

Alexander, Rani

1998 Afterword: Toward an Archaeological Theory of Culture Contact. In *Studies in Culture Contact: Interaction, Culture Change, and Archaeology,* edited by James G. Cusick, pp. 476–495. Occasional Paper, vol. 25. Center for Archaeological Investigations, Southern Illinois University, Carbondale.

Allen, Ngapine

1998 Maori Vision and the Imperialist Gaze. In *Colonialism and the Object: Empire, Material Culture, and the Museum,* edited by Tim Barringer and Tom Flynn. Routledge, London.

Anderson, Benedict

1983 *Imagined Communities: Reflections on the Origin and Spread of Nationalism.* Verso, London.

Appadurai, Arjun

1986 Introduction. In *The Social Life of Things: Commodities in Cultural Perspective.* Cambridge University Press, Cambridge.

Axtell, James

1988 *After Columbus: Essays in the Ethnohistory of Colonial North America.* Oxford University Press, New York.

1992 *Beyond 1492: Encounters in Colonial North America.* Oxford University Press, New York.

Ayer, Mrs. Edward (translator)

1900–1901 *The Memorial of Fray Alonso de Benavides, 1630.* Horn and Wallace, Albuquerque, N.M.

Bagley, Christopher

1973 *The Dutch Plural Society: A Comparative Study in Race Relations.* Oxford University Press, London.

Barber, Ruth Kerns

1932 *Indian Labor in the Spanish Colonies.* Publications in History 6. University of New Mexico Press, Albuquerque.

Barrett, Elinore

1997 *The Geography of Rio Grande Pueblos Revealed by Spanish Explorers, 1540–1598.* University of New Mexico Press, Albuquerque.

Barringer, Tim, and Tom Flynn (editors)

1988 *Colonialism and the Object: Empire, Material Culture, and the Museum.* Routledge, London.

Barth, Fredrik (editor)

1969 *Ethnic Groups and Boundaries: The Social Organization of Cultural Difference.* Brown University Press, Boston.

Basso, Keith H.

1996 *Wisdom Sits in Places: Landscape and Language among the Western Apache.* University of New Mexico Press, Albuquerque.

Bayer, Laura, and Floyd Montoya

1994 *Santa Ana: The People, The Pueblo, and the History of Tamaya.* University of New Mexico Press, Albuquerque.

Baxter, John O.

1993 Livestock on the Camino Real. In *El Camino Real de Tierra Adentro,* Gabrielle G. Palmer, ed., pp. 101–112. Cultural Resources Series No. 11. Bureau of Land Management, Santa Fe, N.M.

Beck, Warren
1962 *New Mexico: A History of Four Centuries.* University of Oklahoma Press, Norman.

Beidelman, Thomas O.
1982 *Colonial Evangelism: A Socio-Historical Study of an East African Mission at the Grassroots.* Indiana University Press, Bloomington.

Bender, Susan J., and Edward V. Curtin
1990 *A Prehistoric Context of the Upper Hudson Valley, Report of the Survey and Planning Project.* New York State Office of Parks, Recreation, and Historic Preservation, Albany.

Biblioteca Nacional de Mexico Archivo Franciscano
Documentos Nuevo Mexico. Legajo 1, no. 34, pp. folios 1–24v.

Bielinski, Stefan
1991 The New Netherlands Dutch: Settling in and Spreading Out in Colonial Albany. In *The American Family: Historical Perspectives,* edited by Jean E. Hunter and Paul T. Mason, pp. 1–15. Duquesne University Press, Pittsburgh, Pa.

Billington, Ray Allen
1967 The American Frontier. In *Beyond the Frontier: Social and Cultural Change,* edited by Paul Bohannan and Fred Plog, pp. 3–24. Natural History Press, New York.

Binford, Martha R.
1979 Spatial Patterning and Content Variability in Four Historic Faunal Assemblages, edited by Jan V. Biella and Richard C. Chapman, pp. 247–268. Office of Contract Archaeology, Department of Anthropology, University of New Mexico, Albuquerque.

Blusse, Leonard
1986 *Strange Company: Chinese Settlers, Mestizo Women, and the Dutch in VOC Batavia.* Foris Publications, Dordrecht, Holland.

Bogaert, Harmen Meyndertsz van den, Charles T. Gehring, and William A. Starna
1988 *A Journey into Mohawk and Oneida Country, 1634–1635: The Journal of Harmen Meyndertsz Van den Bogaert.* Iroquois Books. Syracuse University Press, Syracuse, N.Y.

Bohannan, Paul, and Fred Plog
1967 *Beyond the Frontier: Social Process and Cultural Change.* American Museum Sourcebooks in Anthropology. Natural History Press, Garden City, N.Y.

Bolton, Herbert E.
1921 *The Spanish Borderlands: A Chronicle of Old Florida and the Southwest.* Yale University Press, New Haven, Conn.

Bourdieu, Pierre
1984 *Distinction: A Social Critique of the Judgement of Taste.* Harvard University Press, Cambridge, Mass.

Boxer, Charles Ralph

1965 *The Dutch Seaborne Empire, 1600–1800.* The History of Human Society. Knopf, New York.

Bradley, James W.

1987 *Evolution of the Onondaga Iroquois: Accommodating Change, 1500–1655.* Iroquois Books. Syracuse University Press, Syracuse, N.Y.

Brandon, William

1990 *Quivira: Europeans in the Region of the Santa Fe Trail, 1540–1820.* Ohio University Press, Athens.

Brooks, James

2002 *Captives and Cousins: Slavery, Kinship, and Community in the Southwest Borderlands.* University of North Carolina Press, Chapel Hill.

Bruijn, J. R., F. S. Gaastra, and Ivo Schoffer

1987 *Dutch-Asiatic Shipping in the 17th and 18th Centuries.* Rijks geschied kundige. I. Martinus Nijhoff, The Hague.

Brumbach, Hetty Jo, and Susan J. Bender

1986 Winney's Rift: A Late Woodland Village Site in the Upper Hudson River Valley. *Bulletin and Journal of Archaeology for the State of New York* 92(Spring):1–8.

Burke, Thomas Jr.

1991 *Mohawk Frontier: The Dutch Community of Schenectady, New York 1661–1710.* Cornell University Press, Ithaca, N.Y.

Bustamante, Adrian

1989 Espanoles, Castas, y Labradores: Santa Fe Society in the Eighteenth Century. In *Santa Fe: History of an Ancient City,* edited by David Grant Noble, pp. 65–78. School of American Research Press, Santa Fe, N.M.

1991 "The Matter Was Never Resolved": The Casta System in Colonial New Mexico, 1693–1823. *New Mexico Historical Review* 66(2): 143–163.

Butzer, Karl W.

1992 The Americas before and after 1492: An Introduction to Current Geographical Research. *Annals of the Association of American Geographers* 82(3):345–368.

Calloway, Colin

1994 *The World Turned Upside Down: Indian Voices from Early America.* Bedford Series in History and Culture. St. Martin's Press, Boston.

1997 *New Worlds for All: Indians, Europeans, and the Remaking of Early America.* Johns Hopkins University Press, Baltimore, Md.

Cameron, Catherine, and Steve Tomka

1993 *Abandonment of Settlements and Regions: Ethnoarcaheologcial and Archaeological Approaches.* Cambridge University Press, Cambridge.

Campbell, Colin

1987 *The Romantic Ethic and the Spirit of Modern Consumerism.* B. Blackwell, Oxford.

Cantwell, Anne Marie, and Diana diZerega Wall

2001 *Unearthing Gotham.* Yale University Press, New Haven, Conn.

Capone, Patricia

1996 Dynamics of Culture Contact at the Pueblo Mission of Abo Viewed through Ceramic Petrography. Paper presented at the 61st Annual Meeting of the Society for American Archaeology, New Orleans, La.

Carrillo, Charles M.

1997 *Hispanic New Mexican Pottery: Evidence of Craft Specialization, 1790–1890.* LPD Press, Albuquerque, N.M.

Carter, Douglas B.

1966 Climate. In *Geography of New York State,* edited by John H. Thompson, pp. 54–78. Syracuse University Press, Syracuse, N.Y.

Cassedy, Daniel F., Paul A. Webb, and James Bradley

1996 The Vanderwerken Site: A Protohistoric Iroquois Occupation on Schoharie Creek. *The Bulletin: Journal of the New York State Archaeological Association* Spring/Fall(111, 112):21–34.

Cather, Willa

1990 *Death Comes for the Archbishop.* In *Later Novels, 1923–1940,* pp. 273–459. Library of America, 49, New York.

Ceci, Lynn

1977 *The Effect of European Contact and Trade on the Settlement Pattern of Indians in Coastal New York, 1524–1665: The Archaeological and Documentary Evidence,* City University of New York.

Chapman, Richard C., Jan V. Biella, Jeanne A. Schutt, James G. Enloe, Patricia J. Marchiando, A. H. Warren, and John R. Stein

1977 Description of Twenty-Seven Sites in the Permanent Pool of Cochiti Reservoir. In *Archaeological Investigations in Cochiti Reservoir, New Mexico,* vol. 2: *Excavation and Analysis 1975 Season,* edited by Jan V. Biella, Richard C. Chapman, and Stanley D. Bussey, pp. 119–496. Office of Contract Archaeology, Department of Anthropology, University of New Mexico, Albuquerque.

Chilton, Elizabeth S.

1998 The Cultural Origins of Technical Choice: Unravelling Algonquian and Iroquoian Ceramic Traditions in the Northeast. In *The Archaeology of Social Boundaries,* edited by Miriam Stark, pp. 132–60. Smithsonian Institution Press, Washington, D.C.

Chrisman, Laura, and Patrick Williams

1993 *Colonial Discourse and Post-Colonial Theory.* Harvester Wheatsheaf, New York.

Church, Minette

1999 The Grant and the Grid: Homestead Landscapes in the Landscapes in the Late 19th-Century Borderlands of Southern Colorado. Paper presented at the 64th Annual Meeting of the Society for American Archaeology, Chicago, Ill.

Cohen, Ronald

1993 Conclusion: Ethnicity, the State, and the Moral Order. In *Ethnicity and the State,* vol. 9, edited by Judith D. Toland, pp. 231–258. Transaction Publishers, New Brunswick, N.J.

Cohn, Bernard S.

1996 *Colonialism and Its Forms of Knowledge: The British in India.* Princeton Studies in Culture/Power/History. Princeton University Press, Princeton, N.J.

Comaroff, Jean, and John Comaroff

1991 *Of Revelation and Revolution: Christianity, Colonialism, and Consciousness.* Vols. 1, 2. University of Chicago Press.

1992 *Ethnography and the Historical Imagination.* Studies in the Ethnographic Imagination. Westview Press, Boulder, Colo.

Cooley, Charles H.

1894 *The Theory of Transportation.* American Economic Association, Baltimore, Md.

Cooper, Frederick, and Ann Stoler

1997 *Tensions of Empire: Colonial Cultures in a Bourgeois World.* University of California Press, Los Angeles.

Cordell, Linda S.

1979 *A Cultural Resources Overview of the Middle Rio Grande Valley, New Mexico.* : USDA Forest Service, Southwestern Region, Albuquerque; Bureau of Land Management, New Mexico State Office, Santa Fe.

1980 (editor) *Tijeras Canyon: Analyses of the Past.* Maxwell Museum of Anthropology. University of New Mexico Press, Albuquerque.

1984 *Prehistory of the Southwest.* New World Archaeological Record. Academic Press, Orlando, Fla.

1989 Durango to Durango: An Overview of the Southwest Heartland. In *Columbian Consequences,* vol. 1, edited by David Hurst Thomas, pp. 17–40. Smithsonian Institution Press, Washington, D.C.

Cordell, Linda S., and Amy Earls

1984 The Rio Grande Glaze "Sequence" and the Mogollon. In *Recent Research in Mogollon Archaeology,* edited by Stedman Upham, Fred Plog, David G. Batcher, and Barbara Kauffman, pp. 90–97. New Mexico State University Occasional Papers No. 10, University Museum, Las Cruces.

Cornell, Stephen E.
1988 *The Return of the Native: American Indian Political Resurgence.* Oxford University Press, New York.

Courlander, Harold (editor)
1982 *Hopi Voices: Recollections, Traditions, and Narratives of the Hopi Indians.* University of New Mexico Press, Albuquerque.

Creamer, Winifred
1996 Developing Complexity in the American Southwest: Constructing a Model for the Rio Grande Valley. In *Emergent Complexity: The Evolution of Intermediate Societies,* edited by Jeanne E. Arnold, pp. 91–106. Archaeological Series 9. International Monographs in Prehistory, Ann Arbor, Mich.
1999 Regional Integrations and Regional Systems in the Protohistoric Rio Grande. In *The Archaeology of Regional Interaction: Religion, Warfare and Exchange across the American Southwest and Beyond,* edited by Michelle Hegmon, pp. 99–118. University Press of Colorado, Boulder.

Creamer, Winifred, Catherine M. Cameron, and John D. Beal
1993 *The Architecture of Arroyo Hondo Pueblo, New Mexico.* Arroyo Hondo Archaeological Series 7. School of American Research Press, Santa Fe, N.M.

Creamer, Winifred, Jonathan Haas, and Lisa Renken
1994 Testing Conventional Wisdom: Protohistoric Ceramics and Chronology in the Northern Rio Grande. Paper presented at the 59th Annual Meeting of the Society for American Archaeology, Anaheim, Calif.

Crerar, Jacqueline E. M.
1992 Assets and Assemblages: The Neutral Economic Approach to Inter-Cultural Relations. Paper presented at the People to People Conference, Rochester Museum and Science Center, Rochester, N.Y.

Cressey, George B.
1966 Land Forms. In *Geography of New York State,* edited by John H. Thompson, pp. 19–53. Syracuse University Press, Syracuse, N.Y.

Cronon, William
1983 *Changes in the Land: Indians, Colonists, and the Ecology of New England.* Hill and Wang, New York.

Crosby, Alfred
1986 *Ecological Imperialism: The Biological Expansion of Europe 900–1900.* Studies in Environment and History. Cambridge University Press, Cambridge.

Crown, Patricia L.
2000 Gendered Tasks, Power, and Prestige in the Prehispanic American Southwest. In *Women and Men in the Prehispanic Southwest,* edited by

Patricia L. Crown, pp. 3–42. School of American Research Press, Santa Fe, N.M.

Cushman, David
1983 A Description and Analysis of the Jackson-Everson Site Lithic Assemblage. In *Faunal Remains from the Jackson-Everson (NYSM 1213) Site,* edited by Robert D. Kuhn and David H. Snow, pp. 67–74. State University of New York, Albany.

Cusick, James G. (editor)
1998 *Studies in Culture Contact: Interaction, Culture Change, and Archaeology.* 25. Center for Archaeological Investigations, Southern Illinois University, Carbondale.

Dart, Al (editor)
1980 *Archaeological Investigations at San Antonio de Padua, LA 24, Bernalillo County, New Mexico.* Laboratory of Anthropology Note 167, Santa Fe, N.M.

Dawdy, Shannon Lee
2000 Preface to Special Issue of Historical Archaeology on Creolization. *Historical Archaeology* 34(3):1–4.

Deagan, Kathleen A. (editor)
1983 *Spanish St. Augustine: The Archaeology of a Colonial Creole Community.* Academic Press, New York.
1995 *Puerto Real: The Archaeology of a Sixteenth-Century Spanish Town in Hispaniola.* Ripley P. Bullen Series; Columbus Quincentenary Series. University Press of Florida, Gainesville.
1998 Transculturation and Spanish American Ethnogenesis: The Archaeological Legacy of the Quincentenary. In *Studies in Culture Contact: Interaction, Culture Change, and Archaeology,* vol. 25, edited by James G. Cusick, pp. 23–43. Center for Archaeological Investigations, Southern Illinois University, Carbondale.

Deeds, Susan
1991 Mission Villages and Agrarian Patterns in a Nueva Vizcayan Heartland, 1600–1750. *Journal of the Southwest* 33(3):345–364.

Delage, Denys
1991 *Le Pays Renverse: Amerindiens et Européens en Amerique de Nord-Est 1660–1664.* Boreal, Quebec, Canada.

De Laubenfels, David J.
1966 Soil. In *Geography of New York State,* edited by John H. Thompson, pp. 104–112. Syracuse University Press, Syracuse, N.Y.

Dennis, Matthew
1993 *Cultivating a Landscape of Peace: Iroquois-European Encounters in Seventeenth-Century America.* Cornell University Press, Ithaca, N.Y.

Denton, Daniel

1966 *A Brief Description of New York.* March of America Facsimile Series No. 26. University Microfilms, Ann Arbor, Mich.

de Rasière, Issac

1924 *Documents Relating to New Netherland, 1614–26 in the Henry E. Huntington Library.* Translated by Arnold J. F. Van Laer. Henry Huntington Library and Gallery Press, San Marino, Calif.

[1909] 1990 Letter to Samuel Blommaert, 1628. In *Narratives of New Netherland, 1609–1664,* edited by J. F. Jameson, pp. 97–116. Heritage Books, Bowie, Md.

de Roever, Margaret

1996 Merchandises for New Netherland. In *One Man's Trash Is Another Man's Treasure,* edited by A. V. Dongan, pp. 71–93. Museum Boymanns Van Beuningen, Rotterdam.

de Sille, Nicasius

1920 Letters of Nicasius de Sille, 1654. Translated by Arnold J. F. Van Laer. *New York History* (1):98–108.

Dickens, Charles

[1875] 1931 *American Notes.* Chapman and Hall, London.

Dirks, Nicholas B.

1992 *Colonialism and Culture.* Comparative Studies in Society and History Books Series. University of Michigan Press, Ann Arbor.

2001 *Castes of Mind: Colonialism and the Making of Modern India.* Princeton University Press, Princeton, N.J.

Dominguez, Fray Francisco Anastasio

1956 *The Missions of New Mexico, 1776.* Translated by Eleanor B. Adams and Fray Angelico Chavez. University of New Mexico Press, Albuquerque.

Donnan, Hastings, and Thomas M. Wilson

1999 *Borders: Frontiers of Identity, Nation, and State.* Berg, Oxford.

Douglas, Mary, and Baron C. Isherwood

1996 *The World of Goods: Towards an Anthropology of Consumption; With a New Introduction.* Routledge, London.

Duff, Andrew I.

1998 The Process of Migration in the Late Prehistoric Southwest. In *Migration and Reorganization: The Pueblo IV Period in the American Southwest,* edited by K. A. Spielmann, pp. 31–52. Anthropological Research Papers 51, Arizona State University, Tempe.

Dunn, Shirley

1994 *The Mohicans and Their Land, 1609–1730.* Purple Mountain Press, Fleischmanns, N.Y.

Earls, Amy C.
1982 *An Archaeological Assessment of "Las Huertas," Socorro, New Mexico.* Bureau of Land Management, U.S. Department of the Interior, Washington, D.C.
1986 *The Organization of Piro Pueblo Subsistence, AD 1300–1680.* Unpublished Ph.D. dissertation, University of New Mexico.

Edwards, Charles S.
1981 *Hugo Grotius, The Miracle of Holland: A Study in Political and Legal Thought.* Nelson-Hall, Chicago.

Eggan, Fred
1950 *Social Organization of the Western Pueblos.* University of Chicago Press, Chicago, Ill.

Elliott, Michael J.
1983 *Large Pueblo Sites Near Jemez Springs, New Mexico.* Santa Fe National Forest. Cultural Resources Report 3. On file at New Mexico State Museum.
2002 Mission and Mesa: Some Thoughts on the Archaeology of Pueblo Revolt Era Sites in the Jemez Region, New Mexico. In *Archaeologies of the Pueblo Revolt: Identity, Meaning, and Renewal in the Pueblo World,* edited by Robert W. Preucel, pp. 45–60. University of New Mexico Press, Albuquerque.

Espinosa, Manuel J.
1988 *The Pueblo Indian Revolt of 1696 and the Franciscan Missions in New Mexico: Letters of the Missionaries and Related Documents.* University of Oklahoma Press, Norman.

Ewers, John C.
1981 The Use of Artifacts and Pictures in the Study of Plains Indian Prehistory. In *The Research Potential of Anthropological Museum Collections,* edited by Anne-Marie Cantwell, James B. Griffin, and Nan A. Rothschild, pp. 247–266. Annals of the New York Academy of Sciences, vol. 376. New York Academy of Sciences.

Fabian, Johannes
1983 *Time and the Other: How Anthropology Makes Its Object.* Columbia University Press, New York.

Farriss, Nancy
1984 *Maya Society under Colonial Rule: The Collective Enterprise of Survival.* Princeton University Press, Princeton, N.J.

Fayden, Meta
1993 *Indian Corn and Dutch Pots: Seventeenth-Century Foodways in New Amsterdam/New York.* Unpublished Ph.D. dissertation, City University of New York.

Fenton, William N., and Elisabeth Tooker
1978 Mohawk. In *Handbook of North American Indians,* vol. 15, edited by Bruce G. Trigger, pp. 466–480. Smithsonian Institution Press, Washington, D.C.

Ferg, Alan
1984 *Historical Archaeology on the San Antonio de las Huertas Grant, Sandoval County, New Mexico.* CASA Papers 3.

Ferguson, Leland
2000 Introduction. *Historical Archaeology* 34(3):5–9.

Ferguson, T. J., Richard E. Hart, Ron Stauber, and Troy Lucio
1985 *A Zuni Atlas.* Civilization of the American Indian Series 172. University of Oklahoma Press, Norman.

Fish, Suzanne K.
2000 Farming, Foraging, and Gender. In *Women & Men in the Prehispanic Southwest,* edited by Patricia L. Crown, pp. 169–196. School of American Research Press, Santa Fe, N.M.

Fisher, Charles L.
1992 *Catlinite and Red Slate Ornaments from the Enders House Site, Schoharie Crossing State Historic Site, Montgomery County, New York.* New York State Parks, Recreation and Historic Preservation, Bureau of Historic Sites, Albany.

Fitzhugh, William W.
1985 *Cultures in Contact: The Impact of European Contacts on Native American Cultural Institutions, A.D. 1000–1800.* Anthropological Society of Washington Series. Smithsonian Institution Press, Washington D.C.

Forbes, Jack D.
1968 Frontiers in American History and the Role of the Frontier Historian. *Ethnohistory* 15(2):203–235.

Frank, Ross
1998 Demographic, Social and Economic Change in New Mexico. In *New Views of Borderlands History,* edited by Robert H. Jackson, pp. 41–71. University of New Mexico Press, Albuquerque.

Funk, Robert E.
1965 The Archaic of the Hudson Valley: New Evidence and New Interpretations. *Pennsylvania Archaeologist* 35:139–160.

1978 Hudson Valley Prehistory: Current State, Problems and Prospects. In *Neighbors and Intruders: An Ethnohistorical Exploration of the Indians of the Hudson River,* edited by Laurence M. Hauptman and Jack Campisi, pp. 6–75. Mercury Series, Paper (Canadian Ethnology Service) No. 39. National Museums of Canada, Ottawa.

Funk, Robert E., and William A. Ritchie

1973 *Aboriginal Settlement Patterns in the Northeast.* Memoir 20, New York State Museum and Science Service. University of the State of New York, State Education Department, Albany.

Furnivall, John S.

[1941] 1978 *Progress and Welfare in Southeast Asia: A Comparison of Colonial Policy and Practice.* International Research Series. Institute of Pacific Relations, New York.

Gehring, Charles T., and William A. Starna

1992 Dutch and Indians in the Hudson Valley: The Early Period. *Hudson Valley Regional Review* 9(2):1–25.

1988 (editors) *A Journey into Mohawk and Oneida Country, 1634–1635: The Journal of Harman Meyndertsz van den Bogaert.* Syracuse University Press, Syracuse, N.Y.

Gehring, Charles, William Starna, and Dean R. Snow (editors)

1996 *In Mohawk Country: Early Narratives about a Native People.* Syracuse University Press, Syracuse, N.Y.

Goddard, Ives

1978 Delaware. In *Handbook of North American Indians,* vol. 15, edited by Bruce G. Trigger, pp. 213–239. Smithsonian Institution Press, Washington, D.C.

Godelier, Maurice

1977 *Perspectives in Marxist Anthropology.* Cambridge Studies in Social Anthropology No. 18. Cambridge University Press, Cambridge.

Gosden, Chris, and Yvonne Marshall

1999 The Cultural Biography of Objects. *World Archaeology* 31(2):169–178.

Grant, Anne MacVicar

1808 *Memoirs of an American Lady: With Sketches of Manners and Scenery in America, As They Existed Previous to the Revolution.* 1 & 2. Longman, Hurst, Rees, London.

Grayson, Donald K.

1984 *Quantitative Zooarchaeology: Topics in the Analysis of Archaeological Faunas.* Academic Press, Orlando, Fla.

Green, Stanton W., and Stephen M. Perlman (editors)

1985 *The Archaeology of Frontiers and Boundaries.* Academic Press, New York.

Greenhalgh, Wentworth

1996 Observations of Wentworth Greenhalgh in a Journey to Albany, to the Indians Westward, 1677. In *In Mohawk Country: Early Narratives about Native People,* edited by William A. Starna, Dean R. Snow, and Charles T. Gehring, pp. 188–192. Iroquois and Their Neighbors Series. Syracuse University Press, Syracuse, N.Y.

Guldenzopf, David B.

1984 Frontier Demography and Settlement Patterns of the Mohawk Iroquois. *Man in the Northeast* 27:79–94.

1986 *The Colonial Transformation of Mohawk Iroquois Society.* Unpublished Ph.D. dissertation, University of the State of New York.

Gutiérrez, Ramon A.

1991 *When Jesus Came the Corn Mothers Went Away: Marriage, Sexuality, and Power in New Mexico, 1500–1846.* Stanford University Press, Stanford, Calif.

Haas, Jonathan, and Winifred Creamer

1992 Demography of the Protohistoric Pueblos of the Northern Rio Grande, A.D. 1450–1680. In *Current Research in the Late Prehistory and Early History of New Mexico,* edited by Bradley J. Vierra, pp. 21–27. Special Publication 1. Archaeological Council, Albuquerque, N.M.

Habicht-Mauche, Judith

1995 Changing Patterns of Pottery Manufacture and Trade in the Northern Rio Grande Region. In *Ceramic Production in the American Southwest,* edited by Barbara J. Mills and Patricia L. Crown, pp. 167–199. University of Arizona Press, Tucson.

Habicht-Mauche, Judith A., Richard W. Lang, Anthony Thibodeau, and Carl James Phagan

1993 *The Pottery from Arroyo Hondo Pueblo, New Mexico: Tribalization and Trade in the Northern Rio Grande.* Arroyo Hondo Archaeological Series 8. School of American Research Press, Santa Fe, N.M.

Hackett Jr., Charles Wilson (editor)

1923 *Historical Documents Relating to New Mexico, Nueva Vizcaya, and Approaches Thereto, to 1773.* 1. Carnegie Institution, Washington, D.C.

1926 (editor) *Historical Documents Relating to New Mexico, Nueva Vizacaya, and Approaches Thereto, to 1773.* 2. Carnegie Institution, Washington, D.C.

1937 (editor) *Historical Documents Relating to New Mexico, Nueva Vizacaya, and Approaches Thereto, to 1773.* 3. Carnegie Institution, Washington, D.C.

Hall, Martin

1997 Patriarchal Facades: The Ambivalences of Gender in the Archaeology of Colonialism. In *Our Gendered Past: Archaeological Studies of Gender in Southern Africa,* edited by Lyn Wadley, pp. 221–236. Witwatersrand University Press, Johannesburg.

Hall, Thomas D.

1989 *Social Change in the Southwest, 1350–1880.* Studies in Historical Social Change. University Press of Kansas, Lawrence.

Hallenbeck, Cleve

1926 *Spanish Missions of the Old Southwest.* Doubleday, Page, Garden City, N.Y.

Hamell, George R.

1980 Gannagaro State Historic Site: A Current Perspective. In *Studies on Iroquoian Culture,* edited by Nancy Bonvillian, pp. 91–108. Occasional Publications in Northeastern Anthropology No. 6, Rindge, N.H.

1983 Trading in Metaphors: The Magic of Beads. In *Proceedings of the 1982 Glass Trade Bead Conference, Sponsored by the Arthur C. Parker Fund for Iroquois Research,* edited by Charles F. Hayes III, pp. 5–28. Research Record No. 16. Research Division Rochester Museum and Science Center, Rochester, N.Y.

Hamilton, Milton W.

1961 Diary of the Reverend John Ogilvie, 1750–59. *Bulletin of Fort Ticonderoga Museum* X(5):331–385.

Hammond, George P., and Agapito Rey

1924 *The Rodriguez Expedition to New Mexico, 1581–1582.* Historical Society of New Mexico, Publications in History IV.

1927 *The Gallegos Relation of the Rodriguez Expedition to New Mexico.* Historical Society of New Mexico, Publications in History 4.

Hanlon, Don

1992 The Spanish Mission Church in Central New Mexico: A Study in Architectural Morphology. *Anthropologica* 34:203–229.

Hatley, Tom

1993 *The Dividing Paths: Cherokees and South Carolinians through the Era of Revolution.* Oxford University Press, New York.

Hayes, Alden C., Jon Nathan Young, and A. H. Warren

1981 *Excavation of Mound 7 Gran Quivira National Monument New Mexico.* National Park Service Publications in Archaeology 16.

Hays-Gilpin, Kelly

2000 Gender Ideology and Ritual Activities. In *Women and Men in the Prehispanic Southwest,* edited by Patricia L. Crown, pp. 91–135. School of American Research, Santa Fe, N.M.

Hegmon, Michelle (editor)

2000 *The Archaeology of Regional Interaction: Religion, Warfare, and Exchange across the American Southwest and Beyond.* University of Colorado Press, Boulder, Colo.

Hemming, John

1978 *Red Gold: The Conquest of the Brazilian Indians.* Harvard University Press, Cambridge, Mass.

Hodge, Frederick Webb, George P. Hammond, and Agapito Rey
1945 *Fray Alonso de Benavides' Revised Memorial of 1634; With Numerous Supplementary Documents Elaborately Annotated.* Coronado Cuarto Centennial Publication 1540–1940 IV. University of New Mexico Press, Albuquerque.

Horvath, Steven M.
1979 *The Social and Political Organization of the Genizaros of Plaza de Nuestra Senora de los Dolores de Belen, New Mexico, 1740–1812.* Unpublished Ph.D. dissertation, Brown University.

Howell, Todd L.
1995 Tracking Zuni Gender and Leadership Roles across the Contact Period in the Zuni Region. *Journal of Anthropological Research* 51:125–147.

Howell, Todd L., and Keith W. Kintigh
1996 Archaeological Identification of Kin Groups Using Mortuary and Biological Data: An Example from the American Southwest. *American Antiquity* 61:537–554.

Huey, Paul R.
1967a *Cultural Patterns of Beef, Pork, and Mutton Consumption in Britain and North America before 1800.* Ms. in author's possession.
1967b *Pork, Beef, and Mutton Consumption in Colonial Boston: 1675–1725.* Ms. in author's possession.
1984 Dutch Sites of the 17th Century in Rensselaerswyck. In *Scope of Historical Archaeology: Essays in Honor of John L. Cotter,* edited by John L. Cotter, David G. Orr, Daniel G. Crozier, and Laboratory of Anthropology Temple University. Occasional Publication of the Department of Anthropology, Temple University, Philadelphia, Pa.
1988 *Aspects of Continuity and Change in Colonial Dutch Material Culture at Fort Orange. 1624–1664.* Unpublished Ph.D. dissertation, University of Pennsylvania.
1990 *Early Occupation of Crailo Site, Memorandum to Dr. Gordon.* New York State, Office of Parks, Recreation, and Historic Preservation, Albany.
1991 The Dutch at Fort Orange. In *Historical Archaeological in Global Perspective,* edited by Lisa Falk, pp. 21–68. Smithsonian Institution Press, Washington, D.C.

Hunter-Anderson, Rosalind, James G. Enloe, and Martha R. Binford
1979 *LA 10114,* edited by New Mexico Archaeological Investigations in Cochiti Reservoir, vol. 3: *1976–1977 Field Seasons,* pp. 55–73. Office of Contract Archaeology, Department of Anthropology, University of New Mexico, Albuquerque.

Huntley, Deborah L., and Keith W. Kintigh
2000 Archaeological Patterning and Organizational Scale of Late Prehistoric

Settlement Clusters in the Zuni Region of New Mexico. Paper presented at the 66th Annual Meeting of the Society of American Archaeology, New Orleans, La.

Ivey, James E.

1988 *In the Midst of a Loneliness: The Architectural History of the Salinas Missions, Salinas Pueblo Mission National Monument Historic Structure Report.* National Park Service Professional Paper 15. Submitted to Southwest Cultural Resource Center, Santa Fe, N.M.

1994 The Greatest Misfortune of All: Famine in the Province of New Mexico, 1667–1672. *Journal of the Southwest* 36(1):76–100.

Ivey, James E.

1993 Seventeenth-Century Mission Trade on the Camino Real. In *El Camino Real de Tierra Adentro,* edited by Gabrielle G. Palmer, pp. 101–112. Cultural Resources Series No. 11. Bureau of Land Management, Santa Fe, N.M.

Jackson, Robert H. (editor)

1998 *New Views of Borderlands History.* University of New Mexico Press, Albuquerque.

1999 *Race, Caste, and Status: Indians in Colonial Spanish America.* University of New Mexico Press, Albuquerque.

Jameson, John Franklin (editor)

1990 (1909) *Narratives of New Netherland, 1609–1664.* Heritage Books, Bowie, Md.

Jennings, Francis

1984 *The Ambiguous Iroquois Empire: The Covenant Chain Confederation of Indian Tribes with English Colonies from Its Beginnings to the Lancaster Treaty of 1744.* Norton, New York.

1988 *Empires of Fortune: Crowns, Colonies, and Tribes in the Seven Years War in America.* Norton, New York.

John, Elizabeth

1975 *Storms Brewed in Other Men's Worlds: The Confrontation of Indians, Spanish, and French in the Southwest, 1540–1795.* Texas A & M University Press, College Station.

Johnson, Gregory A.

1989 Dynamics of Southwestern Prehistory: Far Outside Looking In. In *Dynamics of Southwest Prehistory,* edited by Linda S. Cordell and George J. Gumerman, pp. 371–389. Smithsonian Institution Press, Washington, D. C.

Jojola, Theodore S.

1997 Pueblo Indian and Spanish Town Planning in New Mexico. In *Anasazi Architecture and American Design,* edited by Baker H. Morrow and Vincent Barrett Price, pp. 171–185. University of New Mexico Press, Albuquerque.

Jordan, Kurt

2002 *The Archaeology of the Iroquois Restoration: Settlement, Housing, and Economy at a Dispersed Seneca Community ca A.D. 1715–1754.* Unpublished Ph.D. dissertation, Columbia University.

Jordan-Bychkov, Terry G. Kaups, and Matti E. Kaups

1989 *The American Backwoods Frontier: An Ethnic and Ecological Interpretation.* Creating the North American Landscape. Johns Hopkins Press, Baltimore, Md.

Junker-Anderson, C.

1986 Faunal Remains from the Jackson-Everson (NYSM 1213) Site. In *The Mohawk Valley Project: The Jackson-Everson Excavations,* edited by Robert D. Kuhn and David H. Snow, pp. 93–160. State University of New York, Albany, N.Y.

Kessell, John L.

1978 *Kiva, Cross, and Crown: The Pecos Indians and New Mexico, 1540–1840.* Department of Interior, National Park Service, Washington D.C.

1989 Spaniards and Pueblos: From Crusading Intolerance to Pragmatic Accommodation. In *Columbian Consequences: Archaeological and Historical Perspectives on the Spanish Borderlands West,* vol. 1, edited by David Hurst Thomas, pp. 127–138. Smithsonian Institution Press, Washington D.C.

Kessell, John L., Rick Hendricks, and Meredith D. Dodge (editors)

1992a *Letters to the New World: Selected Correspondence of Don Diego de Vargas to His Family.* University of New Mexico Press, Albuquerque.

1992b (editors) *By Force of Arms: The Journals of Don Diego de Vargas, New Mexico, 1691–1693.* University of New Mexico Press, Albuquerque.

1995 (editors) *To the Royal Crown Restored: The Journals of Don Diego de Vargas, New Mexico, 1692–1694.* University of New Mexico Press, Albuquerque.

Kestler, Frances Roe

1990 *The Indian Captivity Narrative: A Woman's View.* Women's History and Culture, 2, Garland Reference Library of the Humanities, vol. 1179. Garland, New York.

Kidder, Alfred Vincent

1924 *An Introduction to the Study of Southwestern Archaeology with a Preliminary Account of the Excavations at Pecos.* Yale University Press, New Haven, Conn.

Kiernan, V. G.

1986 *The Lords of Human Kind.* Columbia University Press, New York.

Kintigh, Keith W.

1984 Measuring Archaeological Diversity by Comparison with Simulated Assemblages. *American Antiquity* (49):44–54.

1990 Protohistoric Transitions in the Western Pueblo Area. In *Perspectives on Southwestern Prehistory,* edited by Paul E. Minnis and Charles L. Redman, pp. 258–275. Investigations in American Archaeology. Westview Press, Boulder, Colo.

2000 Leadership Strategies in Protohistoric Zuni Towns. In *Alternative Leadership Strategies in the Prehistoric Southwest,* edited by Barbara J. Mills, pp. 95–116. University of Arizona Press, Tucson.

Kipp, Rita S.

1990 *The Early Years of a Dutch Colonial Mission: The Karo Field.* University of Michigan Press, Ann Arbor.

Knaut, Andrew

1995 *The Pueblo Revolt of 1680: Conquest and Resistance in the Seventeenth-Century New Mexico.* Oklahoma University Press, Norman.

Kohler, Timothy A., Matthew W. Van Pelt, and Lorene Y. I. Yap

2000 Reciprocity and Its Limits: Consideration for a Study of the Prehistoric Pueblo World. In *Alternative Leadership Strategies in the Prehistoric Southwest,* edited by Barbara J. Mills, pp. 180–206. University of Arizona Press, Tucson.

Kopytoff, Igor

1986 The Cultural Biography of Things: Commoditization as Process. In *The Social Life of Things: Commodities in Cultural Perspective,* edited by Arjun Appadurai, pp. 64–94. Cambridge University Press, Cambridge.

Kroeber, Alfred (editor)

1939 *Culture and Nature Areas of Native North America.* University of California Press, Berkeley.

Kroskrity, Paul

1993 *Language, History, and Identity: Ethnolinguistic Studies of the Arizona Tewa.* University of Arizona Press, Tucson.

Kuhn, Robert D.

1985 *Trade and Exchange among Mohawk-Iroquois: A Trace Element Analysis of Ceramic Smoking Pipes.* Unpublished Ph.D. dissertation, State University of New York at Albany.

1986a Indications of Interaction and Acculturation through Ceramic Analysis. In *The Mohawk Valley Project: The Jackson-Everson Excavations,* edited by Robert D. Kuhn and David H. Snow, pp. 75–92. State University of New York, Albany.

1986b Interaction Patterns in Eastern New York: A Trace Element Analysis of

Iroquoian and Algonkian Ceramics. *Bulletin and Journal of Archaeology for the State of New York* (92):9–21.

Kuhn, Robert D., and Robert E. Funk

1994 Mohawk Interaction Patterns during the Late Sixteenth Century. In *Proceedings of the 1992 People to People Conference,* edited by Charles F. III Hayes, pp. 77–84. Rochester Museum and Science Center Research Records No. 23, Rochester, N.Y.

2000 Boning Up on the Mohawk: An Overview of Mohawk Faunal Assemblages and Subsistence Patterns. *Archaeology of Eastern North America* 28:29–62.

Kuhn, Robert D., and Martha L Sempowski

2001 A New Approach to Dating the League of the Iroquois. *American Antiquity* 66(2):301–314.

Lambert, Marjorie F., and Spencer L. Rogers

1954 *Paa-ko, Archaeological Chronicle of an Indian Village in North Central New Mexico.* School of American Research, Santa Fe, N.M.

Lamphere, Louise

2000 Gender Models in the Southwest: A Sociocultural Perspective. In *Women & Men in the Prehispanic Southwest,* edited by Patricia L. Crown, pp. 379–402. School of American Research Press, Santa Fe, N.M.

Lang, James

1975 *Conquest and Commerce: Spain and England in the Americas.* Academic Press, New York.

Lang, Richard W., and Arthur H. Harris

1984 *The Faunal Remains from Arroyo Hondo Pueblo, New Mexico: A Study in Short-Term Subsistence Change.* Arroyo Hondo Archaeological Series. School of American Research Press, Santa Fe, N.M.

Lange, Charles H.

[1959] 1990 *Cochiti: A New Mexico Pueblo, Past and Present.* University of New Mexico Press, Albuquerque.

Lenig, Donald

1977 On Dutchman, Beaver Hats, and Iroquois. *New York State Archaeological Association, Current Perspectives in Northeast Archaeology: Essays in Honor of William A. Ritchie* 17(1):71–84.

Leonard, Robert D., and George T. Jones (editors)

1989 *Quantifying Diversity in Archaeology.* Cambridge University Press, Cambridge.

Le Page du Pratz, Antoine

[1774] 1947 *The History of Louisiana—Translated from French.* J. S. W. Harmonson, New Orleans, La.

Levine, Frances

1996 Reorganized Intensification and Accommodation: Altering Pueblo Responses to Spanish Contact. Paper presented at the 61st Annual Society for American Archaeology, New Orleans, LA.

Lévi-Strauss, Claude

1969 *The Elementary Structures of Kinship.* Beacon Press, Boston.

Lewis, Kenneth E.

1984 *The American Frontier: An Archaeological Study of Settlement Pattern and Process.* Studies in Historical Archaeology (New York, N.Y.). Academic Press, Orlando, Fla.

Liebmann, Matthew J.

2002 Signs of Power and Resistance: The (Re)Creation of Christian Imagery and Identities in the Pueblo Revolt. In *Archaeologies of the Pueblo Revolt: Identity, Meaning and Renewal in the Pueblo World,* edited by Robert W. Preucel, pp. 132–144. University of New Mexico Press, Albuquerque.

Lord, Philip Jr.

1996 Taverns, Forts, and Castles: Rediscovering King Hendrick's Village. *Northeast Anthropology* Fall (52):69–94.

Loren, Diana D. P.

2000 The Intersection of Colonial Policy and Colonial Practice: Creolization on the Eighteenth-Century Louisiana/Texas Frontier. *Historical Archaeology* 34(3):84–98.

Lycett, Mark

1995 *Archaeological Implications of European Contact: Demography, Settlement, and Land Use in the Middle Rio Grande Valley, New Mexico.* Unpublished Ph.D. dissertation, University of New Mexico.

Macleod, William C.

1928 *The American Indian Frontier.* A. A. Knopf, London.

MacNeish, Richard S.

1976 The In Situ Iroquois Revisited and Rethought. In *Culture Change and Continuity: Essays in Honor of James Bennett Griffin,* edited by C. E. Cleland, pp. 79–98. Academic Press, New York.

Malinowski, Bronislaw

1922 *Argonauts of the Western Pacific: An Account of Native Enterprise and Adventure in the Archipelagos of Melanesian New Guinea.* Studies in Economics and Political Science No. 65. G. Routledge and Sons, London.

Marshall, Michael P.

1987 *Qualacu, Report to the Department of Fish and Wildlife.* U.S. Department of the Interior, Office of Contract Archaeology, University of New Mexico.

Marshall, Michael P., and Henry J. Walt

1984 *Rio Abajo: Prehistory and History of a Rio Grande Province.* New Mexico Historic Preservation Society, Santa Fe.

Martien, Jerry

1996 *A Shell Game: A True Account of Beads and Money in North America.* Mercury House, San Francisco.

Marx, Karl

1976 *Capital: A Critique of Political Economy.* Translated by Ben Fowkes. Penguin Books, London.

Mauss, Marcel

1990 *The Gift: The Form and Reason for Exchange in Archaic Societies.* W.W. Norton, New York.

McConnell, Michael

1992 *A Country Between: The Upper Ohio Valley and Its Peoples, 1724–1774.* University of Nebraska Press, Lincoln.

McGuire, Randall H., and Robert Paynter (editors)

1991 *The Archaeology of Inequality.* Blackwell, Oxford.

McKusick, Charmion R.

1981 The Faunal Remains of Las Humanas. In *Contributions to Gran Quivira Archaeology: Gran Quivira National Monument/New Mexico,* edited by Alden C. Hayes, pp. 39–66. Publications in Archaeology No. 17. National Park Service, U.S. Department of the Interior, Washington, D.C.

Mera, H. P.

1940 *Population Changes in the Rio Grande Glaze-Paint Area.* Technical Series 9. Laboratory of Anthropology; Archaeological Survey, Santa Fe, N.M.

Merrill, James H.

1989 Our Bands of Peace: Patterns of Intercultural Exchange in the Carolina Piedmont. In *Powhatan's Mantle: Indians in the Colonial Southeast,* edited by Peter H. Woods, Gregory A. Waselkov, and Thomas M. Hatley, pp. 196–222. Indians in the Southeast Series. University of Nebraska Press, Lincoln.

Merwick, Donna

1990 *Possessing Albany, 1630–1710: The Dutch and English Experiences.* Cambridge University Press, Cambridge.

Mick-O'Hara, Linda

n.d. *Identification and Analysis of the Faunal Remains from the 1984 Excavations at Rowe Pueblo.* Unpublished ms.

Miller, Daniel

1987 *Material Culture and Mass Consumption.* Social Archaeology. Blackwell, Oxford.

1998 *A Theory of Shopping.* Cornell University Press, Ithaca, N.Y.

Miller, Daniel, Michael Rowlands, and Christopher Y. Tilley

1995 *Domination and Resistance.* Routledge, London.

Miller, Henry M.

1984 *Colonialization and Subsistence Change in the 17th-Century Chesapeake Frontier.* Unpublished Ph.D. dissertation, Michigan State University.

Mills, Barbara J.

1995a Assessing Organizational Scale in Zuni Ceramic Production: A Comparison of Protohistoric and Historic Collections. *Museum Anthropology* 19(3):37–46.

1995b The Organization of the Protohistoric Zuni Ceramic Production. In *Ceramic Production in the American Southwest,* edited by Barbara J. Mills and Patricia L. Crown, pp. 200–230. University of Arizona Press, Tucson.

2000a Alternative Models, Alternative Strategies. In *Alternative Leadership Strategies in the Prehistoric Southwest,* edited by Barbara J. Mills, pp. 3–18. University of Arizona Press, Tucson.

2000b Gender, Craft Production, and Inequality. In *Women & Men in the Prehispanic Southwest,* edited by Patricia L. Crown, pp. 301–344. School of American Research Press, Santa Fe, N.M.

2001 The Archaeology of Inalienable Possessions: Social Valuable and Formation of Collective Prestige Structures in the Greater Southwest. Paper presented at the 66th Annual Meeting of the Society of American Archaeology, New Orleans, La.

Mills, Barbara J., and Patricia Crown (editors)

1995 *Ceramic Production in the American Southwest.* University of Arizona Press, Tucson.

Moore, James L. (editor)

n.d. *Historic Occupation of the Glorieta Valley in the Seventeenth and Nineteenth Centuries: Excavations at LA 76138, LA 76140, and LA 99029.* Office of Archaeological Studies, Museum of New Mexico, Albuquerque.

Moore, James L., Jeffrey L. Boyer, and Daisy F. Levine

n.d. *Adaptation of the Anasazi and Spanish Frontiers: Excavations of Five Sites near Abiquiu, Rio Arriba County, New Mexico.* Archaeological Note 187. Office of Archaeological Studies, Museum of New Mexico, Albuquerque.

Mullin, Molly H.

1999 Mirrors and Windows: Sociocultural Studies of Human-Animal Relationships. *Annual Review of Anthropology* (28):201–224.

Munn, Nancy

1986 *The Fame of Gawa: A Symbolic Study of Value Transformation in a*

Massim (Papua New Guinea) Society. Cambridge University Press, Cambridge.

Nabokov, Peter (editor)
1991 *Native American Testimony: A Chronicle of Indian-White Relations from Prophecy to Present, 1492–1992.* Viking, New York.

Neitzel, Jill E.
2000 Gender Hierarchies: A Comparative Analysis of Mortuary Data. In *Women and Men in the Prehispanic Southwest,* edited by Patricia L. Crown, pp. 137–168. School of American Research Press, Santa Fe, N.M.

Nequatewa, Edmund
1936 Truth of a Hopi and Other Clan Stories of Shungopovi. *Museum of Northern Arizona Bulletin.*

Niemczycki, Mary Ann Palmer
1984 *The Origin and Development of the Seneca and Cayuga Tribes of New York State.* Rochester Museum and Science Center Research Records No. 17, Rochester, N.Y.

O'Callaghan, Edmund Bailey (editor)
1849–51 *Documentary History of the State of New York,* 4 vols. Weed, Parson, Albany, N.Y.

O'Crouley, Pedro Alonso
1972 *A Description of the Kingdom of New Spain,* Sean Galvin, transl. John Howell Books, San Francisco, Calif.

Ortíz, Alfonso
1969 *The Tewa World: Space, Time, Being, and Becoming in a Pueblo Society.* University of Chicago Press, Chicago, Ill.

Palmer, Gabrielle G. (editor)
1993 *El Camino Real de Tierra Adentro.* Bureau of Land Management, Santa Fe, N.M.

Perttula, Timothy K.
1992 *The Caddo Nation: Archaeological and Ethnohistoric Perspectives.* Texas Archaeology and Ethnohistory Series. University of Texas Press, Austin.

Pilkington, William
1880 *The Journals of Samuel Kirkland.* Hamilton College, Clinton, N.Y.

Prakash, Gyan
1995 *After Colonialism: Imperial Histories and Postcolonial Displacements.* Princeton University Press, Princeton, N.J.

Preucel, Robert W.
2002 Writing the Pueblo Revolt. In *Archaeologies of the Pueblo Revolt: Identity, Meaning, and Renewal in the Pueblo World,* edited by Robert W. Preucel, pp. 3–29. University of New Mexico Press, Albuquerque.

Quinn, David

1979 *New American World: A Documentary History of North America to 1612,* 5 vols. Arno Press, New York.

Quintana, Frances Leon Swadesh, and David Kayser

1980 The Development of the Tijeras Canyon Hispanic Communities. In *Tijeras Canyon, Analyses of the Past,* edited by Linda S. Cordell, pp. 41–59. Maxwell Museum of Anthropology and University of New Mexico Press, Albuquerque.

Radisson, Peter Esprit

[1885] 1967 *Voyages of Peter Esprit Radisson, Being and Account of His Travels and Experiences among the North American Indians, from 1652–1684.* Reprint of 1885 ed. Burt Franklin, New York.

Ramenofsky, Ann F.

1996 The Problem of Introduced Infectious Diseases in New Mexico AD 1540–1680. *Journal of Anthropological Research* (52):161–184.

2001 *Summary Report of Archaeological Research at San Marcos Pueblo (LA 98) by the University of New Mexico.* University of New Mexico, Albuquerque.

Ramenofsky, Ann F., and James K. Feathers

2002 Documents, Ceramics, Tree-Ring, and Luminescence: Estimating Native Abandonment from the Lower Rio Chama. *Journal of Anthropological Research* 58(2):121–160.

Ray, Arthur J.

1974 *Indians and the Fur Trade: Their Role as Trappers, Hunters, and Middlemen in the Lands Southwest of Hudson Bay, 1660–1870.* University of Toronto Press, Toronto, Canada.

Rice, Prudence

1998 Contexts of Contact and Change: Peripheres, Frontiers, and Boundaries. In *Studies in Culture Contact: Interaction, Culture Change, and Archaeology,* vol. 25, edited by James G. Cusick, pp. 44–66. Center for Archaeological Investigations, Carbondale, Ill.

Richter, Daniel K.

1992 *The Ordeal of the Longhouse: The Peoples of the Iroquois League in the Era of European Colonization.* University of North Carolina Press, Chapel Hill.

Rick, Anne M.

1980 *Behind the Barracks: Analysis of Animal Remains from the Rear of the Soldiers Barracks, Crown Point State Historic Site, New York.* New York State Office of Parks, Recreation and Historic Preservation, Albany.

1991 *Faunal Remains from the Enders House: An Historic Mohawk Dwelling.* Zooarchaeological Identification Centre of the Canadian Museum of Nature, Ottawa, Ont.

Riley, Carroll L.
1987 *The Frontier People: The Greater Southwest in the Protohistoric Period.* University of New Mexico Press, Albuquerque.

Rink, Oliver A.
1986 *Holland on the Hudson: An Economic and Social History of Dutch New York.* Cornell University Press, Ithaca, N.Y.
1994 Private Interest and Godly Gain: The West India Company and the Dutch Reformed Church in New Netherland, 1624–1664. *New York History* 75(3):245–264.

Ritchie, William A., and Robert E. Funk
1973 *Aboriginal Settlement Patterns in the Northeast.* Memoir 20, New York State Museum and Science Service, University of the State of New York, Albany.

Rogers, J. Daniel
1990 *Objects of Change: The Archaeology and History of Arikara Contact with Europeans.* Smithsonian Institution Press, Washington D.C.

Rosendale, Simon
1895 The Involution of Wampum as Currency: The Story Told by the Colonial Ordinances of New Netherland. *New York Times,* July 28.

Rothschild, Nan A.
1990 *New York City Neighborhoods: The 18th Century.* Academic Press, San Diego, Calif.
1991 *Prehistoric Dimensions of Status: Gender and Age in Eastern North America.* Evolution of North American Indians Series. Garland, New York.
1996 Social Distance between Dutch Settlers and Native Americans. In *One Man's Trash Is Another Man's Treasure,* edited by Alexandra Van Dongan, pp. 189–202. Museum Boymanns-Van Beuningen, Rotterdam.

Rothschild, Nan A., and Susan Dublin
1995 *The Zuni Farming Village Study and Excavations at Lower Pescado Village: A Report on the Columbia University and Barnard College Field School, 1989–91.* Submitted to the Tribal Council, Zuni, N.M.

Rothschild, Nan A., Barbara Mills, Susan Dublin, and T. J. Ferguson
1993 Abandonment at Zuni Farming Villages. In *Abandonment of Settlements and Regions: Ethnoarchaeological and Archaeological Approaches,* edited by Catherine Cameron and Steve A. Tomka. New Directions in Archaeology. Cambridge University Press, Cambridge.

Rubertone, Patricia
1989 Landscape as Artifact: Comments on the "The Archaeological Use of Landscape Treatment in Social, Economic, and Ideological Analysis." *Historical Archaeology* 23(1):50–54.

Rumrill, Donald A.
1985 An Interpretation and Analysis of the 17th Century Mohawk Nation: Its Chronology and Movements. *Bulletin and Journal of Archaeology for New York State* (90):1–39.

Ruttenber, Edward Manning
[1872] 1971 *History of the Indian Tribes of Hudson's River: Their Origins, Manners and Customs, Tribal, and Sub-Tribal Organizations, Wars, Treaties, etc.* J. Munsell, Albany, N.Y.

Sackett, James R.
1977 The Meaning of Style in Archaeology. *American Antiquity* 42:369–80.

Sahagún, Berardino de
1978 *The War of Conquest: How It Was Waged Here in Mexico.* Translated by Arthur J. O. Anderson and Charles E. Dibble. University of Utah Press, Salt Lake City.

Sahlins, Marshall, and Patrick Kirch
1992 *Anahulu: The Anthropology of History in the Kingdom of Hawaii.* Historical Ethnography One. University of Chicago Press, Chicago, Ill.

Sampson, C. Garth
1988 *Stylistic Boundaries among Mobile Hunter-Foragers.* Smithsonian Institution Press, Washington, D.C.

Sando, Joe S.
1979 The Pueblo Revolt. In *Handbook of North American Indians,* vol. 9, edited by Alfonso Ortiz, pp. 194–197. Smithsonian Institution Press, Washington, D.C.

Santley, Robert S., and Rani T. Alexander
1992 The Political Economy of Core-Periphery Systems. In *Resources, Power, and Interregional Interaction,* edited by Edward M. Schortman and Patricia A. Urban. Interdisciplinary Contributions to Archaeology. Plenum Press, New York.

Saunders, Nicholas J.
1999 Biographies of Brilliance: Pearls, Transformations of Matter and Being, c. A.D. 1942. *World Archaeology* 31(2):243–257.

Schama, Simon
1995 *Landscape and Memory.* A. A. Knopf, New York.

Scholes, France V.
1929 Documents for the History of the New Mexican Missions in the Seventeenth Century. *New Mexico Historical Review* 4:45–58.
1930 The Supply Service for the New Mexican Missions in the Seventeenth Century. *New Mexico Historical Review* V:93–115, 186–210, 386–404.
[1942] 1977 *Troublous Times in New Mexico 1659–70.* University of New Mexico Press, Albuquerque.

Scholes, France V., and Lansing B. Bloom

1944 Friar Personnel and Mission Chronology, 1598–1629. *New Mexico Historical Review* 19:319–336.

1945 Friar Personnel and Mission Chronology, 1598–1629. *New Mexico Historical Review* 20:58–82.

Schortman, Edward M., and Patricia A. Urban (editors)

1992 *Resources, Power, and Interregional Interaction.* Plenum Press, New York.

Schrire, Carmel

1995 *Digging through Darkness: Chronicles of an Archaeologist.* University of Virginia Press, Charlottesville.

Schrire, Carmel, and Donna Merwick

1991 Dutch-Indigenous Relations in New Netherland and the Cape in the Seventeenth Century. In *Historical Archaeology in Global Perspective,* edited by Lisa Falk, pp. 11–20. Smithsonian Institution Press, Washington, D.C.

Schroeder, Albert H.

1979 Pueblos Abandoned in Historic Times. In *Handbook of North American Indians,* vol. 9, edited by Alfonzo Ortiz, pp. 236–254. Smithsonian Institution Press, Washington, D.C.

Schroeder, Albert H., and Dan S. Matson

1965 *A Colony on the Move: Gaspar Castaño de Sosa's Journal: 1590–1591.* School of American Research, Santa Fe, N.M.

Schuyler, Robert S. (editor)

1980 *Archaeological Perspectives in Ethnicity in America: Afro-American and Asian American Culture History.* Baywood, Farmington, N.Y.

Seed, Patricia

1995 *Ceremonies of Possession in Europe's Conquest of the New World, 1492–1640.* Cambridge University Press, New York.

Sharp, Joanne P. et al.

2000 *Entanglements of Power: Geographies of Domination/Resistance.* Routledge, London.

Sider, Gerald

1986 *Culture and Class in Anthropology and History: A New Foundland Illustration.* Cambridge University Press, Cambridge.

Simmel, Georg

1978 *The Philosophy of Money.* Routledge and Kegan Paul, London.

Simmons, Marc

1969 Settlement Patterns and Village Plans in Colonial New Mexico. *Journal of the West* 8:7–21.

1991 *Coronado's Land: Essays on Daily Life in Colonial New Mexico.* University of New Mexico Press, Albuquerque.

Smith, Bernard
1992 *Imagining the Pacific: In the Wake of the Cook Voyages.* Yale University Press, New Haven, Conn.

Smith, Richard
1906 *A Tour of Four Great Rivers: The Hudson, Mohawk, Susquehanna, and Delaware in 1769,* edited by Francis W. Halsey. C. Scribner's Sons, New York.

Snow, Cordelia T.
1979 The Evolution of a Frontier: An Historical Interpretation of Archaeological Sites. In *Archaeological Investigations in Cochiti Reservoir, New Mexico,* vol. 4: *Adaptive Change in the Northern Rio Grande,* edited by Jan V. Biella and Richard C. Chapman, pp. 217–234. Office of Contract Archaeology, Department of Anthropology, University of New Mexico, Albuquerque.

1993 "A Headdress of Pearls": Luxury Goods Imported over the Camino Real during the Seventeenth Century. In *El Camino Real de Tierra Adentro,* edited by Gabrielle G. Palmer, pp. 69–76. Cultural Resources Series No. 11. Bureau of Land Management, Santa Fe, N.M.

Snow, David H.
1976 *Archaeological Excavations at Pueblo de Encierro, LA 70 Cochiti Dam Salvage Project, New Mexico Final Report: 1964–1965 Field Seasons.* Museum of Anthropology, Laboratory of Anthropology, Notes No. 78a. Santa Fe.

1981 Protohistoric Rio Grande Pueblo Economics: A Review of Trends. In *The Protohistoric Period in the North American Southwest, A.D. 1450–1700,* edited by David R. Wilcox and W. Bruce Masse, pp. 354–377. Anthropological Research Paper No. 24. Arizona State University, Tempe.

1984 Spanish American Pottery Manufacture in New Mexico: A Critical Review. *Ethnohistory* 31(2):93–113.

1990 Tener Comal y Metate: Protohistoric Rio Grande Maize and Diet. In *Perspectives on Southwestern Prehistory,* edited by Paul E. Minnis and Charles L. Redman, pp. 289–300. Westview Press, Boulder, Colo.

1992a (editor) *The Native American and Spanish Colonial Experience in the Greater Southwest,* vol. 9 of *Spanish Borderlands Sourcebooks,* edited by David H. Snow. Garland, New York.

1992b A Note on Encomienda Economics in Seventeenth-Century New Mexico. In *The Native American and Spanish Colonial Experience in the Greater Southwest,* vol. 10 of *Spanish Borderlands Sourcebooks,* edited by David H. Snow, pp. 469–480. vol. 10. Garland, New York.

1992c A Review of Spanish Colonial Archaeology in Northern New Mexico.

In *Current Research on the Late Prehistory and Early History of New Mexico,* edited by Bradley J. Vierra, pp. 185–193. Special Publication 1. Archaeological Council, Albuquerque, N.M.

1993 "Purchased in Chihuahua for Feasts." In *El Camino Real de Tierra Adentro,* edited by Gabrielle G. Palmer, pp. 133–146. Cultural Resources Series No. 11. Bureau of Land Management, Santa Fe, N.M.

Snow, David H., and A. H. Warren

May 1969, May 1973 *Cochiti Dam Salvage Project: Archaeological Excavation and Pottery at the Torreon Site, LA 6178 Cochiti Dam, New Mexico.* Laboratory of Anthropological Note. No. 76, 76A.

October 1969, April 1973 *Cochiti Dam Salvage Project: Archaeological Excavation and Pottery of the Las Majadas Site LA 591, Cochiti Dam, New Mexico.* Laboratory of Anthropology Note No. 75.

Snow, Dean R.

1992 Societies in Eclipse: Eastern North America at the Dawn of Colonization. Paper presented at the 57th Annual Meeting for the Society for American Archaeology, Pittsburgh, Pa.

1994 *The Iroquois.* Peoples of America. Blackwell, Oxford.

1995 *Mohawk Valley Archaeology: The Collections.* Occasional Papers in Anthropology No. 22. Matson Museum of Anthropology, Pennsylvania State University, University Park.

1996 Mohawk Demography and the Effects of Exogenous Epidemics on American Indian Populations. *Journal of Anthropological Archaeology* (15):160–182.

Snow, Dean R., Charles Gehring, and William A. Starna

1996 *In Mohawk Country: Early Narratives about Native People.* Iroquois and Their Neighbors Series. Syracuse University Press, Syracuse, N.Y.

Snow, Dean R., and William A. Starna

1989 Sixteenth-Century Depopulation: A View from the Mohawk Valley. *American Anthropologist* 91(1):142–148.

Socci, Mary

1995 *The Zooarchaeology of the Mohawk Valley.* Unpublished Ph.D. dissertation, Yale University.

Spicer, Edward H.

1962 *Cycles of Conquest: The Impact of Spain, Mexico, and the United States on the Indians of the Southwest, 1533–1960.* University of Arizona Press, Tucson.

Spielmann, Katherine A.

1991 *Subsistence and Exchange at Gran Quivira Pueblo,* vol. 1. Submitted to the Southwest Regional Office of the National Park Service, Santa Fe, N.M.

1992 *Subsistence and Exchange at Gran Quivira Pueblo.* Submitted to the Southwestern Regional Office of the National Park Service, Santa Fe, N.M.

1993a *Preliminary Report for the 1992 Excavation Season at Quarai Pueblo, New Mexico.* Submitted to the Southwestern Regional Office of the National Park Service, Santa Fe, N.M.

1993b *The Evolution of Craft Specialization in Tribal Societies.* 2 vols. Submitted to the Southwestern Regional Office of the National Park Service, Santa Fe, N.M.

1994a *Preliminary Report for the 1993 Excavation Season at Quarai Pueblo, New Mexico.* Submitted to the Southwestern Regional Office of the National Park Service, Santa Fe, N.M.

1994b Clustered Confederacies: Sociopolitical Organization in the Protohistoric Rio Grande. In *The Ancient Southwestern Community: Models of Methods for the Study of Prehistoric Social Organization,* edited by W. H. Wills and Robert D. Leonard, pp. 45–54. University of New Mexico Press, Albuquerque.

1998 *Economy and Society at Pueblo Colorado, New Mexico.* Report of the 1989 Excavations, submitted to USDA Forest Service, Albuquerque, N.M.

2000 Gender and Exchange. In *Women and Men in the Prehistoric Southwest,* edited by Patricia L. Crown, pp. 345–377. School of American Research Press, Santa Fe, N.M.

Spielmann, Katherine A., and William M. Graves

1998 *Concluding Discussion.* USDA Forest Service, Albuquerque, N.M. Submitted to Report of the 1989 Excavations.

Spielmann, Katherine A., Jeannie Mobley-Tanaka, and James M. Potter

1999 Style and Resistance in the Seventeenth-Century Salinas Province. Paper presented at the 64th Annual Meeting of the Society for American Archaeology, Chicago, Ill.

Stark, Miriam

1998 *The Archaeology of Social Boundaries.* Smithsonian Series in Archaeological Inquiry. Smithsonian Institution Press, Washington, D.C.

Starna, William

1991 Indian Dutch Frontiers. *De Halve Maen* 64:21–25.

Stern, Peter

1998 Marginals and Acculturation in Frontier Society. In *New Views of Borderlands History,* edited by Robert H. Jackson, pp. 157–188, University of New Mexico Press, Albuquerque.

Stoler, Ann L.

1992 Rethinking Categories: European Communities and the Boundaries of Rule. In *Colonialism and Culture,* edited by Nicholas B. Dirks, pp. 319–352. University of Michigan Press, Ann Arbor.

Strathern, Marilyn
1988 *The Gender of the Gift: Problems with Women and Problems with Society in Melanesia.* Studies in Melanesian Anthropology 6. University of California Press, Berkeley.

Strout, Clevy L.
1978 The Resettlement of Santa Fe; 1695: The Newly Found Muster Roll. *New Mexico Historical Review* (53):261–270.

Sutton, Wendy
n.d. *The Effects of Indirect Contact on the High Plains: A Study of the Process of Tribal Formation during the Protohistoric Period.* Ms. in possession of author.

Szuter, Christine
2000 Gender and Animals: Hunting Technology, Ritual, and Subsistence in the Greater Southwest. In *Women and Men in the Prehispanic Southwest,* edited by Patricia L. Crown, pp. 197–220. School of American Research Press, Santa Fe, N.M.

Szuter, Christina, and Steve Bayham
1989 Sedentism and Animal Procurement among Desert Horticulturists of North American Southwest. In *Farmers and Hunters: The Implications of Sedentism,* edited by Susan Kent, pp. 80–95. Cambridge University Press, Cambridge.

Tarr, Ralph S.
1902 *The Physical Geography of New York State.* Macmillan, New York.

Taylor, Jean Gelman
1983 *The Social World of Batavia: European and Eurasian in Dutch Asia.* University of Wisconsin Press, Madison.

Taylor, William B., and Franklin Pease
1994 *Violence, Resistance, and Survival in the Americas.* Smithsonian Institution Press, Washington, D.C.

Thiel, Homer
1998 The Effects of Sedentism on Faunal Resources at Pueblo Colorado. In *Economy and Society at Pueblo Coilorado, N.M.,* edited by K. A. Spielmann, pp. 186–212. USDA Forest Service, Albuquerque, N.M.

Thomas, David Hurst
1989 Columbian Consequences: The Spanish Borderlands in Cubist Perspective. In *Columbian Consequences: Archaeology and Historical Perspectives on the Spanish Borderlands West,* vol. 1, edited by David Hurst Thomas. Smithsonian Institution Press, Washington, D.C.

Thomas, Nicholas

1991 *Entangled Objects: Exchange, Material Culture, and Colonialism in the Pacific.* Harvard University Press, Cambridge, Mass.

1994 *Colonialism's Culture: Anthropology, Travel, and Government.* Princeton University Press, Princeton, N.J.

Thompson, John H. (editor)

1966 *Geography of New York State.* Syracuse University Press, Syracuse, N.Y.

Thwaites, Reuben Gold (editor)

1959 *The Jesuit Relations and Allied Documents, Travels and Explorations of the Jesuit Missionaries in New France.* Pagent Books, New York.

Tjarks, Alicia

1978 Demographic, Ethnic and Occupational Structure of New Mexico, 1790. *Americas: A Quarterly Review of Inter-American Cultural History* (35):45–88.

Todorov, Tzvetan

1984 *The Conquest of America: The Question of the Other.* Harper and Row, New York.

Toulouse, Joseph H. Jr.

1949 *The Mission of San Gregorio de Abo: A Report on the Excavation and Repair of a Seventeenth-Century New Mexico Mission.* School of American Research Monograph Series No. 13. University of New Mexico Press, Albuquerque.

Trigg, Heather B.

1999 *The Economy of Early Colonial New Mexico AD 1598–1680: An Investigation of Social Structure and Human Agency Using Archaeological and Documentary Data.* Unpublished Ph.D. dissertation, University of Michigan.

Trigger, Bruce G.

1971 The Mohawk-Mahican War (1624–28): The Establishment of a Pattern. *Canadian Historical Review* 52:276–286.

Tuck, James

1971 *Onondaga Iroquois Prehistory: A Study in Settlement Archaeology.* A New York State Study. Syracuse University Press, Syracuse.

Turner, Frederick Jackson

1986 *The Frontier in American History.* University of Arizona Press, Tucson.

Twitchell, Ralph Emerson

1914 *The Spanish Archives of New Mexico.* Torch Press, Cedar Rapids, Iowa.

Upham, Steadman

1982 *Polities and Power: An Economic and Political History of the Western Pueblo.* Studies in Archaeology. Academic Press, New York.

Upham, Steadman, and Lori S. Reed

1989 Regional Systems in the Central and Northern Southwest: Demography, Economy, and Sociopolitics Preceding Contact. In *Columbian Consequences: Archaeological and Historical Perspectives on the Spanish Borderlands,* vol. 1, edited by David Hurst Thomas, pp. 57–76. Smithsonian Institution Press, Washington, D.C.

Van den Bogaert, H. M.

1988 *A Journey into Mohawk and Oneida Country, 1634–1635.* Translated by Charles L. Gehring and William A. Starna. Syracuse University Press, Syracuse, N.Y.

Van der Zee, Henri, and Barbara Van der Zee Van

[1977] 1978 *A Sweet and Alien Land: The Story of Dutch New York.* Viking Press, New York.

Van Laer, Arnold J. F. (translator and editor)

1908 *Van Rensselaer Bowier Manuscripts.* University of the State of New York, Albany.

1920 (editor) *Minutes of the Court of Fort Orange and Beverwyck, 1652–1656.* 1. University of the State of New York, Albany.

1922 (editor) *Minutes of the Court of Rensselaerswyck, 1648–1652.* University of the State of New York, Albany.

1923 (editor) *Minutes of the Court of Fort Orange and Beverwyck, 1657–1660.* 2. University of the State of New York, Albany.

1924 (editor) *Documents Relating to New Netherland, 1624–1626, in the Henry E. Huntington Library.* Henry E. Huntington Library and Art Gallery, San Marino, Calif.

1927–1928 (editor) *Arent Van Curler and His Historic Letter to the Patroon.* Dutch Settlers Society of Albany, Albany, N.Y.

1928 (editor) *Minutes of the Court of Albany, Rensselaerswyck, and Schenectady, 1675–1680.* 2. University of the State of New York, Albany.

1930–31 (editor) *Albany Wills and Other Documents.* 6.

1932 (editor) *Minutes of the Court of Albany, Rensselaerswyck, and Schenectady, 1680–1685.* 3. University of the State of New York, Albany.

Van Rensselaer, Jeremias

1932 *Correspondence of Jeremias van Rensselaer, 1651–1674.* University of the State of New York, Albany.

Vargas, Diego de

1995 To the Royal Crown Restored: The Journals of Don Diego de Vargas, New Mexico, 1692–1694. In *To the Royal Crown Restored: The Journals of Don Diego de Vargas, New Mexico, 1692–1694.* University of New Mexico Press, Albuquerque.

Vargas, Diego de

1992 By Force of Arms: The Journals of Don Diego de Vargas, New Mexico, 1691–93. In *By Force of Arms: The Journals of Don Diego de Vargas, New Mexico, 1691–93,* edited by John L. Kessell, Rick Hendricks, and Meredith D. Dodge. University of New Mexico Press, Albuquerque.

Vernon, Howard

1978 The Dutch, The Indians and the Fur Trade in the Hudson Valley, 1609–1664. In *Neighbors and Intruders: An Ethnohistorical Exploration of the Indians of the Hudson River,* edited by Laurence M. Hauptman and Jack Campisi, pp. 198–209. Mercury Series, Canadian Ethnology Service Paper No. 39. National Museums of Canada, Ottawa, Canada.

Vierra, Bradley J.

1989 *A Sixteenth-Century Spanish Campsite in the Tiquex Province.* Laboratory of Anthropology Note, Santa Fe, N.M.

1992 (editor) *Current Research in the Late Prehistory and Early History of New Mexico.* Archaeological Council, Albuquerque, N.M.

Vincent, Joan

1990 *Anthropology and Politics: Visions, Traditions, and Trends.* University of Arizona Press, Tucson.

Wade, Edwin, and Lea S. McChesney

1981 *Historic Hopi Ceramics: The Thomas V. Keam Collection of the Peabody Museum of Archaeology and Ethnology, Harvard University.* Peabody Museum Press, Cambridge, Mass.

Wallerstein, Immanuel M.

1974 *Capitalist Agriculture and the Origins of the European World-Economy in the Sixteenth Century.* Academic Press, New York.

Walt, Henry J.

1990 *Style as Communication: Early Historic Pueblo Pottery of New Mexico.* Unpblished Ph.D. dissertation, University of New Mexico Press.

Ware, John A.

1984 Man on the Rio Grande: Introduction and Overview. In *Rio Grande Rift: Northern New Mexico,* edited by W. Scott Baldridge et al., pp. 271–273. New Mexico Geological Society 35th Annual Field Conference, Socorro, N.M.

Warren, Helene A.

1979 The Glaze Paint Wares of the Upper Middle Rio Grande. In *Archaeological Investigations in Cochiti Reservoir, New Mexico,* vol. 4, edited by Jan V. Biella and Richard C. Chapman, pp. 187–216. Office of Contract Archaeology, University of New Mexico, Albuquerque.

Warren, Helene, Meliha S. Duran, David M. Brugge, David T. Kirkpatrick, and Archaeological Society of New Mexico

1995 *Of Pots and Rocks: Papers in Honor of A. Helene Warren.* Papers of the Archaeological Society of New Mexico. University of New Mexico Press, Albuquerque.

Warren, A. Helene, and David H. Snow

1976 Formal Descriptions of Rio Grande Glazes from LA 70. In *Archaeological Excavations at Pueblo del Encierro, LA 70.Cochiti Dam Salvage Project, Cochiti, New Mexico: Final Report 1864–65 Field Seasons,* edited by David H. Snow, pp. C1–C34. Laboratory of Anthropology Notes 78, Santa Fe.

Weber, David J.

1992 *The Spanish Frontier in North America.* Yale Western Americana Series. Yale University Press, New Haven, Conn.

Webster, Laurie D.

1997 *The Effects of European Contact on Textile Production and Exchange in the North American Southwest: A Pueblo Case Study.* Unpublished Ph.D. dissertation, University of Arizona.

Weiner, Annette

1992 *Inalienable Possessions: The Paradox of Keeping while Giving.* University of California Press, Berkeley.

Weissner, Polly

1983 Style and Social Information in Kalahari San Projectile Points. *American Antiquity* 49:253–76.

Welkowiz, Joan, Robert Ewen, and Jacob Cohen

1971 *Introduction Statistics for the Behavioral Sciences.* Academic Press, New York.

White, Leslie

1932 *The Pueblo of San Felipe.* Memoirs of the American Anthropological Association No. 38. American Anthropological Association, Menasha, Wis.

White, Luise

1990 *The Comforts of Home: Prostitution in Colonial Nairobi.* University of Chicago Press, Chicago.

White, Richard

1991 *The Middle Ground: Indians, Empires, and Republics in the Great Lakes Region, 1650–1815.* Cambridge Studies in North American History. Cambridge University Press, Cambridge.

Wilcox, David R., and W. Bruce Masse (editors)

1981 *The Protohistoric Period in the North American Southwest, A.D. 1450–1700.* Arizona State University, Tempe.

Wobst, H. Martin

1977 Stylistic Behavior and Information Exchange in Anthropological Papers. In *Museum of Anthropology, University of Michigan for the Director: Research Essays in Honor of James B. Griffin,* edited by Charles E. Cleland, pp. 317–342. Anthropology Papers No. 317–342, vol. 61. Regents of the University of Michigan, the Museum of Anthropology, Ann Arbor.

Wolf, Eric R.

1982 *Europe and the People without History.* University of California Press, Berkeley.

Wray, Charles

1985 The Volume of Dutch Trade Goods Received by the Seneca Iroquois, 1600–1687 A.D. *New Netherland Studies* 84(2 and 3):100–112.

Wray, Charles F., and Harry L. Schoff

1953 A Preliminary Report on the Seneca Sequence in Western New York, 1550–1687. *Pennsylvania Archaeologist* 23:53–63.

Wray, Charles F., Martha L. Sempowski, Lorraine P. Saunders, and Gian Carlo Cervone

1987 *The Adams and Culbertson Sites.* Rochester Museum and Science Center Research Records No. 19, Rochester, N.Y.

1991 *Tram and Cameron: Two Early Contact Era Seneca Sites.* Rochester Museum and Science Center Research Records No. 21, Rochester, N.Y.

Yentsch, Anne

1987 Why George Washington's China Is His and Not Martha's. Paper presented at the 54th Annual Meeting for the Society for Historical Archaeology, Savannah, Ga.

Young, Robert

1995 *Colonial Desire: Hybridity in Theory, Culture, and Race.* Routledge, London.

Index

O

P